Daily Life in Turkmenbashy's Golden Age:

A Methodologically Unsound Study of Interactions Between the
Tribal Peoples of America and Turkmenistan

By

Sam Tranum

The names and identifying details of many of the people in this book have been changed to protect them from their government.

Contents

Part I: From Palm Beach to Central Asia

1.
The Pit of Fire

The sun was low in the sky by the time I found a taxi to take me to the pit of fire. A creaky, old, olive-drab minivan with a jacked-up suspension meant for off-road travel, it was parked outside the bazaar. Its owner, Murat, was planning to leave Ashgabat, Turkmenistan's capital city, drive across the Karakum Desert during the cool of the night, and arrive in the morning at an oasis town on the other side. He agreed to drop me off halfway – at Darvaza, a village among the sand dunes that I'd been told was near the pit. I squeezed into Murat's minivan with ten other passengers, my rolled-up carpet and plastic grocery bag of belongings jammed between my knees. It was August and my white, button-down shirt was soaked with sweat.

I knew I shouldn't have gone. Turkmenistan hadn't changed much since its days as part of Stalin's Soviet Union. The government did not allow people to come and go as they pleased. The roads were clogged with checkpoints where men in uniforms asked questions, demanded passports, and searched trunks. Huge swaths of the country were "restricted zones," which meant that only people with special permits were allowed to visit. Foreigners faced particularly tight restrictions, since the government assumed they were all spies. Most tourists were required to travel with "guides" from state-run tourist agencies. Hopping into a minivan one afternoon for a jaunt into the desert to track down a mysterious burning crater was just not allowed. I didn't care. I was fed up with following all the rules.

I'd arrived in Turkmenistan nearly a year earlier to serve as a Peace Corps Volunteer, assigned to teach health classes. I had expected the typical live-in-a-mud-hut, walk-three-miles-for-water Peace Corps challenges. I had not expected to find myself living in a place so repressive that the *Economist* magazine predicted it would be the worst country in the world to live in during 2004 – the year I'd arrived. To keep himself in power, Turkmen president-for-life Saparmurat Niyazov used the internal security police (the

KNB) to restrict Turkmen citizens' rights to speak, publish, assemble, participate in politics, associate with whom they wished, and worship as they pleased. The KNB used "torture and psychotropic drugs on its prisoners, and stage[d] show trials in which the perceived enemies of the state confess[ed] and beg[ged] forgiveness from the great leader," according to the *Economist*.[1]

A high-school dropout with a longstanding problem with authority, I didn't adjust well to life under this totalitarian regime. After 27 years in the United States, it was just hard to get used to not having any rights. It was hard to get used to the idea that I couldn't criticize the president in public or go wherever I wanted, whenever I wanted. I'd done a poor job following the rules, and in return, the KNB had watched me, harassed me, and interfered with my work. I was frustrated and bitter. I wasn't ready to walk into the Peace Corps office in Ashgabat and ask for an airplane ticket home, but the prospect of being *sent* home was no longer an effective deterrent to keep me from breaking misguided Peace Corps rules and absurd Turkmen laws. I began taking more risks. Maybe I was even half-hoping I'd get caught and deported. I was being stupid. At the time, I didn't understand the country well enough to realize what the consequences would be.

My minivan fought its way north through Ashgabat's rush-hour traffic, toward the desert. It was still 95 degrees outside, even though it was 4:30 p.m., and the real heat of the day had passed. Inside, we sweated, squashed together so tightly that we could doze off without slumping over. There was a man with a melon and a mouth full of gold teeth. A woman in a long dress, her head covered with a colorful scarf, sat in the back with her one-year-old daughter on her lap. Every square inch was packed with bags of clothing and produce. The minivan – called a *marshrutka* – rolled past row after row of nearly identical Soviet-era concrete apartment buildings, built from unpainted concrete.

At the edge of the city, we spent a half-hour waiting at a checkpoint while three sulky teenagers in uniforms wrote information from our passports into their logbooks. Then we were on the open highway, rumbling off into the desert at the *marshrutka*'s top speed – about 45 miles an hour. The capital's apartment towers receded behind us. The radio blared Russian pop music. A hot breeze tried, mostly unsuccessfully, to squeeze in through the window. Flat, scrub-covered desert stretched to the horizon in every direction.

After an hour we stopped at another checkpoint. The driver collected our passports and trudged across the road to a concrete-block house, where three soldiers lounged in the shade. I dozed off, sleepy from the heat. The driver reappeared at the *marshrutka*'s door. With a concerned look, he told me someone wanted to talk to me and motioned for me to follow him. The other passengers stared. I left my carpet and my bag on my seat and crossed the road, squinting against the blowing sand. A tall, blond man in a polo shirt and jeans was waiting for me outside the building, leafing through my passport.

"Hello," I said in my stilted Russian. "How are you? My name is Sam, I'm a Peace Corps Volunteer ..."

"Yes, yes, and you live in Abadan with the Plotnikov family," he interrupted in Russian. "You teach at School No. 8. I know who you are."

"Oh," I said. I didn't know who *he* was.

"How camp Charjou?" he asked me, switching to broken English to inquire about the English immersion camp where I'd been teaching until the day before.

"It was great," I replied, trying to act unconcerned that this stranger in the middle of the desert seemed to know everything about me. "We're having another camp – in Chuli – starting the day after tomorrow. You should come down, practice your English."

"Yes, of course," he said in Russian, laughing. "So where are you going?"

"To Darvaza, to see the eternal flame," I told him in Russian, using vocabulary I'd learned to describe the war memorial near my apartment.

"To see the eternal flame?" he asked skeptically.

When *he* said it, it sounded ridiculous.

"Yes, yes. The place where the gas comes from under the ground," I said, grinning stupidly. "Fire."

He looked at me for a long moment. He paged through my passport. The wind blew a dead thorn bush across the highway.

The man with the melon and the gold teeth watched me through the minivan's window. I scuffed my feet on the pavement, looked up the highway into the wind, and tried to seem harmless.

"Okay," he said and handed my passport back.

Two hours later a village appeared from around a bend in the road, and I thought we had arrived at Darvaza – after all, the driver had said the trip would take three hours. Several dozen concrete-block houses and round felt tents (*yurts*) were sprinkled among the dunes. Next to almost every structure were a few camels or sheep, milling about in corrals that looked like they'd been pieced together from driftwood.

"Is this Darvaza?" I asked.

"No," the driver said and climbed out to negotiate with the boys selling gasoline from dirty plastic jugs on the side of the road.

No one else got out. The mother in the colorful scarf passed her daughter forward, hand-to-hand. A woman sitting near the *marshrutka*'s door opened it, pulled down the little girl's pants, held her out the door, and waited while she peed into the sand. Then she pulled the girl's pants back up and passed her back to her mother. The driver, meanwhile, had found an urchin offering a good price. We rumbled off again.

As the sun fell, the world outside the *marshrutka* got smaller and smaller until all I could see were the two strips of pavement lit by the van's headlights. In the dark, my plan no longer seemed like such a good one. I had no place to stay in Darvaza and no way to get back to Ashgabat. All I had in my bag was a packet of peanuts and raisins, a small bottle of water, a sweater, and a book. The driver had turned off the music. The further we got from the capital, the worse the road got. He needed to concentrate so he could dodge the wandering sand dunes that crept across the road and the ubiquitous, wheel-eating potholes. I dozed off, leaning on my sweaty seatmates.

It was almost midnight when the *marshrutka* pulled off the highway and the driver told me quietly that we had reached Darvaza. The three-hour trip had taken more than seven hours. Groggy with sleep, I gathered my belongings and pushed my way out the door. The minivan struggled back onto the road and I watched as its headlights disappeared into the distance.

The "village," it turned out, consisted of two *yurts* and one brick hut. A man named Nurmurat, who did not seem to have shaved or bathed in three or four days, owned all three structures. He ran a sort of truck stop, offering travelers a place to stop for a few minutes for a bite to eat and a bathroom break. His brightly lit compound was like a lone ship on the dark sea of sand dunes; no other sign of human habitation was visible in any direction.

I sat cross-legged on a carpet outside one of the *yurts* with Nurmurat, his wife, and his son. They were watching a Russian movie on TV with the volume turned way up so they could hear it over the chugging of the generator (the satellite dish was hidden behind one of the *yurts*). Two Russian soldiers were guiding an injured American soldier to safety through rugged, forested mountains. They kept making him drink his own urine for some reason. Nurmurat loved this. He couldn't stop laughing. His wife went to the kitchen and returned with a beer for me. She also brought a plate of fried, salted mutton chunks and a loaf of bread, which we all shared. We sat for a long time, watching TV, eating with our hands. Every once in a while, a black beetle as big as a golf ball would crawl onto the carpet and one of us would bat it away, back into the sand.

"Will you take me to see the eternal flame?" I asked after I had finished eating and paid for my share.

"It's midnight," Nurmurat said. "We'll go tomorrow."

"Is it far?"

"Only fifteen kilometers."

"Let's go tonight. I want to see it at night. I can pay."

"It's midnight. You can stay in one of the *yurts*. Two dollars."

Nurmurat stood up, turned off the TV, and went to bed. It wasn't the reaction I'd expected. I had assumed I was doing him a favor by offering him work and that, regardless of the hour, he'd be glad to take me for the right price. After all, he lived in a yurt in the middle of a desert in a developing country. I'd offered to do him a favor and he'd turned me down flat. Not only that, I'd come a long way and now I'd have to just turn around and go home without seeing the pit of fire since I couldn't go see the pit the next day — I had to get back to the Ashgabat area in time for the English camp

7

in Chuli. Annoyed, I finished my beer, grabbed my carpet and my grocery bag, and stalked out past the *yurts* into the darkness. I stumbled through the bushes and up a 50-foot-tall sand dune, wishing I'd brought a flashlight.

On top of the dune, I spread out my carpet and lay down. To my left were the lights of Nurmurat's compound. To my right, there was an orange glow on the horizon, which I assumed was from the pit of fire. The crater, which was big enough to hide a three-bedroom house, had been gouged from the desert by a Soviet natural gas-drilling explosion in the 1970s. It had been burning ever since. By 2005, the firestorm had died down, leaving only a sprinkling of flames – some a few inches high, some a few feet high – sprouting from the pit's floor and walls. It looked as if, a few hours earlier, a meteor had crashed into the earth and exploded.[2] But I couldn't see any of that from where I lay.

In the sky above my dune, there were so, *so* many stars. Not just the few scattered pinpricks I was used to seeing in the US. In the middle of this Central Asian desert, seven hours from the nearest city, the sky was a blackboard sprinkled with glitter and split by the wide, chalky smudge of the Milky Way. I was dazzled. I finally understood why, for all those millennia before the glare of electric lights began to hide the stars, people had made such a big deal about the night sky. This was why people had written poems about the stars, had cobbled them together into constellations and created legends about them.

If I had stretched out on that sand dune a few weeks later, I could have spent my evening searching among all those stars for Niyazov's book, the *Rukhnama*. The "sacred" pink and green text contained Niyazov's history of the Turkmen people, his spiritual guidance for Turkmen citizens, and his ramblings. In places, it read like a pep talk for the Turkmen nation, acknowledging that things hadn't gone well for a few centuries, but asserting that, nevertheless, Turkmenistan was one of the greatest nations on earth.[3] It was required reading for all Turkmen – all 400 pages of it. Children studied it in school. Young adults studied it in universities. Most government buildings and schools had special "*Rukhnama* rooms" where copies of the book were displayed next to golden busts of Niyazov. In one of his many moments of bizarre inspiration, Niyazov paid the Russian Space Agency to launch a copy into orbit. "The book that conquered the hearts of millions on Earth is now conquering space," a state-run Turkmen newspaper announced.[4] That wouldn't happen until late August, though. Since I was a few weeks too early to search for the president's orbiting book, I had to content myself with gazing at the real stars. I soon dozed off, wrapped in my carpet for warmth.

I woke before dawn. I watched as the stars and crescent moon faded away and the earth appeared around me. Apart from the highway and Nurmurat's place, there was nothing but desert as far as I could see in every direction. The dunes were like massive ocean swells, sprinkled with thorn bushes, clumps of dried grasses, and scrubby saksaul trees. I could still see the pit's orange glow on the horizon. It might be 15 kilometers away along the winding road, but it was probably only two or three kilometers away directly through the desert, I thought. The locals probably only took the long way around by jeep because they were lazy – but *I* could walk. I checked my water bottle (half full) and set off, leaving my carpet spread out on the dune. After all, who was going to take it?

It did occur to me that wandering off into the Karakum Desert alone with half a bottle of water, some peanuts and raisins, no map, and no compass was a bad idea. My business-style loafers left a clear trail in the sand, though, and there was no wind to wipe it away. So off I went, climbing the fronts of dunes and sliding down the backs, investigating trails of tiny footprints, taking photographs. The sun began to rise, bloated and orange over the dunes. Soon the sky was bright blue and cloudless and the orange glow was gone. The sun had bleached it from the sky. I'd lost my beacon. I couldn't continue the way I'd been going, because I had to climb over and around sand dunes and I would inevitably lose track of which way I'd been going. I realized I wasn't going to see the pit of fire.

I was disappointed, but wasn't surprised. Most things I'd tried in Turkmenistan had ended in failure. There was a pattern: I would come up with an idea without consulting any of my local friends or colleagues and attempt to put it into action. Locals would warn me that my plan wouldn't work and I'd ignore them, assuming that their can't-do attitude was rooted in laziness or apathy. Then, as I'd been warned, I'd run into obstacles and, instead of adjusting my plan to reality, I'd tried to bull my way through, assuming energy, persistence, creativity, and a can-do attitude was all it would take. In the end, I would accomplish nothing; I would have just worn myself out, puzzled the locals, and pissed off the government.

Frustrated, I turned back. The temperature began to rise. I started to sweat, and the blowing sand stuck to my face. I trudged through the sand toward the highway. I collected my carpet, slid down the giant sand dune where I had slept, passed Nurmurat's yurts, and crossed the highway. I sat on my rolled-up carpet on the shoulder and waited. The sun climbed higher in the sky and the temperature continued to rise. Every 15 or 20 minutes, I would hear a car in the distance, watch as it grew larger and larger, and curse as it passed. Bored, I took photos of myself next to the highway with my thumb out, hitchhiking in the desert. I counted how many seconds it took from the time I heard each car until it appeared. I drank the last of my water. Finally, an ancient truck pulled over and the two guys in the cab motioned for me to climb in. We rattled along the highway in the burning heat, the world outside the windshield almost too bright to look at. I chatted with the truckers a little but the heat made me sleepy – the temperature was well over 100 degrees – and I dozed off, bathed in sweat.

The truck was even slower than the *marshrutka* had been. It took eight or nine hours to reach the checkpoint where I had met the blond man the previous day. He was gone. In his place was a man in a khaki uniform with a belly that spilled over his belt. He was standing outside the concrete-block building, eating sunflower seeds and spitting the shells into the sand. I handed him my passport. He took it inside and made a phone call. When he returned, he looked angry.

"Where did you go?" he asked me, in Russian.

"To Darvaza. To see the eternal flame. Fire where gas comes out of the ground."

"Why?"

"Because I wanted to see the eternal flame. I wanted to see the desert, too. It's interesting to me. Where I am from, we don't have desert like this."

"You are a teacher?"

"Yes."

"Do you have students in the desert?"

"No."

"Then don't go to the desert. Go to school."

He shoved my passport at me and went back inside.

When I got back to Ashgabat, I found a cheap hotel, took a long shower, and went to bed, exhausted, dirty, and frustrated. Unfortunately, that night in the hotel, I took only one lesson from my experience: next time, leave Ashgabat earlier in the day. It took me almost a year to learn the lessons I should have learned from that trip, but when I eventually did, my life got easier, my friends and acquaintances grew less frustrated, and things I tried to do actually started working.

The next morning I went to Chuli, a resort area in the mountains outside Ashgabat where some Peace Corps Volunteers were running an English-language Model United Nations camp for several dozen teenagers. For three days I helped with Model UN debates, taught journalism, and led camp songs. I began to think my unauthorized trip to Darvaza had gone unnoticed. Then, on the fourth day, my friend Geldy showed up.

I worked with Geldy at my real job – the job I did when it wasn't summer and I wasn't traveling around the country teaching at Peace Corps Volunteer-organized summer camps. He'd just found out his fiancée, Maral, was pregnant, despite the fact that she faithfully used her birth control every time they had sex (a half a tab of aspirin applied directly). His response had been to go out to a bar with his girlfriend Gözel. After some beer and vodka, they'd decided to take a taxi to Chuli to find me.

"I miss you," Geldy slurred in Russian, his arm slung around my shoulders for balance. "I haven't seen you all summer. You're my friend, right? We're friends, right?"

It was about 11 p.m. when they arrived. The kids were asleep in the broken-down little hotel where we were holding the camp. I took Geldy and Gözel, who were both in their early twenties, to the bar next door. We lounged on a raised, wooden platform covered with carpets and cushions – a *tapjan* – and drank

11

big bottles of Baltika (Russian beer). Geldy filled me in on the news from home.

The KNB had come to work looking for me three times in the past few days. My boss, Aman, had told them he didn't know where I was or what I was doing and that he wasn't responsible for whatever I had done wrong. A KNB man had also visited my host family's apartment, questioned my host father, and ordered him to come to the KNB office once a week to report on me. Geldy assured me he had "taken care of it"— that he had smoothed everything over. I wondered, though, if he really had. Maybe I would get sent home after all, I thought, almost hopefully.

After a few more beers, Gözel was drunk enough to stand up, pull her dress over her head, and jump into the swimming pool. She refused to get out, spinning slowly in neck-deep water with her arms outstretched, much to the amusement of the groups of Turkmen men lounging on *tapjan*s nearby. Geldy wanted to leave her in the water and go to bed, but I climbed in, pulled her out, and put her dress back on her.

I didn't want to bring my two drunken friends into the hotel where the campers were sleeping, but it was midnight, and there was no way for them to get home. So we all stumbled over to the hotel. I left them in an upstairs hallway while I went to my room, changed into dry clothes, and scavenged for spare mattresses and sheets. When I got back, Gözel had passed out on the thin hotel-hallway carpet. Geldy and I stripped off her wet clothes, wrapped her in sheets, and settled down on our own mattresses to get some sleep.

I lay there in the hotel hallway, a little drunk, staring at the ceiling and thinking about how strangely things had turned out. When I had signed up to become a Peace Corps Volunteer, I had been hoping to travel, learn a language, and do some good. I'd seen the photos on the Peace Corps web site of the fresh-faced female Volunteer walking down dusty village streets, mobbed by smiling black children; of the preppy young man standing at the chalkboard in front of rows of attentive brown students who were sitting cross-legged on the floor. I had not expected to be hounded by internal security police. I had not expected to spend my time fighting the local government to be allowed to do my job. I *had* expected I would make local friends, but not that they would be womanizers whose drunken, naked girlfriends I would have to help to put to bed on mattresses in the hallways of shabby hotels.

2.
From Palm Beach to Central Asia

I joined the Peace Corps in the spring of 2004, while I was working as a newspaper reporter in South Florida. I was 27 years old, and the life I saw stretching out before me was one I didn't want: daily commutes to work along I-95, congratulatory holiday form-emails from corporate headquarters, articles about condo association disputes. The most exciting part of each day would be choosing whether to get Thai food or Jamaican food for lunch. I would spend my life as a professional observer, standing aside and scribbling on my notepad while things happened in front of me. I wanted to get involved in the world, have some adventures, and try to be of use.

When I applied for a two-year Peace Corps assignment, I wrote on one of the endless forms that I wanted to go to Latin America or the Middle East. Peace Corps offered me Central Asia. Although I had spent the previous four or five years working as a journalist, Peace Corps offered me an assignment as a health teacher. But Peace Corps told me Turkmenistan had asked the US government to send health teachers. I agreed to go. I figured it was less important to go where I wanted than to go where I was needed.

When I took the assignment, I didn't really know where Turkmenistan was – just that it was over near all the other "stans." I did a little research on the Internet and started daydreaming. I would live with a Turkmen family in a *yurt* in the desert. They would be shepherds. I would work in a school, teaching important things to eager little kids. I sat in the newsroom in my button-down shirt and khakis, computer screens glowing on desks all around me, and told my co-workers that from then on the only commute I'd be making would be across sand dunes on a camel. I bought a guitar, planning to learn how to play it while leaning against my *yurt* in the evenings, after long, fulfilling days.

After a short stay in a hotel in Washington, D.C. filling out forms and listening to speeches, I boarded a plane to Turkmenistan with four dozen other Peace Corps trainees. We stopped first in

14

Germany and then in Azerbaijan, where almost all the passengers got off the airplane. The plane took off again, climbing out over the Caspian, over the oil rigs pumping black crude out from under the waves. We had no idea what we were getting ourselves into.

It was the middle of the night, and outside the airplane's window everything was black except the light at the end of the wing. I stared into the darkness, exhausted from flying across the Atlantic Ocean and across Europe and now across the Caspian Sea and into Central Asia. Some trainees stood in the nearly empty plane's aisles, talking. Others read, slept, or listened to their iPods. Below us the Caspian ended and Turkmenistan began.

The plane landed in Ashgabat around midnight. We shuffled through the deserted airport half asleep, cleared customs under flickering fluorescent lights, and collected our bags. We climbed onto a shabby tour bus with soft, red seats. It rolled along the city's wide, empty boulevards, past block after block of identical four-story, bare-concrete apartment buildings. A smooth, modern highway took us through a police checkpoint and out of the capital. The road got narrower, rougher, and twistier as we climbed into the mountains. The bus stopped about 3:30 a.m., and we piled out into a leafy valley sprinkled with broken-down cabins. I found a bed inside one, curled up under a blanket I'd taken from the airplane, and went to sleep.

As I slept, Turkmenistan stretched out around me like an oversized Death Valley. About the size of California, it was almost completely covered in desert. There was cracked-mud desert, scrub desert, and sand-dune desert. It was all called the Karakum, and in the summer it was scorching hot, with temperatures that hovered around 115 degrees for weeks at a time. The country was sparsely populated; while nearly 34 million people lived in California, only about 5 million lived in Turkmenistan. Most of the population was concentrated in a few oases around the edges of the nearly empty Karakum.

On Turkmenistan's western border, the desert's barren sands slipped under the Caspian Sea's waves. To the south, the crumbly, nearly treeless Kopetdag Mountains rose up to divide Turkmenistan from Iran and Afghanistan. To the north and east, the Amudarya River valley marked the border with Uzbekistan.

15

There was a time when the land that is now Turkmenistan was covered with evergreen forests and lush grasslands, but that was millions of years ago. When the glaciers of the last ice age started to melt and recede, it was already a giant sandbox; the rivers that poured in torrents from the melting ice swept out across a landscape nearly as barren as the one that exists today. Flowing across a flat plain, with no natural barriers to guide their paths, they shifted their routes from time to time, cutting new channels through the sand.

The mountains – where temperatures were a little cooler – were forested with juniper, pistachio, and ash trees back then. But for millennia, people cut them to build fires and houses and, by the time I arrived, there were precious few left. As time passed, Turkmenistan dried up, its rivers receding, its natural oases shrinking. About 8,000 years ago, the area's ancient inhabitants began building irrigation systems. Nearly everything that grows in Turkmenistan today (besides desert scrub) has been planted and watered by human hands.

Although, these days, Turkmenistan is the middle of nowhere, it used to be the middle of the world. Missionaries, merchants, diplomats, and adventurers crisscrossed the Karakum on the Silk Road and other trade routes that connected Europe, Persia, India, and China. They rested in the great oasis cities of Merv and Konye-Urgench and died in the scorching desert sands. Massive armies swept through: Alexander the Great's troops brought Greek language and culture to the region; Chinggis Khan's army brought terror and destruction; Arab armies brought Islam; Turkic armies brought nomadic traditions from the northern steppe. The great empires of the Seljuks, the Parthians, and the Khoresmshahs bloomed and faded. Turkmenistan dropped off the map around the 16th century, when travelers and conquerors began to make their journeys by ship, and the overland routes through the heart of Asia became obsolete.

Once a great center of science and learning, from that point on, Central Asia began to fall behind the rest of the world. When tsarist Russian troops conquered and colonized Turkmenistan in the 1880s, they found Turkmen tribes living more or less as they had been since the Middle Ages. Meanwhile, the first skyscraper

16

was being built in the United States and the automobile was being invented in Germany. The Turkmen lived under Russian rule for more than a century (first tsarist and then Soviet). The Soviets ended the partially nomadic Turkmen way of life, dragging the tribes into modernity, for better or worse. They built cities, factories, and schools; they trained scientists, engineers, and bureaucrats. Then, in 1991, the Soviet Union crumbled, and the Turkmen were suddenly on their own.

It was in this troubled, independent Turkmenistan that I found myself when I woke under my airline blanket inside my little cabin in the mountains. The wallpaper was peeling and yellowed and there was a bare light bulb hanging from the ceiling. It was early September. The temperature was in the low 90s. A soft breeze blew through the oasis valley, rustling the leaves of walnut, box elder, and Osage-orange trees (the same varieties common in southwestern Ohio, where I'd gone to college). A stream rushed through, feeding the irrigation ditches that kept the valley green. Through the leafy canopy I could see barren, taupe hills. I climbed out of the shade and onto the top of one of them. I could feel the desert sun bearing down on me, cooking my skin, sapping my energy. I looked out across the Kopetdag Mountains. Everything was dirt brown. There wasn't a single tree anywhere except in the valley from which I'd come.

The valley was called Chuli. It was a resort where people from Ashgabat liked to go on weekends to escape the city's heat. They would picnic, drink vodka, and dance until the early hours. We stayed there for a few days, recovering from jet lag and getting oriented. Peace Corps staff took the time to review some rules: stay out of local politics; make sure Peace Corps knows where you are at all times; file your tri-annual activity reports on schedule. We had Turkmen and Russian language lessons. We learned that Turkmen sit cross-legged on the floor to eat, and that they sleep on *dushek*s, which are like futons. We had some practical lessons, getting tips on how to use pit latrines ("squatters") and wash our clothes by hand. We had cultural sensitivity lessons, too: don't ever set a loaf of bread upside down; don't walk on carpets while wearing shoes; and don't ask too many questions or you might get pegged as a spy and dogged by the KNB.

17

* * *

After a few days, we took a field trip into Ashgabat. We piled back onto the tour bus and rolled down the curvy mountain road, along the broad new highway and into the capital. I didn't know what to expect. Relatively few Westerners have visited the city. In the 19th century, most foreigners avoided Turkmen lands, afraid they would be either robbed and killed, or captured and sold into slavery.[5] When Turkmenistan was part of the Soviet Union, access was tightly restricted, perhaps because it was an "underdeveloped" area, and Moscow wanted the outside world to see the USSR's best side. One of the few outsiders to spend time in Ashgabat during the Soviet era was the American writer Langston Hughes.

He arrived in the early 1930s, when the Soviet Union was doing its best to embarrass the United States for its racism. Moscow invited about 40 African American performers to the USSR to make a film called *Black and White* about racism in the US. Hughes went along to work on the script. After the Americans arrived, though, Washington-Moscow relations improved, and the Soviets dropped the project. The members of the movie crew were told they could go home, tour the USSR and then go home, or stay forever – their choice. Hughes decided he wanted to visit the parts of the USSR where "the majority of the colored citizens lived, namely Turkmenistan in Soviet Central Asia." The Soviet government initially resisted, since Turkmenistan was closed to foreigners, but eventually relented, perhaps feeling guilty about inviting him to the USSR to make a movie and then abruptly canceling it.[6]

Hughes took the train south from Moscow. "Suddenly, almost without warning, the train came to a stop in the middle of a sandy plain, and there on a sign above a little wooden station was the word: Ashkhabad [sic]," he wrote later. He checked into a hotel meant for traveling Soviet government officials; there were, of course, no facilities for tourists. He was in his room one night, playing jazz records on a portable phonograph he'd brought with him, when there was a knock at the door. Thinking it was the man

18

the government had assigned to keep an eye on him, he yelled for the visitor to come in. The door opened and "an intense-looking young white man, in European clothing, with a sharp face and rather oily dark hair stepped in."

It was the Hungarian writer Arthur Koestler, who at the time was a Communist but would later become disillusioned and write *Darkness at Noon*, a haunting condemnation of the Soviet system. He was writing about traveling to the USSR's northernmost and southernmost points – Turkmenistan being the southernmost. They introduced themselves. Koestler, who had read and admired Hughes's work, was dumbfounded. "It was difficult not to say 'Dr. Livingstone, I presume,'" he recalled. Hughes didn't know Koestler's work, but was glad to invite him in to listen to records, eat camel sausage, drink vodka, and talk about Koestler's recent trip to the North Pole in a zeppelin. After this chance meeting, the two writers spent weeks exploring Central Asia together. Hughes was especially amused to snap photos of Koestler picking cotton.

Back in 1933, Koestler noted that Ashgabat, like most Turkmen cities, was grim and completely lacking in local color and architecture. Most Turkmen preferred to live in the countryside – they generally didn't build cities. So southern Turkmenistan's cities (including Ashgabat) mostly began their lives as severe and utilitarian Russian garrison towns. When the Soviets took over the Russian Empire, they made things even worse. They built row upon row of soul-crushing, bare-concrete, multi-story dominoes. "The natives were drawn into the towns, educated, Russified and Stalinised by the pressure-cooker method ... All national tradition, folklore, arts and crafts, were eradicated by force and by propaganda," Koestler wrote.[7]

Turkmenistan's gloomy totalitarian cities didn't begin to change until after independence. Niyazov wanted to turn *his* Ashgabat into a model city, a source of national pride. He ordered huge swaths of the old Soviet buildings torn down. In the late 1990s and early 2000s, he replaced them with parks, monuments, banks, theaters, museums, apartment towers, government offices, and a presidential palace. He also built an elaborate theater for

19

puppet shows and a skating rink called the "ice palace," which drew amused articles from the international press, which apparently assumed it was an actual palace made of ice. He also commissioned some even more eccentric projects, such as a 25-foot-tall *Rukhnama*, which opened on special occasions to show episodes from Turkmen history on its oversized, movie-screen pages. It was this new, hybrid Tsarist-Soviet-Niyazovite capital that I explored on my first trip out of Chuli.

All of Niyazov's new buildings shared a similar architectural style, which might be described as Walmart-meets-desert-emirate. They were boxy, white marble constructions with vast, gleaming, reflective windows, topped by shallow, turquoise-tiled or golden domes. They looked impressive: spectacular and lavish. They were not made from solid white marble, though. The builders had simply glued white marble tiles to concrete buildings and the tiles soon began to fall off. Some of the new apartment towers were built on soft foundations and began to lean. Others stood mostly empty because few Turkmen could afford to live there.

An army of women with short-handled brooms made from bunches of brush kept Ashgabat's wide boulevards immaculate. Soldiers and policemen stood on street corners, watching over the city's 700,000 or so residents. Concrete irrigation ditches ran between the streets and the sidewalks, carrying water to rows of trees and lush rose gardens. Boxy old Soviet Ladas and brand-new Toyota sedans vied for space on the roads. Unlike most cities in the world, there were few signs of American influence: no McDonald's, no Pizza Hut, and no posters for Hollywood movies. In most of the city, the only shops were dreary, state-run food-marts and an occasional tailor or shoe repair stall. There was only one Western-style grocery store in the entire city, which had been built by a Turkish company and boasted what was perhaps the country's only escalator.

Most of Ashgabat's commerce took place in open-air markets. The central ("Russian") bazaar was the first place I visited. It was as big as a football field and was covered by a roof some 30 feet above the ground. Its rows of concrete tables were piled with fresh tomatoes, cucumbers, cabbages, carrots, squash, potatoes, scallions, radishes, dill, basil, parsley, pomegranates, apples, oranges, pears, bananas, dried apricots, raisins, walnuts, spices, teas, cookies and candies. There were dried meats, smoked fish, imported sausages, freshly butchered lamb, cheeses, sour cream, and ice cream. There were piles of fresh, flat Turkmen bread called *chorek* wrapped in cloths to keep them warm. Around the bazaar's edges there were long buildings filled with stores offering meat pastries, *shawarma*, furniture, toys, rugs, alarm clocks, bootleg CDs, clothing, and computers. I bought a pastry filled with mutton, fat, gravy, and onions – a *somsa* – and headed for the exit.

As I left, three women with shopping bags of cash called to me: "Change dollar? Change dollar?" The local currency was the *manat*, which was nearly worthless. Officially, at the bank, one *manat* was worth about 1/5,000 of a dollar. But no one changed money at the bank. At the bazaar, one *manat* was worth about 1/25,000 of a dollar. Turkmen often took their *manat* to the bazaar and bought dollars to save in closets or under carpets – or to use for big purchases. It was just more practical. The biggest *manat* denomination was 10,000, which was worth about 40 cents. Buying a $2,000 car or an $8,000 apartment would require bags full of 10,000-*manat* bills. The economy was essentially all-cash; credit cards and checks weren't options.

Munching on my *somsa* and enjoying the sunshine, I left the bazaar and walked across the street to a two-story, white marble mall with towering, reflective glass windows. On its roof there was a giant globe featuring a Turkmenistan that spread across most of the eastern hemisphere. Inside I found a Turkmen version of the Gap with American-style clothes, tiled floors, bright lights, and carefully designed floor displays. Among the giddy, skimpily dressed teenaged girls browsing for jeans and t-shirts was a traditionally dressed older couple. The woman wore a handmade, brightly embroidered dress that fell to her ankles and a scarf covering her hair. The man wore a lightweight, shin-length, olive-drab coat, a long white beard, high rubber boots, and a poofy wool hat. His hands were gnarled and weathered and scarred and used. The couple looked lost. The teenagers didn't seem to even notice them.

Ashgabat was not what I had expected. I had pictured

something dirtier and poorer. What I found was a nice surprise, and I enjoyed my chance to explore the city after being sequestered for days in Chuli. As I wandered, though, I began to get a little worried. Everywhere I went there were signs glorifying Niyazov, who called himself Turkmenbashy, which means, roughly, "father of all Turkmen." Many said "Halk, Watan, Turkmenbashy" ("people, nation, Turkmenbashy"), which echoed Hitler's "Ein Volk, Ein Reich, Ein Fuhrer" ("one people, one state, one leader"). Niyazov's portrait hung on the wall of nearly every store and office. There were golden statues of him in parks and in front of government ministries. Atop a 165-foot-tall tower presiding over the city center, a gilded statue of him stood, arms raised, on a platform that rotated so that it would always face the sun.

I knew a little about Niyazov and his personality cult. I'd read several newspaper stories about him before leaving the US. I had read that getting a driver's license in Turkmenistan required taking a test on the *Rukhnama*. I had read that he had renamed January, April, and September after himself, his mother, and the *Rukhnama*. I had read that when he dyed his gray hair black, it caused a small national crisis because everyone had to replace their old, gray-haired portraits of him with new, younger-looking portraits. He'd even commissioned "Turkmebashi" merchandise: cologne, vodka, and watches. Before arriving, though, I had been more focused on my *yurt*, my camel, and escaping my prematurely middle-aged life in South Florida. I had taken the whole crazy dictator thing as a joke – something that would add some humor to my letters home.

During my first trip to Ashgabat, though, I began to realize it was serious. Human Rights Watch began its 2004 report on Turkmenistan this way: "The regime of president-for-life Saparmurat Niyazov is one of the most repressive in the world. It crushes independent thought, controls virtually all aspects of civic life, and actively isolates the country from the outside world... Turkmen law bans criticism of any policies initiated by President Niyazov and equates it with treason." The consequences for stepping out of line? According to a 2004 US State Department report on human rights in Turkmenistan, "there were credible reports that security officials tortured, routinely beat, and used

22

excessive force against criminal suspects, prisoners, and individuals critical of the Government." Only a few months earlier, the United Nations Human Rights Commission had adopted a resolution expressing concern about the human rights situation in Turkmenistan.

Still, in those early days, I didn't see how any of that could possibly affect *me*.

3.
Welcome to the Gulag

I was assigned to live in Abadan, an industrial city about a half-hour outside Ashgabat, in an apartment in one of the ubiquitous Soviet four-story concrete dominoes. There would be no *yurt*, no desert, no shepherds, and no camel. For the first 10 weeks (the "training" period), four other Peace Corps trainees would live in Abadan, too. Then they would move to far-flung corners of the country and I would be stuck, safe and sound, near the capital. I was in a bad mood on the morning our little group piled into a *marshrutka* in Chuli and headed for Abadan. I kept telling myself I had come to Turkmenistan to do what was needed, not what I wanted to do. It didn't help. I was still disappointed.

We rode the *marshrutka* down from the mountains and along the main highway toward Ashgabat. When we reached a massive electrical plant flanked by two red- and white-striped smokestacks and surrounded by a tangle of high-tension wires, we turned onto what at first seemed to be its access road. We passed the plant's gate and there, in the shadow of the smokestacks, was my new neighborhood. In contrast to shiny, clean Ashgabat, Abadan looked gritty and bombed-out. Between the drab, gray apartment buildings, there were empty lots heaped with rubble and trash.

Abadan had once been a little Turkmen village named Bizmein. Residents grew grapes and cotton, lived in one-story family compounds, and shopped at a sleepy bazaar. Then, during World War II, a bureaucrat in an office in Moscow made a decision and everything changed. At the time, the Soviet government was moving industrial plants and workers to Central Asia, which was far from the front lines.[8] Officials ordered the electric plant built in Bizmein, along with factories to produce concrete, carpets, wine, and other goods. Thousands of workers streamed into the city from Russia, the Caucasus, and other parts of Turkmenistan. Dozens of apartment buildings sprouted overnight to house the newcomers. The population reached 35,000, a cosmopolitan mix of Turkmen,

24

Russians, Georgians, Armenians, Azeris, Kurds, Chechens, Ossetians, Koreans, and others.

At the time, Turkmenistan was one of the Soviet Union's far, exotic edges. Young people from Russia moved there to seek their fortunes, in sort of the same way that young East Coast Americans once moved West to see what they could make of themselves. Many of the people who moved to Bizmein were of this type – full of ambition and hope. But not all of them arrived voluntarily. Some of them, prisoners in the Soviet gulag system, were sent to Bizmein as punishment. In the 1970s there was a "strict-regime" camp in Bizmein where some 2,000 prisoners lived while they worked at the local factories.[9]

Bizmein's boom days were long gone by the time I arrived. Since then, the Soviet Union had fallen, most of the factories had closed, unemployment had soared, heroin use had exploded, paint had peeled, many of the non-Turkmen had moved away, and Niyazov had renamed the city Abadan, which meant "prosperous."

Our minivan stopped at a low, four-room schoolhouse on a street lined with Osage orange trees. We got out and walked through a gate and into the dirt schoolyard. About 30 people were waiting for us – elementary school-aged children and a few adults. I stood there in my tie in that schoolyard, sweating in the morning heat, nervous and overwhelmed, a big smile plastered on my face, just trying not to do or say anything too stupid. I was sure I was going to offend someone by stepping on a carpet in my shoes or turning the bread the wrong way up. The adults made speeches and the children – wearing shiny yellow, green, purple, and blue costumes – demonstrated traditional Turkmen dances. A woman offered us a disc of golden-brown *chorek* and we each broke off a piece.

The crowd led us into the schoolhouse, which was called Dom Pionerov. Decades of children's footsteps had worn the paint from its floorboards. A hot breeze drifted through the windows. I sat at a desk built for an eight-year-old, next to a gaunt Russian woman with tired eyes. It took me a few minutes to understand that she was my host mother. I'd been assigned to live with her and her family. I'd missed her name. She gave me a kind smile, flashing a gold tooth, and passed me a sprig of green grapes. She didn't speak

English and I knew only a few words of Russian.

Local dignitaries in dark suits made speeches. I watched their mouths move, not understanding a word, and ate grapes. After they finished, a small group of teenaged students stood up, looking only slightly less nervous than I felt, and recited a Langston Hughes poem. Then, clapping their hands and stomping their feet, they launched into Queen's "Vee Vill Rock You." After that, they sang along to a staticky recording of the John Lennon's "Imagine." The room erupted in applause after each number. Some of the teens wore modest, ankle-length Turkmen dresses with brightly embroidered necklines – *koyneks*. One girl, who looked about 12 and was dressed in a tiny t-shirt and skin-tight jeans, lip-synched and writhed her way through a Shakira song. When the kids were done, the other trainees and I took turns introducing ourselves in a mix of English and halting Russian – whatever we could manage. "Hello. My name is Sam. I am 27. I am from America," I told the crowd in Russian (I think).

When the program ended, my host mother took my arm and guided me across the room to one of Abadan's English teachers. Still holding my elbow, she looked at me, smiling, and said something in Russian to the teacher. "She says you are a good boy," the teacher translated. "She says she can tell. She has a .... a special sense for these things."

My new home was only a few blocks from Dom Pionerov. I hauled my bags up to the second floor of a dirty gray apartment building. The stairwell had no lights, no paint, and no glass in its windows. My host mother opened a steel door and motioned for me to enter. I found myself in a normal, Western-style apartment. I was surprised. There were beds to sleep on, there was a table to eat at, and there was a television with hundreds of channels beamed in via satellite to watch. I stashed my bags in my room and then joined my host family – Olya, her husband Misha, their 17-year-old son Denis, and their 10-year-old grandson, Sasha – at the kitchen table for tea. We shared family photographs. Then I gave them some little gifts that, on the instructions of Peace Corps staff, I had randomly selected from a hotel gift shop in Washington, D.C., for this occasion.

I gave Olya a key chain decorated with the seal of the

President of the United States. For Misha, I had chosen a frosted shot glass emblazoned with the same design. He was about 5-foot-9, slight and worn. His face was wrinkled, his shoulders slumped, his pale blond hair gone except for a fringe above his ears. He said he was a carpenter, but he spent most of his time lying on the living room floor shirtless, chain-smoking and watching Russian World War II movies on satellite TV. Olya brought in most of the family's income with her job as a bookkeeper at a paint factory. I thought a shot glass would be a good choice for a Russian man; I'd learned everything I knew about Russians from the movies. Misha took the glass, thanked me, and gave it to Olya, who put it away in a cupboard with a tight smile.

For Denis, I had picked out some pencils decorated with an American flag pattern. From the photo of the family I had seen while I was at Chuli, I had thought he would be a child. In fact, he had already graduated from high school and was biding his time until spring, when he would start his two years of mandatory military service. Blond with a crew cut and acne, he was built like a bear. He looked at me like I was an idiot and thanked me for the pencils. I had nothing for Sasha, since I hadn't known he would even be there. He'd come from Russia only a few weeks earlier. His mother was trying to get an accounting degree there and had asked her parents, Olya and Misha, to look after him for a year so she could focus on school. Blond and hyperactive, he was just as confused by Turkmenistan as I was. I dug through my backpack and found a deck of cards to give him.

It was still morning, but I was exhausted and overwhelmed so I went to my room, lay down, and fell asleep. When I woke up an hour later, I wandered into the kitchen and sat down across from Olya at the table, which was covered with a purple- and white-checked tablecloth. She had a lump of dough and a bowl of seasoned, ground meat and she was making Russian tortellini — *pelmini* — one by one. Wordlessly, she showed me how. We sat in silence, folding pasta, and sweating. It was well over 90 degrees outside, and the apartment's un-insulated concrete walls radiated heat. Misha lay on the floor shirtless, watching TV and smoking. I was relieved that no one was trying to talk to me. My brain hurt from trying all morning to speak and understand a language I had been studying for only a few days. Olya boiled a few handfuls of *pelmini* in a pot on the stove and served them in bowls with sour cream, salt, and pepper. It was delicious. I had seconds.

That evening, Sasha knocked on the door to my room and asked if I wanted to *goolyat* with him and Olya. I didn't understand, so while he stood there in the doorway impatiently, I paged through my yellow Russian-English dictionary. It took me a while to find the word, since I barely knew the Russian alphabet. It turned out he was asking if I wanted to go out for a walk. I put on a long-sleeved shirt, sat on the floor, and pulled on my shoes. Outside, night was falling but it was still about 85 degrees. People escaping their stifling apartments for the cool of the evening filled the streets. Women walked in groups, little children tugging at their skirts. Men squatted in rows on curbs, eating sunflower seeds and spitting the husks into the gutters. Smoke from burning trash piles drifted among the buildings.

We walked toward the mountains, passing among row upon row of concrete apartment buildings just like ours. Satellite dishes sprouted from nearly every window, all facing the same direction, like rows of giant, gray sunflowers. Each first-floor apartment had its own garden. I peeked over hedges and through fences at them as we passed. In the gardens, men lounged under grape arbors drinking tea on *tapjans*. Women baked *chorek* in clay ovens and fried *somsas* in cast-iron cauldrons over wood fires. We passed a man butchering a sheep that was hanging by its back legs from the side of a concrete telephone pole.

Six blocks or so from our apartment, we came to the town's main bazaar. Roofed with a patchwork of canvas and plastic, its tables were laden with pyramids of fruits and vegetables. The street in front of the bazaar was crowded. Turkmen women with long black braids and *koyneks* walked with Russian bottle-blonds in mini-skirts and high heels. Most men – Turkmen and Russian alike – wore black pants and white, button-down shirts. In the buildings around the bazaar, there were convenience stores, a dressmaker's shop, and a barber's shop the size of a phone booth. We passed an arcade where a crowd of kids clamored to rent time on two Sony PlayStations. When it got dark, families hauled beds from their apartments onto the sidewalks so they could sleep outside where it was cool. Olya, Sasha, and I headed home. Back at the apartment, I read for a few minutes and then fell asleep, exhausted.

I had expected Turkmenistan to be extremely poor. After exploring Ashgabat and now Abadan, though, I was beginning to realize that it was not as underdeveloped as places I'd visited in Latin America and Africa. On international scales of development, Turkmenistan ranked somewhere in the middle (although that still meant that 58 percent of Turkmen lived in poverty and 60 percent were unemployed).[10] The frustrating thing was that it should have ranked much higher. It had a small population, some of the world's largest natural gas reserves, and small but significant oil reserves.[11] After independence, Niyazov promised that this fortuitous combination would turn the country into the "Kuwait of Central Asia" and "promised every family free bread and a new Mercedes."[12] But a combination of factors kept the people of Turkmenistan relatively poor.

Bad government was certainly part of the problem. The nongovernmental organization Transparency International ranked Turkmenistan among the ten most corrupt countries in the world in 2005, worse than Nigeria and on par with Haiti. Turkmenistan made about $2 billion a year off of its natural gas, according to one estimate. But "...Niyazov [kept] most of the gas revenues under his effective control in overseas and off-budget funds...no money from the sale of Turkmen gas even [made] it into the national budget."[13] He spent tens of millions on prestige projects like the reconstruction of downtown Ashgabat, which didn't do much to improve life for the Turkmen people or strengthen the country's economy. It's not clear where the rest went.

Bad government wasn't the only factor keeping Turkmenistan poor, though. Pipeline politics also played a role. During the Soviet days, Turkmenistan's gas flowed north, through Soviet pipelines. It was provided at artificially low prices to other Soviet republics. While the other republics got cheap gas, Turkmenistan stayed poor. After independence, not much changed: most of Turkmenistan's gas continued to flow through the same pipelines. Russia used the leverage that arrangement provided – it could close its pipelines, virtually shutting down the country's ability to export gas – to buy Turkmen gas for artificially low prices. Turkmenistan remained relatively poor. Niyazov had looked for ways to break Russia's stranglehold on Turkmenistan's ability to export its gas, investigating the possibility of building pipelines across Afghanistan to Pakistan and India, across the Caspian Sea and the Caucasus to Turkey, and across Kazakhstan to China, but he had not managed to solve the problem.

* * *

Almost every morning for the first 10 weeks, I had language classes at Dom Pionerov with the other trainees who lived in Abadan. We had been assigned to live in cities where there were lots of Russian speakers, so we were learning Russian. All the other Peace Corps trainees were learning Turkmen. The schoolhouse and everything in it had been designed for children; for class, we squeezed into miniature chairs, around a miniature table. Flies buzzed in and out of the open windows. We struggled to conjugate verbs and memorize vocabulary, sweating in the late-summer heat.

Sitting around the table were Matt, a metro-sexual from New Hampshire who had just graduated from law school; Allen, a distracted Korean American guy fresh out of Yale who rarely talked; Laura, a kindhearted woman from suburban Miami who looked a little like Sandra Bullock and had a good story about an NBA player grabbing her ass; and Kellie, a good Christian girl from Washington state who often looked like she was about to burst into tears and occasionally did. Our teacher, Tanya, had worked for Peace Corps for nearly a decade. She was patient and good at her job. We learned fast.

Every day after class, our little group would walk from Dom Pionerov through the dust and glaring late-summer heat to Aunt Olga's apartment for lunch. A full, gray-haired woman of about 65, she would kiss our cheeks, tell us what good boys and girls we were, pile our plates with stuffed peppers and push us to eat more and more because we were "too skinny."

After lunch, we'd trudge out the door, down the grimy

stairwell, and back out into the heat, trying to avoid the emaciated, mangy cat that was dying in the stairwell, day-by-day. One afternoon, just outside the building, I found a boy and a girl – they looked like they were three or four years old – playing in a mud puddle. They were sucking up the stagnant water with dirty plastic syringes and squirting it at each other, giggling. At a loss, I checked to make sure there were no needles attached to the syringes, returned them to the kids, and went on my way.

At first I was assigned to spend several hours a week at a clinic – a standard training assignment for health teachers. Soon, though, I got permission to skip my clinic time, since I wouldn't be working at a clinic after training, anyway. Instead, I was to spend a few hours a week at the local branch of the Red Crescent (the Red Cross of the Islamic world).

This turned out to be difficult to arrange, since I couldn't find the Red Crescent office. I couldn't look up its location on the Web, since Internet access was not available in Abadan. I couldn't look it up in the Abadan telephone book, because there didn't seem to be one. Besides, even if I had been able to find Red Crescent's address somehow, it wouldn't have helped because there were few street signs or numbers in Abadan. People in Turkmenistan don't move around much—in part because they aren't allowed to – so almost everyone in Abadan is from Abadan. They don't need yellow pages or street signs to find their ways around. They just know.

With Tanya's help, I asked around for a few days and eventually learned Red Crescent's location: "In the building across from city hall, where the old *pelmini* shop used to be. Everyone knows that." The office was on the first floor of an apartment building. I knocked, but there was no answer. I pushed open the green metal door and found myself in a dark, musty dining hall, about 30 feet square. A few plastic tables and chairs stood on the tile floor and a portrait of Niyazov hung on the wall. I didn't see anyone around, so I crossed the room and ducked through a curtain into a short hallway. On my right, a door opened into a kitchen where a skeleton-skinny 21-year-old was standing by the window smoking a cigarette – one of those slim menthol ones marketed to women – and drinking instant coffee. His name was Geldy. He grinned at me.

Geldy was my official "counterpart," which meant he was supposed to be my guide, interpreter, and primary contact at work. When he was younger he had been a Red Crescent youth volunteer in Ashgabat, teaching health lessons in schools, putting on New Year's shows at orphanages, and going on camping trips in the mountains. He stuck around for so long that they hired him to coordinate the Abadan youth volunteer group. He lived with his parents in Ashgabat and took the bus to Abadan every morning. He led me across the hall and into the main office to introduce me to Aman, our boss.

Aman turned out to be a fat, greasy looking man with a comb-over, sitting behind an empty desk. A portrait of Niyazov hung on the wall behind him. He put down his newspaper and gave me a fake smile. I introduced myself and he welcomed me and said some things in Russian that I didn't understand. Geldy, who was supposed to be my interpreter, stood next to him to facilitate the exchange. It turned out, though, that he only knew a few words of English.

"He bitch," Geldy told me, straight-faced. "He big fat bitch."

Aman spoke again.

"He stupid gravedigger," Geldy explained, helpfully.

Aman concluded his remarks.

"He bad man," Geldy said.

I told Aman I was pleased to meet him and followed Geldy back across the hall to the kitchen, where we both burst out laughing. We spent the next few hours talking, with lots of help from my little yellow dictionary, and drinking coffee. He told me Aman was a greedy, corrupt ex-dentist and asked me a million questions about myself. He turned out to be sharp, funny, and well-read, full of sayings like: "Never be afraid to try new things. Remember, Noah was an amateur and the guys who built the Titanic were professionals." He had a black, cynical sense of humor, which I found hilarious. I didn't realize yet how deep his cynicism ran, though; I thought he was joking when he called himself "the Turkmen Machiavelli." When it was time for me to go, I used my dictionary to try to tell him I had class until noon the next day but would come by after I'd finished. He burst out laughing.

"After you've finished?" he asked, giggling.

"Yes," I said, showing him the word in the dictionary. "After I've finished."

"Don't use that word," he said, laughing so hard he had to put his coffee on the counter so he wouldn't spill it. "We use that word for when a man finishes having sex."

4.
Life in the Gulag

Lying diagonally to fit my six-foot-plus body between the headboard and footboard of my little bed, I would watch the sky lighten through my window each morning. A grape vine as thick as my arm grew up the side of the apartment building. As summer wore into autumn, the leaves browned and fell. I would note the changes as I lay in bed, adjusting to the waking world, listening to Olya clattering around the kitchen, putting together a breakfast of tea and cookies and sometimes – on special days – Russian crepes called *blini*.

After breakfast, I would iron my button-down shirt and slacks, shine my shoes and walk to work. If I wanted to be respected, I'd been told, I had to look good. Turkmen men were obsessive about their shoes, carrying handkerchiefs so they could stop from time to time to wipe the dust off them. Most Turkmen could not understand the American jeans-and-t-shirt aesthetic. I once overheard a teenager who had visited the United States telling a friend in an amused tone that, "in America, even the rich people dress like they're poor."

I would leave my building and cross a ruined playground, a desolate dirt lot with a busted merry-go-round and a swing set with only one swing left. I would turn right onto the main road to the bazaar, which was wide, paved, and flanked by concrete sidewalks. On my right were rows of apartment buildings. On my left was a neighborhood of brick and stucco family compounds. They were walled-in clusters of one-story houses built around central courtyards, which sheltered gardens, livestock, and *tapjan*s. I would often pass a child driving his family's sheep, goats, cows, or camels to the fields to graze. I would follow the road south, up a slight incline, toward the Kopetdag range, which rose up off the flat desert plain like a wall, its highest peaks topping 10,000 feet. Denis, my host-brother, had told me that the tallest mountains, furthest in the distance, were in Iran.

When I reached the war memorial, I would cross the street

and turn left onto the tree-lined road that led to Dom Pionerov. The memorial, an eternal flame surrounded by 15-foot-high concrete fins meant to evoke more flames, honored the soldiers from Abadan who had died in what Americans call World War II and Soviets called the Great Patriotic War. There were similar monuments in nearly every town, village, and hamlet in Turkmenistan. The Soviet Union lost some 23 million souls in the war, more than 13 percent of its population (the United States lost about 418,500 citizens, still a staggering loss, but less than half a percent of its population). The city government had extinguished this particular eternal flame because neighborhood kids kept catching themselves on fire while playing in it.

Some days I would stop at a corner store and buy cookies to eat during the mid-morning break from Russian class. During those early days, I practically lived on the crispy, rectangular, chocolate-covered cookies that were for sale in bulk in every store and at the bazaar. I think my body was craving junk. My diet at the Plotnikovs' apartment was just too plain and wholesome compared to American food. Olga made it all from scratch, with no preservatives and few spices.

Most days, though, I wasn't responsible for the cookies and I would go straight to the schoolhouse, drop my notebook on the table and squeeze into a miniature chair. Sweating in the classroom one morning, flies buzzing around the outside of my head and verb conjugations rattling around the inside, I noticed something had changed. After weeks of mind-numbing Russian classes, I had memorized every object in the room and there hadn't been a two-foot-tall carpet loom leaning in that dusty corner before. I was thrilled to see it. I had wanted to learn to weave Turkmen carpets but I hadn't known how or where. Here was my answer.

Turkmen carpets had been famous for centuries. Long known as "Bukhara" rugs because they were sold at the bazaars in that city, they were lauded by Marco Polo as "the finest carpets in the world, and the most beautiful."[14] The classic Turkmen rug had a burgundy red background. In the center there was a field of repeating medallions called *güls* – different tribes used different *güls* – surrounded by a wide, geometric border. When the Soviets took control of Turkmenistan, they quickly saw the value of the local carpets, organized weavers into cooperatives, and started marketing the rugs abroad. They even sent one to the 1937 Paris World Fair, where it won a prize.[15]

After independence, the carpets became national symbols. The Turkmen flag features a *gül* from each of the country's five *welayats* (states). Niyazov had weavers make the world's biggest carpet, which is housed in a museum in the capital, with a plaque from the Guinness Book of World Records. The Turkmen government considers antique carpets national treasures and protects them with export restrictions. Though the rugs are cheap by Western standards, few Turkmen families can afford them. Most cover their floors with poor-quality, factory made knock-offs.

It took me a week to gather my courage, practice my vocabulary, and ask Dom Pionerov's carpet weaving teacher, Mayhm, to teach me her craft. She was a handsome middle-aged Turkmen woman with streaks of gray in her braided black hair and the smell of sweat, mutton grease, and onions hanging about her clothes. I couldn't understand her reply in Russian, but her gold-toothed smile told me yes. Every day after lunch, I would walk back to Dom Pionerov for carpet weaving class, where I would spend two or three hours squatting on my heels over a little loom, tying knot after tiny knot.

I stood out among the other students in the class. They were all 8- to 10-year-old girls. Sometimes people would stop by to watch "the American" weave a Turkmen carpet. They were all surprised to see a man weaving a carpet. Turkmenistan is the kind of place where women weave the carpets and men just sit on them and ask when their dinners will be ready. I always worked close enough to the window to catch some light; every second or third day the power would go out, despite the fact that we were a half-mile from a power station.

Some days, after working on my carpet, I would go to Red Crescent. Aman and Geldy mostly couldn't figure out what to do with me, so I loafed in the kitchen, drinking coffee and joking with Geldy. As the days passed, I began to suspect that he'd requested a Peace Corps Volunteer because he was bored and wanted a friend, not because he thought I could help with any of Red Crescent's work. Occasionally, I taught lessons about hand washing and

36

nutrition at nearby School No. 8. I taught Geldy's youth volunteers English. I acted as the token American at the Thanksgiving and Halloween parties organized by the English teachers at School No. 8, a quartet of Russian women – Catherine (nèe Yekaterina), Rumia, Natalya, and Natasha – who had been working together for more than two decades.

In those early days, I also spent a lot of time just sitting around and talking to people. They were curious about me and I was curious about them. At first, the conversations didn't go much further than family and work. People in Turkmenistan were careful about what they said and to whom; a few wrong words to the wrong person could mean prison. After a several weeks, though, people got more comfortable with me and started talking politics.

It made me nervous. Peace Corps had warned me again and again to avoid local politics. So I tried to either change the subject or give neutral responses. One day an acquaintance took me out to lunch and, while we were in his car, safe from eavesdroppers, launched into a rant against the government.

"This is a rich country," he said. "There's enough gas and oil money that Niyazov could be paying each and every person $25 a day. Where's all the money going?"

"I don't know," I said.

"Look, one thing you need to understand about Turkmenistan is that our 'president,' Niyazov, is a dictator like Saddam Hussein. He's as bad as Saddam Hussein."

"Really?" I said.

We went on like that for 20 minutes or so, but I refused to engage, to commit – I was afraid it was a trick. Eventually he gave up on me. We never became friends.

Nearly everyone had something bad to say about Niyazov, though few were bold enough tell a near-stranger that he was as bad as Saddam Hussein. Perhaps the only person I knew who was a consistent Niyazov supporter was Geldy. He was a member of Niyazov's political party (the only one in the country). He understood Turkmenistan's problems, but he maintained that Niyazov was doing as good a job as anyone could. He knew the government had made some terrible policies and was absurdly corrupt, but he blamed all that on Niyazov's underlings. He reminded me of the Russians I'd met – including Misha – who maintained that Stalin was a good man surrounded by vicious, greedy incompetents.

After spending my days teaching a little and talking a lot, I would go home and sit at the kitchen table with Denis and Olya while Misha lay on the floor, clicking his false teeth, chain-smoking, and watching TV. Sasha was almost always outside avoiding his homework – throwing firecrackers into apartment building stairwells or playing a game with sheep knuckles and rules similar to marbles. Sometimes I would study my Russian flashcards. Other times Denis, who spoke good English, would serve as translator so we could all chat. They had endless questions about the prices of things in America: clothes, cars, food, toothbrushes, train tickets. I had endless questions about their lives in Turkmenistan, and before that, in the Soviet Union. I was fascinated – everything I knew about the USSR I had learned from *Red Dawn* and *Rocky IV*.

Olya, it turned out, was from Siberia. She didn't bother to tell me which city because it wouldn't have meant anything to me anyway. While she, Misha, and Denis knew American geography in great detail, I knew embarrassingly little about the former Soviet Union. When Olya was in her 20s, a girl she knew moved to Turkmenistan for work and then invited her to visit. She did, and liked it so much she decided to stay. The bazaars were full, the winters were mild – it was "paradise," she told me. She soon met and married Misha, who was an officer in the Soviet air force, posted at a base just outside Abadan.

The base was still there, home to fighter jets and helicopters, its hangars covered with dirt and disguised as hills. Misha had long since retired from the military and become a freelance carpenter. He didn't seem to work much, though. Every morning when Olya went to work and Sasha went to school, Misha and Denis would also leave, supposedly to spend all day building cabinets, chairs, doors, and shelves. Every once in a while, though, I would forget something and return home later in the morning. I would invariably find Misha sleeping or lounging in front of the television. And that was when he wasn't away on his frequent two- and three-day fishing trips. (He would return with a couple dozen hand-sized fish, which he would salt and hang on a clothesline near the window in my room to dry. This meant my room always smelled like old fish. It also meant, however, that we always had something to snack on while we played cards).

The Plotnikovs might have lived for decades in Turkmenistan, but they still considered themselves Russians. Denis, who had been born in Abadan and had spent his entire life there, spoke only the most basic Turkmen. Olya and Misha didn't speak any. This resistance to assimilation wasn't unique to Russians. While many Americans assume that anyone who immigrates to the US can become an American, too, the attitude is different in Turkmenistan. There, nationality is about blood, about history. It doesn't change. Turkmen passports recorded their holders' nationalities and casual descriptions of people invariably included nationalities. The Plotnikovs were friendly with a few Turkmen, but spent their time mostly with other Russians.

I'd usually sit around the living room talking to my host family until the sun began to set and the air cooled off a little. Then I would go for a run. No matter how hot it was I always wore pants. Only young boys wear shorts in Turkmenistan. Some days I would just jog along the streets, passing burning garbage, grazing sheep, women pushing babies in strollers, and men squatting on their haunches in doorways and on curbs, talking in low voices. Other days, I would run on the track at the town's sport center, the "FOK." It was a strange building, a two-story, angular tin turtle. The weight room was stocked with iron bars to which someone had welded paired chunks of scrap metal of various sizes. Outside was a half-kilometer track wrapped around a dirt soccer field. As I ran around and around, children would often chase me, grabbing my clothes, trying to slow me down, giggling. Sometimes I would pick them up and carry them with me for a half-lap, others I would convince them to race me.

While I walked home from the sport center, sweating and trying to catch my breath, the children from the neighborhood would call out to me:

"Hello, hello."

"Hello," I would say.

"HELLO! HELLO! HELLO!" they would chant.

"One hello is enough," I would tell them in Russian.

Most of them spoke only Turkmen.

"HELLO! HELLO! HELLO!" they would respond.

I could still hear them long after I was upstairs in the apartment, lying on the floor, sweating, and chugging water.

A few nights a week, I would go to Tanya's apartment for Russian lessons. She and I would sit at her living room table, drinking tea and eating cookies. She gave me some grammar, vocabulary, and reading assignments, but mostly we just talked. She believed in God, feng shui, and horoscopes. I didn't. We spent hours arguing over whether putting fake gold coins under her refrigerator would make her rich. I was so desperate to win the arguments that I studied hard and strained to make myself understood. Tanya was excellent at baiting me; my Russian improved fast.

5.
Marching for One Man

After about two months of studying, teaching, weaving, card playing, and running, Independence Day arrived – October 27. Someone from the KNB called Tanya and demanded to know where "her Americans" would be during the holiday. We asked what our options were and Tanya laid them out for us. That's how I learned there was a celebration planned in Ashgabat. I was eager for a break from my routine so I arranged to go. Denis, Allen, and I took a *marshrutka* into Ashgabat and joined a river of people flowing through the streets into the new, optimistically named, Olympic Stadium. As the light faded from the sky, we packed into the stands with thousands of other people and waited for the show to begin. Every seat was filled.

Schoolchildren across Turkmenistan had been training for months – they'd often been excused from classes – to dance during the Independence Day celebration. Dressed in color-coordinated outfits, thousands of them filled the field in the center of the stadium. They moved in waves and spirals, spinning and dipping in synchronized dances for hours. It reminded me of videos I'd seen of North Korea's "mass games." The president watched from a skybox. Soldiers patrolled the stands, passing out Turkmen flags and telling spectators to waive them and cheer. A couple hours into the show, two middle-aged women sitting near me tried to leave. A soldier blocked their way, handed them two miniature flags and told them to sit back down and cheer until the performance was over. They obeyed.

Although American independence day celebrations often feature symbols of the American struggle for independence, Turkmenistan's celebration did not dwell on history. That's probably because the reality of the country's history did not fit well with the nationalist narrative that Niyazov was trying to build. Turkmenistan had never existed before the Soviets created it.

When tsarist Russian troops conquered the area in the 1880s, they found it occupied by a mix of sedentary, seminomadic, and nomadic tribes – Yomuts, Choudirs, Goklengs, Tekes, Salirs, Sariks, and Ersaris, among others – which claimed a common ancestry but had little else in common. Some were sheep herders, some fished the Caspian, and others were farmers. The tribes spoke different dialects and were often at war with each other. They had no aristocracy and little government. "We are a nation without a head and we do not need any chiefs. We are all equal, among us each is his own tsar," they said of themselves, according to one report.[16] This "near-anarchic" state of affairs may have been the result of more than three centuries of severe hardship caused by wars and environmental changes. Whatever the cause, the tsarist government did little to alter the situation during its brief period of control of the area.

In 1917, the Bolsheviks took over the Russian empire in and began transforming it into the Soviet Union. Seeing that they could not suppress the desires of different nationalities to have their own homelands, they decided that the best way to hold their multi-ethnic state together was to promote carefully controlled, state-sponsored nationalism. In *Tribal Nation*, Adrienne Lynn Edgar described how, in the 1920s, the Soviets sent ethnographers to map Central Asia's ethnic geography based on factors like language, lineage, dress, and way of life.

In 1924, they drew the borders of a Turkmen homeland. It was meant to be as homogenously Turkmen as possible, but ended up including a large Uzbek minority. Since Turkmen preferred to live in rural areas, they had built few towns. So the Soviets gave them the heavily Uzbek cities of Dashagouz and Charjou. Once the borders were drawn, the Soviets started creating a uniform Turkmen language, a Turkmen school system, and a Turkmen government.[17] The Turkmen began to come together as a nation, though tribal divisions were not forgotten. But they still didn't have an independent state.

Moscow ran the Turkmen government and economy through shell institutions in Ashgabat. The Turkmen Soviet Socialist Republic (SSR) was among the most underdeveloped and conservative parts of the Soviet Union – like the rural South in the US. While elites in some of the other 14 republics that comprised the Soviet Union pushed Moscow for radical changes during the

1980s, elites in the Turkmen SSR did not call for the breakup of the Union or welcome it when it arrived. In fact, 97 percent of Turkmen voted in a March 1991 referendum to preserve the Union. As the Soviet Union's disintegration continued, though, the Turkmen held another referendum later that year. They did an about-face. More than 94 percent voted for independence. The Ashgabat government declared independence October 27, 1991.[18] The Turkmen had an independent state, whether they were sure they wanted it or not.

Not much changed after independence. The Communist Party renamed itself the Democratic Party. Elections were held and Saparmurat Niyazov, the leader of the Communist Party of Turkmenistan since 1985 (and the only candidate for president) was elected with 99.95 percent of the vote. A legislature with almost no powers was created. In 1999, the parliament extended Niyazov's term indefinitely; he became president for life. There was much talk about a transition to capitalism – and there were a few economic reforms – but the economy remained essentially state-directed. By 2004, the private sector accounted for only 25 percent of Turkmenistan's GDP.[19] A 2008 assessment by the Heritage Foundation ranked Turkmenistan's economy as one of the least free in the world – 152nd of 157 – and noted that the government provided most of the jobs in the country.[20]

"Niyazov was willing to create enough of the institutions of modern statehood to be accepted by the international community … but he was never willing to give any of those institutions autonomous authority or power. They serve[d] his interests and whims, reflecting neither themselves as institutions, nor the people they theoretically represent[ed]," one scholar explained.[21]

None of this, of course, was mentioned at the celebration in the stadium on Independence Day, which focused on Turkmenistan's 14 years of independence, its glorious democracy, its United Nations-recognized neutrality, and Niyazov's benevolence and wisdom.

It wasn't mentioned at the parade the next day, either. Tanks, missiles, soldiers, floats, and dancers languished in unmoving queues along Ashgabat's wide boulevards, among the white marble and gleaming glass of the new ministry buildings and presidential palace. They assembled and marched for only one block – the block in front of Niyazov's glassed-in, gold-domed reviewing stand. I stood in a crowd around the corner and we all strained to see the parade as it marched for the president.

6.
A Massacre, a Plague of Locusts, and an Earthquake

Living with the Plotnikovs was chaotic. They seemed never to sleep. They were awake when I went to bed at night and they were awake when I woke in the morning. The only access to the apartment's tiny enclosed balcony, which the family used for storage, was through my room. I would often wake at 3 a.m. to find Misha rummaging around on the balcony, searching for fishing tackle, or Olya rifling through the spare, dorm-sized refrigerator, collecting ingredients for soup. The TV blared day and night, playing Russian movies and variety shows.

It was a good life. It was comfortable. I didn't mind the salted fish drying in my room. I didn't mind that everything I owned smelled like stale cigarettes. I didn't mind being woken up at 3 a.m. sometimes. I loved being part of a family, no matter how messy. Olya would put extra blankets on my bed on cold nights. Denis was always ready to play cards or help me with my Russian. We all suffered Sasha's hyperactivity and pestering together and conspired to make him do his homework.

I had not been part of that sort of crowded, boisterous family life growing up in eastern Massachusetts. My parents divorced when I was a child and I lived with my mother and older brother for most of my school years. We had a big house in the suburbs with plenty of space to live separate lives. We did not eat breakfast and dinner together every day, the way I did with the Plotnikovs. We did not spend each evening talking over the day's events, strategizing about how to get through the next day's challenges. When I was 16, I left home and my life tangled up in my family ended. I moved to Seattle and lived with a cousin, hoping high school would be less miserable there than it had been in Massachusetts. A few months later, I dropped out and left Seattle. I was more or less on my own from then on.

My adoptive Russian family found it hilarious and bizarre that I spent my afternoons learning to weave carpets. To them, not only was that women's work, even worse, it was *Turkmen* women's

45

work. By November I had learned the basics and was helping Mahym teach my young classmates. I finished with my magazine-sized training rug and began planning my next project. Mahym knelt on an ancient-looking carpet scrap while she was working at her loom. It was worn thin, but its geometric pattern and its deep reds and earth tones were still vibrant. She told me it had lain on the floor of the fortress where the Turkmen made their final stand against the tsarist army in 1881.

That battle marked the beginning of 110 years of Russian domination of Turkmen lands and played a prominent role in the nationalist version of Turkmen history promoted by the Niyazov regime. In the early 1800s, Russian forces had started pushing southeast, conquering Central Asia bit by bit. Great Britain, worried the tsar might be planning to march right through Central Asia and into British India, slipped spies into the region to watch the Russians. By 1879, the two empires were deeply tangled in this so-called "Great Game," and Russia made its next move, sending its soldiers to subdue the Turkmen tribes.

They laid siege to the Akhal Teke tribe's stronghold, a mud-brick fortress in Geokdepe. "Used to fighting rabble armies and ill-led and untrained tribesmen," the Russians underestimated their opponents, Peter Hopkirk recounted in *The Great Game*. The Akhal Tekes bested them and sent them scrambling back to their fort at Krasnovodsk, on the Caspian coast. The Russians regrouped and marched on Geokdepe again in 1881, bombarding the fortress with artillery and rockets while tens of thousands of Akhal Teke troops and civilians sheltered inside.

The Akhal Tekes managed to hold out until the Russians tunneled underneath one of the fortress's walls and blew a massive hole in it. Then the carnage began. The Russians reportedly killed some 14,500 Akhal Tekes, bayoneting babies, slaughtering old men, and raping women. Mikhail Skobelev, the Russian general who led the attack, justified the atrocities by saying, "The harder you hit them, the longer they remain quiet."[22] The tsar's troops conquered the rest of the Turkmen lands with little difficulty.

I had friends who lived in Geokdepe. I'd seen the remains of the fortress. As I sat by the window in Dom Pioneerov, copying the pattern from Mahym's carpet scrap, history felt very close. I could almost smell it as I counted the tiny knots with a needle and marked their colors on a piece of graph paper. It took me two afternoons to finish copying the pattern and reproduce the missing bits beyond the scrap's ragged edges.

Then I got started on my next task: finding a loom. Dom Pionerov had two large looms, but I couldn't commandeer one. The kids needed them for their classes. So I asked Denis and Misha whether they would help me build a loom in Misha's workshop. They seemed agreeable but kept putting me off. I didn't want to be too pushy, so I let it drop, thinking they would eventually get around to it.

While I waited for the loom, I went shopping for yarn. I woke early on a Sunday – my only day off, since Turkmenistan had a six-day work week – and rode an ancient, crank-started bus to the Tolkuchka Bazaar, a sprawling jumble of booths and stands, tin and canvas, on a patch of scrub-desert outside Ashgabat. Everything was for sale there, from jeans and CD players to antique Soviet rubles and ancient pottery, from bicycles to books, from wrenches to frying pans. I crossed the parking lot, which was just a patch of empty sand, and followed the crowd through a maze of fruit and vegetable sellers who were squatting in front of piles of tomatoes, cucumbers, pomegranates, kiwis, and basil, laid out on mats on the ground.

Under the tall brick arch that marked the entrance, a chorus of *babushka*s called out: "Change money? Change money?" On my right was a pile of brooms as big as a sleeping elephant, on my left, a woman was telling fortunes with a handful of stones. The air smelled like grilled meat, dust, and garbage. I wandered until I found a woman sitting among stacks of gorgeous Turkmen carpets next to a colorful pile of yarn. Operating from a shopping list Mahym had written for me, I bought skeins of red, orange, black, brown, white, and blue yarn, priced by the kilogram. Back home, I found I'd been cheated. The insides of all the skeins were wet, which made them heavier – and thus, more expensive. For days, I spent my evenings winding the yarn into balls in front of the television while Olya held the skeins between her arms to keep them from tangling.

I had been living in Turkmenistan for nearly two months but I had seen only Ashgabat, Abadan, and Chuli. I was getting restless and curious. I wanted to explore the country. So Allen and I decided to take a trip to an ancient mosque in Anew, on the other side of the capital. We woke early on a Sunday and rode *marshrutka*s and buses for an hour and a half to the bazaar in Anew. I bought some water and some potato-filled pastries called *piroshkis*, and we asked around for directions to the "very, very old mosque." The answer was always a vague gesture toward the east edge of town.

We set off on foot. Although it was November already, the summer heat had barely faded. The sky was clear and the sun beat down on us. At first we followed a two-lane road lined with box elder, locust and Osage orange trees. After a half-hour, we left the road and started hiking through a field of cotton. The waist-high plants had been picked over and were starting to dry out and lose their leaves. The sounds of town faded and soon all I could hear was the wind, an occasional songbird, and my feet crunching in the crumbly soil. Clouds began to gather and the temperature dropped.

In the fields, we came upon a young couple with two little daughters who were gathering leftover cotton – a few stray puffs of pure white from each bush – into canvas bags that hung around their waists. We asked for directions to the mosque and they said we were headed the right way. We walked on. In the distance, between us and the mountains, there were two dirt mounds as big as baseball stadiums and about 50 feet high. To me, they seemed completely out of place on the flat desert plain.

The Russian General A.V. Komarov, the man placed in charge of the newly conquered Turkmen lands after the battle of Geokdepe, thought the same thing. An amateur archaeologist, he figured they were man-made and thought he might find treasure inside them. In 1886, he had his men carve a trench into one. He didn't find gold, but he found evidence of an ancient civilization, which he later published. [23] In 1904, an American geologist/ archaeologist arrived to explore the mounds more carefully.

Already in his late 60s, Raphael Pumpelly had a bushy

white beard that made him look a little like Charles Darwin. His excavations uncovered evidence of human habitation stretching back 7,000 years.[24] During that time, Anew had developed from a small rural settlement into an urban center. From roughly the second through the fifteenth centuries A.D., it had served as a stop for Silk Road caravans traveling between China and India in the east, and Mediterranean ports in the west.[25]

One day while Pumpelly's men were digging, locusts began crawling out of the ground: first a scattered few, then thousands. "The whole surface of the oasis became at once covered with an endless insect army, always twenty or more per square foot ...At last, when they accumulated in our excavation pits faster than men could shovel them out ...we had to stop work and flee," he recalled.[26] As the archaeologists retreated, the locusts gorged themselves on the surrounding wheat fields, creating a regional famine.

***

When Allen and I reached the nearest of the two mounds, we saw no evidence of locusts, trenches, ancient civilizations, or Silk Road caravans. Just a lot of dust, some empty bottles and an old tire. On top, though, we discovered two ragged pillars surrounded by rubble. We'd found the mosque.

Old photographs of the Shaykh Jamal al-Din Mosque show a soaring, arched entrance (a *pishtaq*) inlaid with two sinuous dragons, surrounded by geometric patterns and Arabic script. It looks about five stories tall and might once have been flanked by two minarets reaching even higher into the sky. The mosque was apparently built for a local notable sometime in the mid-fifteenth century. One scholar called it, "one of the most unusual and spectacular monuments of Islamic Central Asia."[27]

By the time we arrived, though, there wasn't much left. The graceful *pishtaq* had collapsed and what remained of the famous dragons had been taken to a museum in Ashgabat. All that remained were the two pillars – the sides of the *pishtaq*. The mosque had been destroyed during a massive earthquake that struck the Ashgabat area in 1948. The quake measured 7.3 on the Richter scale and may have killed as many as 110,000 people in and around the Ashgabat area,[28] making it the ninth most destructive earthquake documented by the US Geological Survey.[29]

Two men kneeled on carpets before the ruined mosque, praying. I squatted on my heels nearby, looking out over the patchwork of vineyards, cotton fields, and villages spread out below the mound. Gray-black clouds swirled overheard and the wind blew down from the mountains. The ruins had become a shrine where people came to make wishes, tying scraps of fabric to the scrubby trees nearby, leaving amulets in niches in the crumbled brick walls, propping fallen bricks up into teepee shapes. I rolled a scrap of cotton I'd pocketed in the field into a piece of yarn, tied it to a shrub, and made a wish.

The earthquake that destroyed the mosque was so powerful, the destruction it caused so complete, that there were rumors an atomic bomb had gone off in Ashgabat. A. Abaev, who lived through the quake, wrote about it years later. He was a child, sleeping on the veranda of his family's one-story home in Ashgabat. The quake woke him. There was silence for a moment and then people started screaming – first a few and then thousands. The earthquake had lasted only a few seconds. In that time, nine of the 17 people in his extended family had been killed.[30]

The 7-year-old Saparmurat Niyazov was among the children orphaned that night. His house collapsed and killed his mother and two brothers, according to the *Rukhnama*. (His father had died a few years earlier, fighting in the Red Army during World War II.) Niyazov sat alone by his ruined home for six days, weeping, before his family was pulled from the wreckage and buried.[31] After the Soviet Union fell and Niyazov became Turkmenistan's president-for-life, he had a massive statue of a bull with a globe on its back built in Ashgabat's center. The globe was split and a woman was reaching up out of the crack, lifting a child out of the destruction. The sculpture was black, except for the child, which was golden.

The afternoon fading, Allen and I left the earthquake-ruined mosque and headed back through the cotton fields toward the highway. On the way, we had to pass one of Turkmenistan's ubiquitous checkpoints. Manned by police or soldiers, they surrounded cities and clogged highways. Intercity journeys could involve clearing 6-10 checkpoints. (Imagine having to stop a half-dozen times while driving from Boston to New York on I-95 so that soldiers could search your car and examine your passport). The policemen at the checkpoint had ignored us on our way out of town, but we caught their attention on the way back – two foreigners appearing from a cotton field.

Two policemen led us into a little guard shack next to the road, told us to sit down, and asked for our passports. At first they were suspicious. They asked who we were, what we were doing, where we had been, and why we had gone there. They demanded to see the photographs on Allen's digital camera. One of them searched Allen's courier bag, pausing to open the crisp white envelope that contained Allen's Peace Corps salary for the month (I have no idea why he had it with him). I held my breath, sure he was going to pocket some of the cash, but he just looked gravely at Allen, closed the envelope and put it back.

As the soldiers questioned us, they calmed down. They must have realized we were hapless teachers, not spies. Soon Allen was showing them how to use his camera and we were all taking pictures of each other and laughing. After 20 minutes, they decided to let us go. One of the soldiers stopped a minivan at the checkpoint and ordered the driver to take us back to Abadan. Grinning, the soldiers waved goodbye as the minivan pulled away. Inside, the driver's wife fed us sweet ruby-colored pomegranates and assured us she would get us home safely, which she did.

7.
Permission Required

For four days, Misha had been drinking vodka by the half-liter, alternately crashing around the house yelling, and passing out on the living room floor. He was an alcoholic and he had just fallen off the wagon, a tri-annual event in the Plotnikov household. My arrival gift, the frosted shot glass, had reappeared and been put to use. I finally understood why Olya had hidden it away right after I'd given it to Misha. I felt like an idiot.

Olya and Sasha slept at a neighbor's house. Denis and I stayed at the apartment with Misha, ignoring his furious outbursts and moving him to the couch when he passed out. He was old and small, more pathetic than scary. One night he went on a long rant about how the US stole Alaska from Russia. To calm him down, I promised we'd give it back. He relaxed a bit and then sunk into a fit of self pity.

"I'm a Soviet officer," he slurred. "I'm a Soviet officer and there's an American living in my home. What happened? I don't understand the world anymore."

Misha was too drunk to work and Olya wasn't around to give him money, so he soon ran out of vodka and sobered up. Olya and Sasha moved back in, and we all went on with our lives. I found it hard to hold the episode against Misha; I felt bad for him. Until 1991, he had lived in one of the two most powerful countries on earth. Then one day the Soviet Union fell apart. The new leaders discarded everything Misha had been brought up to believe in, ended communism and made peace with the United States. It was as if the United States suddenly disintegrated into 50 mini-countries, democracy and capitalism were discredited as viable political and economic systems, and China became the dominant world power. I could see how it would be a little disorienting.

To make things worse, non-Turkmen weren't very welcome in post-independence Turkmenistan. Most ethnically Russian Turkmen citizens had gone to Russia, but the Plotnikovs had stayed for some reason. I never found out exactly why, but I think the problem was money. They were just scraping by from week to week. They didn't have enough saved to transport all their belongings to Russia and buy and apartment there. But they were always planning, always hoping.

Despite Misha's binge, as my 10-week training period wound down, all the trainees became Peace Corps Volunteers, and Allen, Matt, Laura, and Kellie prepared to move to their new homes in the far corners of Turkmenistan, I was glad I was staying with the Plotnikovs. So, as we organized the going away party, I was only a little bit jealous of the others. The party was at Matt's host family's apartment, in a building nearly identical to mine. He lived with Ana and Sesili Burjanadze, a Georgian mother and daughter who sold salads at the Abadan bazaar. Their apartment was on the ground floor, so it had a back porch and a fenced garden.

Ana was in her 40s, cynical and sharp. About five feet tall with short black hair and dark eyes, when she wasn't at work she sat at her kitchen table, chain-smoking, drinking cup after cup of coffee, and telling fortunes for a stream of visitors. She used playing cards, coffee grounds, whatever she could lay her hands on. The medium didn't matter. What she was really doing was counseling people on their financial problems, their love lives, and their jobs. Sesili, barely 20, was shy, quiet, and grounded, a good counter-balance to Ana's raucous volatility. Ana would sit in that crowded kitchen finishing a crossword puzzle and spinning out a story about how she once beat a woman's face bloody with the spiked heel of her shoe. Sesili, looking at the floor, would sigh ("Oh, mom") and stand up to wash some dishes and put on water for more coffee.

I arrived early for the going away party and Ana put me to work. I skewered eggplants, green peppers, and tomatoes. I chopped carrots, cabbage, and hot peppers. I put chicken legs in a massive bowl to marinate in onions, vinegar, salt, and pepper. I carried an empty five-liter bottle down to the bar and had the bartender fill it up with draft beer. Then I built a wood fire in a grill in the back yard and spent the afternoon drinking beer and roasting chicken kebabs (*shashlyk*) and vegetables over the glowing coals.

By the time the kebabs were ready, Ana and Sesili's

apartment and garden were crowded with friends, neighbors, and host families. Everyone had brought a little something to eat and every counter, table, chair, and windowsill in the kitchen was crowded with food: *somsas*, *piroshkis*, cookies, *chorek*, and salads. The house smelled of frying onions, wood smoke, and beer. Ana's two kittens ran around underfoot, looking for someone to pat them, hoping for a scrap of chicken. There wasn't enough room at the kitchen table for all the guests, so we ate Turkmen-style. Ana laid out a long tablecloth – a *klionka* – on the floor in the living room and we all sat around it cross-legged.

The *klionka* was loaded with *plov* (lamb pilaf), chicken *shashlyk*, roasted vegetables, pickled red peppers, salads, *chorek*, *somsas*, cookies, sodas, beer, and vodka. For three hours we ate and took turns making toasts, which in Turkmenistan, are supposed to be sincere and several minutes long. We drank all the vodka so someone ran down to the corner store to buy more. Everyone wished the four departing Volunteers luck and told them to come back and visit soon. Toward the end of the night, Allen's host mother raised her glass.

"I'd never met an American before I met Allen and his friends," she said. "I didn't know much about your country. But now I know that you're good people and I will never forget you."

We all emptied our glasses.

Within a few days, the other Volunteers were gone. Autumn had arrived. The leaves on the box elder and Osage orange trees were turning yellow and falling onto the streets and sidewalks. An army of women with homemade brooms swept them up almost as soon as they touched the pavement. The air smelled like fall and burning leaves. A cold wind blew down from the Kopetdag Mountains, which were already sprinkled with snow. It was sweater weather.

The Plotnikovs' apartment didn't have heat. Instead, we left the oven on, with its door open. On cold nights, we also left the hot water heater on in the *banya* (the room with the bath, which was separate from the room with the toilet). The heater was a five-foot-tall iron tube full of water, welded on top of an iron box into which a gas line had been routed. To light it, I had to turn on the gas, let it run for a moment, throw a match into the box, and jump back. If I waited a few seconds too long, a flame shot out the front and tried to lick my hand.

With the training period over, my job at Red Crescent formally began. No more stopping by the office a few afternoons a week to drink coffee with Geldy. It was time to get serious. On my first official day at work, I arrived at 8 a.m. and went into Aman's office. He lounged behind his desk, which was shaped like a "T," with his chair positioned at the center of the crossbar, facing down the stem. He was fat, greasy, and grinning as usual. I sat nervously in a chair on one side of the stem of the "T." He told me the first thing I should do was to write a day-by-day, hour-by-hour work plan for my first three months at work – in Russian. I told him that was impossible. I had no job description and no specific idea of how I should spend my days at work. (Peace Corps had told me I was supposed to "assess the needs of the community" and then plan projects to address those needs). Furthermore, my Russian wasn't good enough to write a report. Geldy, who had been hovering in the background, stepped in.

"No problem, no problem, he'll write the plan," he told Aman, pulling me out of the office by my elbow.

In the kitchen, Geldy lit the stove and put the scorched old teapot on to boil. The power was out, so the kitchen was dim, lit only by the gray light from the window. He pulled out the instant coffee and two mismatched, chipped old teacups.

"Are you crazy?" I asked Geldy. "How could you say I would write that plan? I can't write it. I don't even know what my job is."

He carefully removed a pane of glass from the window, lit one of his slim cigarettes, took a quick drag, and blew the smoke through the empty frame.

"Calm down," he said. "It makes no difference what you write. You don't have to do any of it. He just wants a plan to show to his boss in Ashgabat."

So, over coffee, we composed a plan. I would teach health seminars at the local schools several days a week. I would hold a weekly meeting with local English teachers to help them practice their language skills. I would draw informational, health-related posters to hang at the local clinic. I would paint a health-related

55

mural at the bus stop. I would write a grant for funds to buy toothbrushes and toothpaste to donate to the local orphanage. I would create and publish a health-related coloring and activity book to use during my lessons in schools. The list went on and on. Geldy's response to each of my proposals was the same: "Great idea, but you'll never get permission."

At the time, I didn't understand what he was talking about – but I learned. The process was different for every situation, but it was always long and tortuous. If I wanted to paint a health mural at a bus stop, for example, I would start by writing a proposal in Russian and submitting it to Aman. After a few rewrites, he might sign it and stamp it with his personal seal. Then, if he was nervous he might get in trouble for approving it – and he surely would be – he would submit it to his boss at the Red Crescent office in Ashgabat, who would put it through the same process. Once everyone at Red Crescent had approved it, I would rewrite the proposal as a grant, in English, which I would submit to an organization that had money to give away – an embassy, an NGO, Peace Corps, etc. If, several months later, one of those organizations approved the grant and gave me the money I needed, I could it with the Ministry of Justice, and, then start trying to get permission to paint the mural. That would mean getting permission from the city government, which (as far as I could tell) owned all the buildings in town, to paint a mural on the side of a building. So I would write a new proposal, in Russian, reflecting all the changes required by Red Crescent and the granting organization, and submit that to the mayor. If the mayor was nervous that he might get in trouble for approving the project – and he surely would be – he would kick it up to a government ministry in Ashgabat for more stamps, and more signatures. If, several months later, the government approved the project, I could start painting.

Even though Geldy knew all this, even though he warned me I would never get permission for my big ideas, he wrote them all down and turned my daydreams into an official-looking report. He typed it up on the computer in Aman's office and gave it to me to give to Aman the next day. Aman, pleased that I'd done as he'd asked, stamped it and went back to reading his newspaper. (This is what he did for most of every day, which was quite impressive, since Turkmen newspapers, which were all government-produced, were rarely longer than eight pages). With my plan approved, Geldy and I put together proposals for the projects on my list and submitted them for permission – to Aman, to the school superintendent, to city hall. Then, when nothing happened, I settled in to wait. I had no job description and no permission to do anything but sit in the office at Red Crescent.

Each morning, I would arrive at the office at 8 a.m. and wait on the front steps for Aman to show up with the keys. My co-workers would come to work one by one and wait with me. There was Vera, the gruff, middle-aged Russian bookkeeper; Aynabat, the young Turkmen nurse who taught health classes in local schools; and, of course, Geldy, who was in charge of the youth volunteers. Aman would arrive around 8:10 a.m. and unlock the door. The rest of us would follow him inside. Vera would hide in her office with the door closed. Aynabat would leave to teach a lesson somewhere. Geldy would make up some errand and skip out, too. I would spend my morning alone with Aman.

I would sit at one end of Aman's desk and he would sit at the other. There was no other place for me to work, except the kitchen counter. Aman would read his newspaper or stare at the wall or talk on the phone. I would, supposedly, work. This was not an ideal arrangement for me, since I didn't really have a job. I would write new project proposals, study Russian, write letters home – anything I could do to look busy. I was right in Aman's line of sight, so when he got bored, he'd grill me about what I was doing, usually concluding that it wasn't enough and that I was lazy. If I asked him what I should do, he would say I should follow my work plan. I would point out that I didn't have permission yet to do any of the things I had proposed in my work plan. We had that same conversation several times every week.

One day, I was trying to look busy by studying Russian when the phone rang. Aman, pleased to have something to do, scooped it up and talked for a few moments. Then he stood, put on his jacket, and hurried out the front door. He returned five minutes later with a balding man in a black leather jacket. They talked and joked for a few minutes in Turkmen, which I didn't understand. Then our guest began asking me questions in Russian: why I had come to Turkmenistan, where I lived, who my local friends were, what I did at work, when I planned to go on vacation, etc. This was not unusual. I was an oddity. People occasionally stopped by just to meet "the American" and pepper me with questions. I didn't mind. I was used to it. After about a half-hour, the man in the leather jacket excused himself and left.

I walked across the hallway to the kitchen to make a cup of tea, feeling proud that I had managed to carry on an entire, 30-minute conversation in Russian. Vera, the bookkeeper, was hovering in the kitchen. A stout, blond woman, she was never friendly, but usually decent. She spent her days sitting in her office with the door closed, behind a desk piled with documents. Given the amount of paperwork involved in running an office in Turkmenistan, she was probably the only one of us who was truly busy. She made me some tea, we sat down at the little table, and she asked if I knew who I'd been talking to. I told her I had assumed the man in the leather jacket was Aman's friend. After all, Aman had been so nice to him.

"He was KNB," she said.

"He seemed nice enough."

"They always do."

8.
Without Permission

The mountains were sprinkled with muddy snow, the trees as bare as skeletons. Everything in the world was either gray or brown: gray concrete buildings, gray streets, gray sky; brown cotton fields, brown mountains, brown trees. The clouds hung low over the city, hiding the sun from view and leaking half-frozen raindrops. I sat in Aman's cold office at Red Crescent, wearing my coat, trying to look busy. The electricity was out again so all the curtains were open to let as much gray light into the room as possible. Aman, in his black leather jacket, alternately read his newspaper and stared at the wall.

I still did not have permission to teach health classes in the schools or to make health posters for the clinic. Aman had not approved the grant proposals I had left on his desk. I was frustrated. There was so much to do; there were so many things to fix. I had the time and ability to make some (small) contributions. I just didn't have permission. So, instead of doing useful things, I was stuck at Aman's desk, studying Russian and writing letters.

When lunchtime mercifully arrived, Aman folded up his newspaper and left the office. I heard his boxy, Soviet-era Lada rattle to life and rumble away down the street. I gathered my papers, put on my hat and scarf, and walked out of the dark office and into the gloom outside. I turned right and walked along a row of anonymous gray apartment buildings, peeking in first-floor windows. In one, a family was sitting around a wood fire they'd built on their apartment's bare concrete floor. Smoke poured from their half-open windows. The heat must have been broken in their building for so long that they just got fed up.

At the end of the row of apartment buildings, I turned right again and walked through the back of the bazaar. In the front of the bazaar, the sellers offered neatly stacked fruits and vegetables at high prices. Clementines were in season – imported from Pakistan, I'd been told. In the back, there were several giant dumpsters and a crew of men who sat on the tailgates of trucks selling cabbages, carrots, and potatoes. There were also the junk shops with piles of everything from bicycles to buckets, bolts to batteries. I stopped for a few moments to browse some books I found stacked between a pile of electrical outlets and an old air conditioner.

At the far side of the bazaar's back lot, I turned left onto a sidewalk and walked past the photo shop, the pharmacy, and the barber's shop. Dodging old Ladas and Volgas, I crossed the street to the bakery. Under a corrugated tin roof, three *tamdur* ovens stood like giant clay eggs half-buried in the ground, smoke rising from holes in their tops. The women who tended the *tamdur*s covered their hair and faces – except for their eyes – with white cloth, to keep from burning their hair or scorching their cheeks as they leaned into the ovens to tend the *chorek*.

A baker reached inside a *tamdur* with her gloved hand, pulled out a golden brown oval of flatbread, and flopped it on the table. I left her 2,500 *manat* (about 10 cents), picked up the *chorek*, broke off a piece to eat right away, and tucked the rest inside my jacket to keep me warm on the walk home. It was two inches thick, crusty on the outside, and soft in the middle – delicious and hot on a winter day.

At home, there was chicken-and-spaghetti soup on the stove. Olya had made it that morning from the previous night's leftovers. The apartment was empty. Misha and Denis were at work for a change. I lit the stove to warm the soup and went into the *banya* to light the pitch. I almost blew myself up by waiting too long with the gas running before throwing a match into the metal box. A flame shot out and there was a loud "whump." I warmed my hands for a few minutes and started removing layers of clothing: hat, scarf, jacket, and sweater.

When the soup was ready, I carried my bowl to the table, and turned on the BBC news. I tore off pieces of fresh *chorek* and dipped them in my soup. When I was full, I made myself a cup of tea. On TV, the anchor was talking in his prim British accent about the latest developments in Ukraine's Orange Revolution. Thousands of Ukrainians in Kiev were protesting the results of an election, which – they believed – pro-Russian Prime Minister Victor Yanukovich had stolen from pro-Western opposition leader Viktor Yushchenko.

After lunch, I went to Dom Pionerov to work on my carpet. I had finally managed to get my own loom, though it hadn't been easy. After weeks of promises and procrastination, Misha had built me a wooden one. When Mahym saw it, though, she said it was too flimsy. If I tried to string it, she said, the tension of the warps would bend it out of shape. She said I needed a metal loom but she had no idea where I could buy one. Husbands made looms, she said. I didn't have a husband, so I took a *marshrutka* to Ashgabat to look for a loom store. With no Internet to consult and no yellow pages to thumb through, I started at a carpet shop. When I asked the man behind the counter where I could buy a loom, he looked surprised.

"A what?" he asked.

"A loom," I said.

"Why do you need a loom?"

"I want to weave a carpet."

"You?"

"Yes. Me."

He sent me to a carpet factory a few blocks away, tucked in among the city's white marble government ministries. It looked like all the other concrete apartment buildings in the city. I couldn't find the front entrance, so I walked around to the back, found an open door, and walked in. I found three women sitting on a blanket on the concrete floor, surrounded by looms holding half-finished carpets. They were drinking tea from little bowls and tearing pieces from a loaf of *chorek*. I greeted them and they – looking quite surprised – invited me to join them for tea. I sat down and the young woman next to me dumped out a tea bowl, rinsed it with tea, scrubbed it a little with her thumb, refilled it with fresh tea, and handed to me. I drank, gratefully.

Her name was Altyn, which means "gold" in Turkmen. She was 27, the same age as me. She said she worked at the carpet factory all day, back aching, tying knot after knot after knot. In the evenings, she went home, ate dinner, and then got to work on the carpet she was weaving at home for extra cash. She could not imagine why I would weave a carpet on purpose – and for free. Still, after we finished our tea, she took me to a ramshackle workshop in the courtyard behind the factory and introduced me to

61

the in-house loom builder. He was a crusty old bearded man whose clothing was streaked with soot and grease. He sold me a six-foot tall, three-foot wide contraption he'd welded from what looked like scraps of pipe and bits of a metal bed frame.

At Dom Pionerov, Mahym helped me string the loom and I started weaving. The carpet was going to be as big as a beach towel. I would weave it in rows, starting at one end and working painstakingly to the other. Each row was 240 knots wide, took me about 45 minutes to finish, and brought me about one millimeter closer to the other end of the carpet. I could only do two or three rows before my back started hurting and my eyes began to strain in the dim light. After a few days, I started to get calluses on my fingertips from handling the taut warps. A real carpet-maker like Altyn could probably finish a medium-sized carpet like the one I was working on in a few weeks. It was going to take me months.

9.
The Road to Tejen

I woke before dawn and walked to Red Crescent in the dark, sleet stinging my face. Geldy and I had arranged to go to Tejen, a small city about three hours east of Abadan, to teach health lessons at a school there. When I arrived at the office, the door was unlocked. I pushed it open and crossed the dining hall, leaving a trail of melting sleet on the floor. Geldy was making tea in the kitchen with Chary, the taxi driver he'd hired. The room was lit only by the stove's blue flames. Geldy, usually boisterous and full of jokes, was quiet – probably hung over. Aynabat, the Red Crescent nurse, was washing a thermos to fill with tea for the road. Chary was 48 and had a wide, flat face and the creased eyes of an East Asian. He was wearing an Addidas track suit, an embroidered skullcap (*tahya*) of the sort popular with Muslims in Central Asia, and a woman's thigh-length suede coat with wide, furry lapels.

"How are you doing?" I asked him.

"Excellent," he said. "We are going to Tejen."

"Oh, you like Tejen?" I asked.

"No, but I love to drive," he replied, grinning.

On the highway, Chary drove intently, flying past other cars, facing down oncoming traffic in the slush of the bumpy two-lane road, sometimes even executing a double pass – passing a car that was passing another car by pulling not just into the oncoming lane, but onto the shoulder of the oncoming lane. With all of us inside drinking tea, the windows were fogged. Now and then, I would wipe mine clean so I could look outside. The road ran along the base of the Kopetdag range. The flat desert plain we were on gave way to rolling hills and then to a wall of craggy mountains. Not a single tree marred the landscape's clean, graceful lines. The sleet had changed to snow; everything was white.

"White is good luck," Geldy said, grinning. "Today must be a very lucky day."

Every twenty minutes or so, we stopped at a checkpoint, showed our passports, popped the trunk so a soldier could look inside, and moved on. After we left Ashgabat and passed through Anew, the countryside emptied out. There was an occasional shepherd, bundled up against the weather, watching from a donkey's back as his sheep foraged for grass hidden under the snow. The only other signs of human habitation were the railroad tracks that ran parallel to the road, followed by a trail of telephone poles.

The Russians had laid the tracks in the late 1800s as part of their efforts to subdue the Turkmen tribes and beat the British in the competition for regional dominance. The Russians had initially thought to conquer the region by camel, but their campaigns against the Akhal Tekes at Geokdepe quickly drove home the need for a better way to move men and munitions across the desert. So they set to work laying rails from the Caspian coast east through Abadan, Ashgabat, Tejen, and Merv. From there, they headed north to Samarkand (in Uzbekistan) and beyond – more than 900 miles in all.[32]

In 1888, George Nathaniel Curzon, a 29-year-old member of the British parliament, rode the railway and returned to give a vivid report to the Royal Geographical Society on what he had seen.[33] The trip from the Caspian Sea to Samarkand took 72 hours, he said. The trains rumbled along at up to 40 miles per hour, through hardpan desert, scrub desert, and the occasional stretch of sand dune desert. "The sand of the most brilliant yellow hue," he wrote, "is piled in loose hillocks and mobile dunes, and is swept hither and thither by powerful winds. It has all the appearance of a sea of troubled waves, billow succeeding billow in melancholy succession, with the sand driving like spray from their summits and great smooth-swept troughs lying between, on which the winds leave the imprint of their fingers in wavy indentations, just like an ebb tide on the sea shore." Curzon found the country drab and ugly, but noted that, "It is only fair to add that the Turckmans [sic] themselves are unaware that so gloomy an impression can at any time be conveyed by their country. They have a proverb which says that Adam, when driven from Eden, never found a finer place for settlement [than Turkmenistan]."[34]

Only a couple of decades later, the British invaded Turkmenistan using this Transcaspian Railway. It was 1918. World War I was raging and the British were worried that the German-Ottoman alliance might launch an offensive through Central Asia and into British-controlled Persia and India. For a while, they were comforted by the fact that the tsar, their ally, controlled Central Asia. But then the Bolsheviks overthrew the tsar and made peace with Germany. It got worse: the Bolsheviks drafted thousands of Austrian and German prisoners of war, who were being held in Central Asia, into their new Red Army, which was fighting remnants of the tsarist forces for control of the Russian empire.[35]

Russian Central Asia no longer stood as a buffer between British possessions in Asia and Ottoman and German forces. Instead, all of a sudden there was an unreliable army including thousands of (former) enemy soldiers practically on the Persian border – and not far from India. As Edwin Montagu, Secretary of State for India, put it: "There is serious danger that [Central Asia] may fall entirely under Turco-German influence, and may be made a base for dispatch of large bodies of armed enemy agents or even organized bodies of armed enemy prisoners into Persia and Afghanistan."[36] So when a motley coalition of Turkmen and Russians deposed the new Bolshevik government in Ashgabat, the British sent troops to support the new anti-Bolshevik government, which called itself the Ashgabat Committee.

For about a year, the Ashgabat Committee and the British controlled western Turkmenistan and the Bolsheviks controlled the east. Since the only practical way to move troops through the Karakum was along the railroad, the opposing forces fought along the track. Mostly, their armored trains would shell each other from a distance. Sometimes soldiers climbed off the trains and fought pitched battles. The conflict was a mix of old and new: the British cavalry used lances; each side had a reconnaissance airplane. When the war ended, the threat to India disappeared and the British withdrew from western Turkmenistan. Within months, the Bolsheviks took control. They ruled until 1991.

Outside my taxi window, the railway snaked through the snowy desert and slipped into the city of Tejen. There wasn't much to see in Tejen: snow, mud, pre-fab concrete Soviet apartment buildings. There was nothing to distinguish it from any other city in Turkmenistan. We stayed just long enough to visit two schools, where Geldy, Aynabat, and I taught high school students how not to get AIDS. The kids sat silently in auditoriums, under their teachers' stern gazes. We lectured, introducing posters and games when it looked like the kids might be losing interest. It felt good to be doing something.

On the ride back to Ashgabat, Chary played his only tape, which included Celine Dion, the Backstreet Boys, and a Turkmen dance remix of "Hava Nagila," until none of us could stand it anymore. Then we gave up and talked to each other. I told Aynabat, who was sitting next to me, about the lesson I was planning on tuberculosis. She read through my pidgin-Russian lesson plan.

"You forgot to put in, under 'treatment,' that eating dog meat cures tuberculosis," she said.

"Dog meat cures tuberculosis? So what kind of meat cures AIDS?" I asked.

"No, it's true," Geldy said, laughing. "It's scientifically proven."

Chary, eyes on the road, broke in: "I don't know if dog meat cures tuberculosis, but it's pretty tasty."

Part II: Corruption, Absurdity, and Paranoia

10.
A New Year

Although the temperature that first winter rarely dipped below freezing, I was cold all the time. My bedroom was unheated. I slept in long underwear and a wool hat. At Red Crescent and Dom Pionerov, miniature electric heaters fought losing battles against the winter wind. At School No. 8, the situation was even worse: windowpanes were missing, snowflakes blew down the hallways, and the kids wore their hats, scarves, and mittens at their desks. In the evenings, I would take long, hot showers in the *banya*, which was the only warm room in the apartment.

The holidays came in a deluge in late December. The Russians in Turkmenistan still had not completed the switch, ordered by Lenin in 1918, from the old Julian calendar to the more accurate Gregorian calendar. They celebrated the holidays according to both calendars: Gregorian Christmas on Dec. 25 and Julian Christmas on Jan. 7; Gregorian New Year's on Jan. 1 and Julian New Year's on Jan. 14. Strangely, Turkmen and Russians alike had adopted the Chinese zodiac, trading little stuffed chickens on Jan. 1 to welcome the Year of the Rooster. The Christian holidays were followed by Gurban Bayram (also known as Eid al-Adha), a three-day Muslim holiday commemorating Abraham's willingness to sacrifice his son for God.[37] Last came Nowruz Bayram, the Persian celebration of the new year.

The most important of all the holidays was "new" New Year's – Jan. 1. Families saved for months to load their holiday tables with huge feasts and buy presents for their friends and relatives. Olya started buying groceries for New Year's in early December, bringing home a couple bottles of soda one day, a bottle of champagne another, and hiding them away in the backs of cabinets and behind sofas. Maybe she did this because she knew what was coming: Niyazov declared that, in the new year, he would raise the salaries of all public employees by 50 percent. Prices at the bazaars shot up. Niyazov ordered the bazaar merchants to stop raising their prices, but they ignored him. The salary increase never materialized.

Work nearly ceased during the buildup to New Year's. Aman rarely showed his face at Red Crescent. I'd spend hours sitting in his office by myself, writing letters and studying Russian. During one of Aman's few appearances, he was tagging along after a confident Turkmen man in a really nice black suit. They sat with me at Aman's big desk and negotiated a price for some *polotki* Aman was selling. I eavesdropped ineffectively – I couldn't remember what *polotki* were. When Aman and the suit finally settled on a price – 3.5 million *manat* per *polotka* (about $140) – they shook hands and stood up to leave the office.

Aman motioned for me to follow. In the dining hall, he unlocked a green door and pulled a long canvas bag painted with a red crescent from a stack of identical bags. The man in the suit took the bag, opened it, pulled out the contents, and unrolled them. It was a tent, a giant tent, big enough to fill the room, meant to house refugees in case of a war or a natural disaster. I translated the assembly instructions from English into Russian for him. The stranger, who was a cotton grower who wanted to house pickers in the tents during the harvest season, seemed satisfied. He bought 10 tents, loaded them into his Toyota 4Runner, and left. I went to the kitchen and made some tea. When Geldy returned to the office from teaching a health lesson at one of the schools, I told him what had happened.

"I didn't know we had any tents left," Geldy said. "He sold 100 of them last year. I thought that was all of them."

"We have to tell someone," I said. "This is really bad."

"Who are we going to tell? The bosses at Red Crescent in Ashgabat already know. They probably get a percentage. They'll just get rid of you and me."

* * *

Since Aman wasn't around most of the time, Geldy, Aynabat, Vera, and I spent our days in the kitchen drinking tea and chatting. The situation seemed to be the same in every office in Turkmenistan. In the midst of all this leisure, I was trying to organize a "mini-camp" to keep the English students from School

No. 8 busy during their winter break. For three days, 50 students would spend their days at the school doing crafts, playing games, singing songs, and taking classes – all in English. I had organized similar events earlier in the year with help from School No. 8's wise quartet of English teachers. They'd been guiding Peace Corps Volunteers through the process of organizing mini-camps for nearly a decade.

Each time I had asked for permission to run an event at School No. 8, I had met more resistance from the superintendent of Abadan's schools, a dapper, barrel-chested man named Ovez. He was wary of private meetings and particularly of meetings organized by foreigners. So when I started planning the winter mini-camp, I expected trouble; I decided to go see Ovez in person instead of just sending him the papers. To enter his office I had to pass through an antechamber crowded with supplicants and then through an airlock-style double set of doors. His office was cavernous. I had time to greet him, introduce myself, and ask about his family and his health before I had managed to cross the room to shake his hand and sit down in front of his desk. Ovez was in a hurry.

"What can I do for you?" he asked.

I told him about my plan for a three-day English immersion camp at School No. 8, asked for his permission, and handed him a proposal that included a daily schedule and rough lesson plans for each class. He read through the documents slowly.

"I can't give you permission to run an English *camp*," he said still looking at the papers. "But I might be able to give you permission to run an English *seminar*."

I was confused for a moment, but then I understood his implication: the term "camp" raised eyebrows; I should call it a "seminar."

Then Ovez launched into a quick speech about how School No. 8's heating system hadn't worked for 12 years, and each winter, the teachers had to shorten their lessons because, even bundled up in their coats, hats, mittens and scarves, the children got too cold to sit through full-length classes. None of this was news to me, I started to tell him. He raised his hand to silence me. Maybe there was something I could do to improve the situation, he suggested.

71

I was thrilled. Finally, I had a substantial project to work on, something that would tangibly improve the lives of the people in my town. And there wouldn't be a problem getting permission – after all, the superintendent had asked me to do it. I told him I could write grants to try to raise money to fix the heating system, but I couldn't guarantee that the grants would be approved. He seemed satisfied. He signed the proposal for my English "seminar," pulled his official seal out of a locked drawer in his desk, inked it, and pressed it over his signature. While he was at it, he also granted me permission (which I had requested months earlier) to teach in the Abadan schools and to meet weekly with Abadan's English teachers to help them improve their language skills.

I told Ovez that, if I was going to fix the heating system, the first thing I needed to do was find out what was wrong with it. He picked up his phone, talked in Turkmen for a minute, and hung up. Then he stood, shook my hand, and walked me to the door, which he closed behind me. An engineer named Bayram was waiting for us outside. Ovez had assigned him to help me figure out exactly what was wrong with the heating system and how to fix it. Standing in the dim hallway, school district employees squeezing by as they carried documents from office to office, I told him what I needed and he agreed to help me.

* * *

A few days later, Geldy and I gathered a half-dozen youth volunteers, 100 bags of candy, and a live sheep, and took a taxi across town to Abadan's orphanage. It was New Year's Eve and Geldy had organized a holiday show for the orphans. I was going to play *Ded Moroz* (Father Frost), the Russian version of Santa Claus, a jolly man with a big white beard who brings children gifts on New Year's. Geldy was going to play *Snegurichka* (Snow Maiden), *Ded Moroz*'s granddaughter. The Red Crescent youth volunteers were our helpers. The sheep was for dinner, after the show.

We'd been rehearsing for weeks. Geldy had written the script himself. Before taking the job at Red Crescent, he had worked at a theater in Ashgabat. When we arrived at the

72

orphanage, we put the sheep out back so it could graze until someone got around to slitting its throat. Inside, we decorated the *yolka* (New Year's tree) and put on our costumes. I wore a red velvet robe trimmed in white and hid my face behind a beard made from cotton balls. Geldy slipped into a lacy white dress he'd borrowed from someone and sat while two teenaged, female volunteers did his makeup.

We entered the great hall to thunderous applause and cheering from a gaggle of children in raggedy, mismatched clothes, ranging in age from kindergarteners to high schoolers. I walked into their midst and delivered my lines, which I'd memorized but didn't understand. The play lasted only five minutes. I was terribly nervous; I hate speaking to groups. It was all a blur. Before I knew it I was sitting on a throne next to the *yolka*, Geldy in a dress at my side, handing out candy to timid children.

* * *

At home, Olya, Sasha and Denis set up a two-foot tall, plastic *yolka* and decorated it with tinsel and scratched CDs. Sasha flipped a switch at its base to make it rotate and play tinny music. Misha watched the TV news, smoking, clicking his dentures, and grumbling. Faced with allegations of fraud and street protests, the Supreme Court in the Ukraine had nullified the election results. There was going to be a new election, under close international scrutiny. It was a huge victory for Yushchenko and the opposition. Misha was annoyed.

"Bush did this," he said. "He paid the court, he made them do this. And as for this fascist Yushchenko – he is no better than Hitler."

New Year's Eve in Turkmenistan was a family holiday. People didn't go out to parties, get drunk, and look for someone to kiss. Instead, they stayed with their families, either receiving neighbors and friends at their houses or going out visiting together. We stayed in for most of the night. We had a New Year's Eve feast that lasted about five hours. Guests would come in twos and threes. We would sit and eat with them, make some toasts, and drink some vodka. Then they would leave, new guests would come, and we would repeat the process. We drank vodka, cognac, wine, and champagne. We ate the *plov*, *piroshkis*, and *pelmini* we'd prepared.

We also ate whatever our guests brought. No one came empty-handed. At one point, a friend of Olya's offered me what looked, in my drunken state, like a bowl of custard drizzled with raspberry sauce. Tempted, I found a spoon and took a big bite. The chef was watching to see how I liked it. I had to turn away so she wouldn't see me gag. Instead of sweet custard, I'd gotten a mouthful of a pickled fish, mashed potatoes, and beets, topped with a layer of mayonnaise, and drizzled with beet juice.

A Russian TV channel played in the background all night, showing a variety show. When the new year arrived in Moscow, we turned up the volume to listen to Russian President Vladimir Putin – who Misha called "our president" – say a few words. An hour later, the new year arrived in Turkmenistan. We raised our glasses, drank to 2005, and cheered. Sasha and Denis leaned out the windows and shot Roman candles into the streets. Children were shooting fireworks from windows all over the neighborhood. Colored sparks rained down the sides of the concrete dominoes. When we ran out of fireworks, we put on our jackets and went out visiting, leaving plates and glasses strewn around the apartment.

I'd promised Ana and Sesili I would stop by their apartment, so I split off from my host family and walked across town to their place. Inside, their home looked like mine, with dishes strewn everywhere and the remains of a feast spread across their table. They were leaning back in their chairs, looking a little stunned. I sat down with them and picked at leftover salads, *plov*, *shashlyk*, fruit, nuts, candies, and cakes. We shared stories about the parties we'd had and made toasts to the new year.

About 3 a.m., I told them it was time for me to leave. Sesili walked me part of the way home to show me the route I should take to avoid the police. The streets were filled with drunken families, calling out holiday wishes to each other, swaying as they hurried home in the cold. At home, I put on my long underwear and my hat, crawled into bed, and fell asleep.

* * *

The first day of 2005 was cold and gray and gloomy. My back hurt from squeezing my body into my miniature bed the wrong way. My head hurt from drinking too much vodka. In the kitchen, we ate leftovers for breakfast and Olya poured us each a shot of vodka for breakfast – to help with the hangover. At first I thought she was kidding, but when she drank hers and chased it with a spoonful of cold *plov*, I followed her example. Then we both went off to work. It was not an auspicious start to the year.

At Red Crescent, no one was working. Aman had come and gone and the others were sitting in the kitchen drinking tea and talking about the big news of the day: Geldy had been fired. None of us knew why, but we didn't puzzle over it for long. There were plenty of good reasons. It didn't matter which one Aman had picked. Luckily for Geldy, he'd immediately found a job at the Red Crescent office in Ashgabat, as an AIDS educator. He was a smooth talker who cultivated friends and connections everywhere, so it was no surprise he'd landed on his feet.

That didn't help me, though. Geldy was the one who had asked Peace Corps for a Volunteer. No one else at Red Crescent Abadan was really interested in working with me. I was on my own. That was bad news, since I hadn't managed to do much of anything without Geldy's help. He'd brainstormed projects with me, told me who to ask for permissions, and helped me translate lesson plans and grant proposals. He wasn't a very ethical person, but he was good at getting things done and he was usually on my side. I felt abandoned.

I met Geldy in Ashgabat that night, and we went out to his regular bar, a place downtown called Ak Gamysh, to celebrate the end of his career at Red Crescent Abadan. He went there because his ex-girlfriend Nastya and her friends, Mehri and Aka, hung out there. They liked it because it had private booths with curtains where they could smoke cigarettes without word getting back to their parents. It was considered unseemly for women to smoke. That night Geldy and I drank coffee and cognac while the girls drank soda. They were aloof and stylish, in high heels and short dresses. They sipped their drinks, drew delicately on their cigarettes, and talked quietly, urgently, into their cell phones.

Geldy didn't seem upset about his recent employment

crisis. I knew he hated Aman and had been miserable working for him, but still, I expected him to be a little sad about leaving Abadan. I began to think maybe he hadn't been fired at all. It just seemed too neat: Geldy had escaped a job he hated for a much better job, with higher pay and more prestige, closer to home. He probably just didn't want to tell me he was taking a job in Ashgabat because he thought I'd be angry that he invited me to come work in Abadan and then abandoned me there a few months later. I didn't say anything to Geldy about my suspicions – I just sat and sipped my coffee and listened to him and his friends talk – but that was the day I stopped trusting him.

Around midnight, we paid our tab and left. Outside, the girls got into one cab and Geldy and I got into another. We went to Geldy's older brother's apartment. He had a key and we slipped in, found a couple *dusheks* and pillows, and laid them out in the living room. He turned on the TV and flipped around until he found a channel showing naked women posing under waterfalls, next to pools, and in showers. He stared at the screen for a few minutes, remote poised. "This is boring," he said and then clicked off the TV and went to sleep.

***

The next day, I went to Dom Pionerov to work on my carpet. I'd been hunched over it tying knots for a couple of hours when Mahym showed up. She walked into the room, came straight to where I was kneeling, and abruptly told me I was no longer welcome. "We don't have room for you to work here anymore," she said sadly. "I need you to move your loom out of here by the end of the day."

It was 4 p.m. and Dom Pionerov closed at 5 p.m. The loom was too big and heavy for me to carry on my own, so I walked home to find Denis. I found him lying in front of the TV, as usual. When I told him what had happened, he didn't seem surprised. He never seemed surprised, no matter how absurd things got. Maybe it was teenaged cynicism; maybe it was the result of living in Turkmenistan all his life. He rummaged through a closet and pulled out a flimsy metal dolly meant for hauling luggage through airports. At Dom Pionerov, we packed up my yarn, my pattern, my tools, and my loom and dragged it all down the street and up the stairs into my little room. I was confused and disappointed. I'd loved working on my carpet. It was something I didn't need permission for, something tangible and I could sit down and just do.

A few days later, Tanya told me what had happened. In typically indirect Turkmen fashion, Mahym had sent me an explanation and apology through Tanya. The local government, it seemed, had decided that I should no longer be allowed to learn to weave Turkmen carpets – that, by doing so, I was stealing a national secret – and told Mahym to throw me out. It was too absurd. I couldn't stay angry. I started laughing.

At the dinner table that night, I told my host family what had happened. Olya was sympathetic. Misha thought it was hilarious.

"What can you expect? The Turkmen have taken over the country. If the Russians were still running things, this never would have happened," he said.

My bedroom was small, but there was space for the loom at the foot of my bed. So I went back to work, adding a millimeter or two per day. When anyone in Abadan asked me how my carpet was coming, I told them I'd given up. I was starting to learn that in Turkmenistan, it's best not to attract attention.

11.
In the Golden Age, There Are No Cold Schools

The school-heating project went well at first. Since Aman wouldn't let me use the phone at Red Crescent, I would make up excuses to leave the office and sneak home to call embassies and non-governmental organizations in Ashgabat, looking for one that was interested in funding the project. I needed $10,000 for materials. Ovez had promised that the school district would provide the labor. While I was calling around, I learned about every available grant program in Ashgabat. The British Embassy, it turned out, was interested in paying me to paint a health-related mural. The American Embassy had a whole bunch of money for Internet centers and nobody to give it to. The Japanese Embassy had just started a grant program and didn't know what it wanted. Neither the Saudi Embassy nor the Iranian Embassy offered grants at all. After a few days on the telephone I found what I was looking for: a non-governmental organization called Counterpart Consortium was interested in my project.

I submitted a preliminary proposal, which Counterpart accepted. At first, local officials were supportive. After all, pretty much everyone in town had a connection to one of School No. 8's 1,000 students or 200 teachers. The mayor promised me that city engineers would help Bayram diagnose the problem with the heating system and draw up a plan to fix it. The principal of the school invited me to her office and thanked me profusely for agreeing to help. I was a local celebrity. Everyone was cheering me on. It felt great.

Then things started to go wrong. I formed a small parent-teacher association to oversee the grant writing and, later, the work on the school. This was a complicated and somewhat risky venture in a country with no freedom of assembly. Aman refused to let the group meet in the dining hall at Red Crescent so the members met in private apartments, moving each week to avoid attracting attention. When the KNB caught on and forbid them from meeting anymore, they talked on the phone, instead.

Then one day, the mayor summoned me to his office. He was a meaty, gray-haired man in a dark suit. Like many government officials, he wore a gold pin of Niyazov's face on his lapel. First he asked me to read the manual for his new cell phone, which was in English, and teach him how to use it. We spent a few minutes taking photos of each other with the phone. Then he put it in his drawer, thanked me, and leaned back in his chair.

"We no longer need your help," he said. "School No. 8 is warm."

"Excuse me, but it's not. I was there yesterday and it was freezing cold."

"Well, today it's warm."

When I pressed him a little bit, he explained that he had simply ordered someone to turn on the heating system. Apparently, for 12 years, no one had bothered to flip the switch. I rushed over to School No. 8, to see if it had, in fact, been that easy – just pressure the local government a little bit and, voila, the school had heat. Inside the school, the steam heating pipes were rattling and hissing. The whole building smelled like hot paint. I found Catherine in the principal's office and she was grinning.

"You did it," she said, and gave me a high five.

Our excitement lasted only a few hours. We waited and waited but the school never warmed up. Over the years, almost all the radiators had been stolen and the pipes that carried hot steam through the building were full of holes. The heating system made a lot of noise but couldn't warm the building by more than a degree or two. Also, the city had diverted the steam to heat the school from a nearby apartment building, which left dozens of families freezing in their apartments. The next day, everything went back to normal: the apartment building got its heat back, and the heating system in the school stopped making such a racket.

A few days later, I went to the weekly meeting of Abadan English teachers that Ovez had given me permission to attend. It was just the Quartet and me. We sat in a cold classroom at School No. 8, drinking tea, and talking in English. The subject, of course, was the school-heating debacle. Their general attitude was: well, what did you expect? Still, they had no intention of giving up – or letting me give up. They were not intimidated by either the KNB or city hall. After all, they had been teaching for nearly 25 years and remembered all the scowling men in dark suits that were causing us such trouble as bratty little kids; they knew their mothers.

Rumia, the most jaded, cynical member of the Quartet, retold the story – which I had heard countless times – of how she had engineered a short, all-expenses paid trip to America for a group of her students and just hours before their flight was to leave Ashgabat, the government had decreed that they couldn't go. After that, she'd given up on ambitious projects. She just taught her classes and kept her head down.

"When I thought this was going to work, it made me believe it might still be possible to do good things here," she said.

I decided to stick with the school-heating project until the bitter end. There wasn't much more I could do, though. The mayor had bowed to reality and admitted the school was cold – an important step – but he still refused to give me official permission to fix it. He told me to write the grant, get the money, and do the work, but he would not provide me with the all-important signed, stamped letter of permission. So Counterpart (wisely) would not accept my grant proposal. Without the letter of permission from the city, I could have ended up winning the grant, buying $10,000 worth of pipes and radiators, and being refused permission to install them.

I spent several days shuttling from Ovez's office to School No. 8 to Counterpart's office to the Peace Corps office to city hall, trying to find a way to convince the mayor to pull his stamp out of his desk drawer and apply it to my proposal. At home, I'd wait until Olya and Denis got home from the paint factory – Denis was helping his mother out, since her secretary had disappeared – and then fill them in on the day's absurdities.

"Are they kidding?" I would rant. "They must be fucking kidding. This whole country must be fucking kidding. The fucking secret police shut down my PTA meetings. I spend my days pleading with city officials to let me give them $10,000 to make their children's school warm. This must be a joke."

Misha would just lie in front of the TV, clicking his dentures. "What did you think would happen?" Denis would ask,

80

laughing. "If they don't want your help, don't help them," Olya would say. But I was so convinced that what I was doing was right – that I should help Abadan heat its school, whether it wanted my help or not – and that if I just stuck with it and bulled my way through, I could get it done, that I didn't even consider following her advice.

After a frustrating week, I went back to the English teachers' meeting. We sat around a table in Catherine's classroom, drinking tea and eating hard candies. I told them I'd made no progress. They discussed the problem. Rumia's former student, Kolya, worked at city hall. The Quartet agreed that he was our last hope. The next day, I called his office and asked for a meeting. He didn't call me back so Rumia went over his head – she called his mother. Within an hour, he had agreed to meet us at Red Crescent.

When Kolya arrived, he greeted Rumia coldly. He was a 30-something Russian man in a black suit with floppy blond hair that spilled over his ears. He wore a golden Niyazov face on his lapel. He told us there was nothing he could do to help us. All the top city officials were scared to approve the project, he explained. Accepting aid from international organizations was hazardous; it could lead to arrest and imprisonment. Two years earlier, he had narrowly escaped going to jail for trying to get a grant from Counterpart to rebuild a playground in town, he said. It could also mean getting fired. Unemployment was at least 60 percent and the government controlled most full-time jobs.[38] That meant that the threat of being blackballed from government work was a powerful tool for social control, since it was really the threat of a lifetime of struggle and poverty.[39]

"This is Turkmenistan's 'Golden Age,'" Kolya said sarcastically, referring to one of Niyazov's slogans. "We don't need help from foreigners. All our schools are already warm. All our playgrounds are already perfect."

And that ended my school-heating project. It also made me question whether Turkmenistan needed me to teach children how to wash their hands and avoid getting AIDS, to try to heat its schools, or to give its children English lessons. After all, how much of a difference could I make when its oil-rich government was closing hospitals, denying the existence of AIDS, letting its schools rot, and leaving teachers' salaries unpaid for months? Maybe what Turkmenistan needed was a new government, I thought.

12.
The Internet Center

All this time, Aman had been getting angrier and angrier at me. It began when Niyazov released the sequel to the *Rukhnama* and everyone in the Red Crescent office was required to buy a copy and sign a statement swearing they'd read it and loved it, but I refused. I pointed out that the book was only available in Turkmen so I couldn't read it. But Aman didn't see that as a valid excuse because, of course, no one else had read it, either. My efforts to heat School No. 8 had made things even worse.

"Why are you spending your time trying to heat that school, when our office is still cold and I still need a new computer and a new Xerox machine?" he asked me one morning from behind his newspaper. "Do that first and then you can go out and start heating schools."

From then on, he rejected all my requests. Could I go teach a class on tuberculosis at School No. 8? No. Could I take a vacation? No. Could I go home to use my phone to call Counterpart? No. As I sat at Red Crescent, I got madder and madder. My boss was blackmailing me. He was punishing me for trying to heat a school where 1,200 people spent their days instead of trying to heat an office where four people worked. There wasn't much I could do, though, so I swallowed my pride and settled on what I thought was a pretty good compromise.

I wrote a proposal to open an Internet center at Red Crescent. It would be the only one in Abadan. My plan was to renovate an unused room, install two computers with Internet service, and run free classes for the community. The grant would cover the center's operating costs for six months. After that, once people in Abadan knew what the Internet was good for, the center would start charging users to cover its operating costs. It would mean Aman's organization would get two new computers and, after six months, a small business that Aman, I was sure, would find a way make a little money from.

It was an edgy project. Internet access in Turkmenistan was

restricted. There was only one service provider – the government phone company Turkmen Telekom– and probably fewer than 10 public Internet centers in the country. A few organizations, including the Red Crescent chapter in Ashgabat, had Internet access, but the government monitored and censored it.

The government restricted Internet access because it hoped to cling to power by stifling political dissent, and isolating Turkmen from each other and from the world. That was the same reason the government controlled all the newspapers and TV channels in the country and ensured that the only "news" they provided was about all the wonderful things "Turkmenbashy the Great" was doing for the people of "independent, neutral, democratic Turkmenistan" in the "Golden Age." It was also the same reason that travel, which could spread uncensored information, was restricted. In 2006, the Committee to Protect Journalists, an American NGO, named Turkmenistan the third most-censored country in the world, after only North Korea and Burma.[40] The same year, the French NGO Reporters sans Frontiers put Turkmenistan third on a list of top violators of press freedom in the world, after North Korea and Eritrea.[41]

The government controlled nearly all information within Turkmenistan's borders. The schools and universities taught students the official party line. The country had a few libraries,[42] but their collections were censored. When I visited the national library in Ashgabat, I found that its massive galleries had been mostly emptied of their contents. Their entrances were blocked with glass cases filled with copies of the *Rukhnama* and Niyazov's other books. I found one gallery with a small clutch of bookshelves that were open to the public. In the back, in an area that was off limits, I could see a messy heap of books that reached almost to the ceiling. A friend of a friend worked at the library and claimed he was allowed to bring home armloads of them to use as toilet paper.

The only gap in the government's control of information was satellite TV. For some reason – whether it was incompetence, inability, or intention – the government allowed nearly everyone in Turkmenistan to own a satellite dish. They could watch everything from BBC news to *The Jerry Springer Show*, Steven Seagal movies to MTV. Still, precious little independent domestic news was available. Even if the foreign press was interested in covering events inside Turkmenistan, government interference, intimidation, and obfuscation made it difficult to produce anything worthwhile or accurate. As far as I could tell, there was only one independent source of information about what was going on inside Turkmenistan that was widely available to Turkmen: a half-hour program called *Azatlyk Radio* (Radio Free Europe/Radio Liberty) that was available via satellite TV. It was a Turkmen language broadcast and almost everyone I knew listened to it.

The fact that the government had near-complete control over all information available in Turkmenistan and used this control to provide the people with lies and half-truths, created an interesting situation. No source of information was definitive. Books, magazines, newspapers, radio shows, television news, and government officials were all likely to provide bad information. So people were more likely to believe what they heard from neighbors, family members, and acquaintances. Conspiracy theories and rumors were treated as if they were just as valid as government statements and news reports (which may well have been the case). Foreign information sources were also assumed to be unreliable. People figured that if domestic news reports were filled with lies, then foreign news reports must be, too. The result: Aynabat was just as likely to believe her neighbor's assertion that dog meat had cured her mother's tuberculosis, as a report from the World Health Organization that found that dog meat would not cure tuberculosis.

My Internet center project was meant, in some small way, to improve this situation. On the Internet, at least, people have some control over the information they consume. They can choose sources they find trustworthy, and they can check one source against another. Despite government restrictions on Internet use, I thought there was a good possibility I would be able to open an Internet center at the Red Crescent office in Abadan for two reasons: the Red Crescent office in Ashgabat had Internet access; and the telephone company, when I had asked, said they'd be glad to provide me with Internet service.

I got Geldy to help me write the proposal for the Internet center. (As part of his new job in Ashgabat, he visited Abadan once or twice a week, so it had turned out, despite my fears, that he hadn't abandoned me entirely). When I handed Aman the finished proposal, he skipped to the last page – the budget. After shopping around in Ashgabat, I had decided I needed $600 for computers. That amount, I had found, would get me two new desktops that would be fast enough for my purposes. Aman didn't even know how to use the computer he had in his office. To him, computers were just status symbols, and he wanted as many as possible.

"You need to double the amount you have budgeted for computers," he told me. "You can't get a decent computer for $300. I won't approve this."

After listening to Aman call me lazy for months, after having him harass me for trying to fix School No. 8's heating system, after having him blackmail me for office equipment, I was fed up. I had tried to compromise, to get along. I had given him an inch and he was trying to take a mile. I grabbed the proposal from Aman's hands, crumpled it up, and threw it into the trash.

"I'm not writing any more grants for Red Crescent," I told him, and stalked out of his office and across the hall to the kitchen. Geldy, who was visiting from Ashgabat, was drinking tea with Vera. I was furious, pacing back and forth in the kitchen.

"I'm quitting," I told them. "I can't work for that fat, greedy man anymore. I'm going to ask Peace Corps to move me to a new job."

Vera got up, walked down the hallway to her office, and shut the door. She didn't want to get involved. Geldy lit a slim cigarette and put the teapot on to boil.

"Why do you take everything so seriously?" he asked me, smiling. "Don't let the undertaker make you so angry."

He made me a cup of coffee and convinced me to call my supervisor at Peace Corps and ask her for help with Aman, instead of asking for a new job. My supervisor was a Turkmen woman named Sachly. She was about 30, elegant, and unflappable. I walked home (since Aman still wouldn't let me use the office phone – "his" phone), called her, and told her what was going on. She agreed to come out the next day and try to smooth things over. I got back to Red Crescent just in time to catch Aman on his way out of the building, holding his car keys in his right hand. I told him to expect a visit from Sachly the next day. His face turned red and he stepped close to me, so that we were almost chest-to-chest.

"What did you tell her?" he asked.

"That you're a bad boss," I said looking down at him. I was easily a head taller.

"Why did you say that?"

"Because you are," I told him. "You're a bad boss and you're greedy."

He pushed past me, got into his car, slammed the door, and roared away. I went inside, packed up my things, and walked back to my apartment.

***

The winter had been cold, dark, and hard. I felt like I hadn't seen the sunshine for months. There were dead fish hanging in my bedroom. I'd been thrown out of carpet weaving class and accused of stealing a national secret. I'd spent weeks begging the government to let me heat School No. 8. My boss was trying to blackmail me by refusing to let me do any work unless I bought him office equipment. Why should I keep trying to help these people? I thought. It was their own damn country. Let them rot in it. I stalked home, looking at the ground, ignoring the kids yelling "hello! hello! hello!" at me, considering the pros and cons of taking a *marshrutka* to Ashgabat and getting on the next plane back to the United States.

My mood soon changed, though. When Olya and Denis came home from the bazaar, arms full of groceries, I told them what had happened with Aman. Olya poured some tea and put a plate of cookies on the table. Denis dealt us each six cards. As we sipped and munched and played, I griped. Olya sympathized, Denis laughed at the absurdity of it all and mocked me for thinking things would turn out differently. Soon, I was laughing, too.

Sachly arrived at Red Crescent at 9 a.m. the next day: slim and attractive, with long black hair and endless patience. Aman welcomed her with a greasy grin and motioned for her to sit down across from him. They talked for a half-hour in Turkmen, which I didn't understand. Aman would go into long explanations, pointing at me, and raising his voice. Sachly, unmoved, would reply to him soothingly, quietly. In the end, Aman agreed to approve my Internet center proposal (with its original budget) and also a proposal I'd written to paint an anti-smoking mural at the town's main bus stop. It was as if Sachly had hypnotized him. She declined his offer of a cup of tea, thanked him, got into her spotless white Peace Corps SUV, and disappeared down the road to Ashgabat.

13.
Doubt

Soon, the winter ended and the weather began to warm. Blades of grass – pale and fragile – sprouted from cotton fields and empty lots and blanketed the craggy Kopetdag. Then came the poppies, like scraps of red crepe paper waving over fields of green. Wild pink tulips pushed up out of the mountainsides. Delicate leaves sprouted from the grape vine outside my bedroom window. Tractors grumbled along the roads on their ways to plow fields, to prepare them for planting. The bazaars began to fill with fresh fruits and vegetables. Winter jackets gave way to sweaters.

After Sachly's visit, since I was no longer grounded by Aman, I went back to work. Although the school-heating project had stalled out, I still had permission from Ovez to teach in the Abadan schools. I gave English classes twice a week at School No. 1. I met with the Quartet weekly at School No. 8. I taught health classes wherever I could. It was good to be busy, to be around kids, who were not yet cynical, corrupt, and broken.

Although my day-to-day work was going well, my bigger projects were going nowhere. I had turned my two Russian language project proposals into English language grant proposals and dropped them off at the American and British embassies. But the American Embassy kept demanding rewrites of my Internet center grant designed to make it as politically inoffensive as possible. And the British Embassy had not made a decision on my health mural project and wasn't returning my calls.

To take my mind off my frustrations, I organized another mini-camp (a "seminar") at School No. 8. That, at least, was something I could accomplish. Geldy offered to get money from Red Crescent to help fund the camp. He also promised to teach a health class. When we gathered all 50 kids at the school and began, though, Geldy found an empty classroom, locked himself in it with a cup of coffee and a pack of cigarettes, and refused to do anything. I banged on the door and swore at him for a while, but I didn't have time to deal with him. Besides, moody, selfish, erratic behavior was nothing new for Geldy. I was used to it. I gave up and found someone else to teach his class.

Geldy told me later he'd never had any intention of teaching. He'd wanted to get involved in the camp because he was deep in debt to the cosmetics company Mary Kay, and the woman who was trying to collect was beginning to scare him. He'd picked up a part-time job selling Mary Kay perfumes, to help pay his bar bills. The problem was, he kept giving away the perfume (to girls he wanted to sleep with), instead of selling it. When I told him about the mini-camp, he saw an opportunity to get himself out of trouble. I told him I needed 2.5 million *manat* for the camp (about $100). He wrote a grant to Red Crescent for more than twice that amount, gave me the 2.5 million *manat* I needed, and used the rest to get Mary Kay off his back.

That kind of corruption was common within Red Crescent and probably at other organizations in Turkmenistan, too. There was a system in place meant to keep it in check; anyone who received a grant was required to submit a spending report once their project was complete, including original receipts for everything purchased with the grant money. However, everyone had a friend in a store who was glad – for a small fee or a future favor – to print up a receipt for any amount. It was common practice to inflate grants, skim a little off the top, and buy receipts to make everything balance out on the final report. By doing so, people paid electric bills, funded New Year's parties, and bought new clothes.

* * *

I was angry at Geldy. He'd used me. But it was hard to blame him. Corruption was a way of life in Turkmenistan at every level. Faced with a corrupt, oppressive, capricious, and marginally legitimate state, people ignored the laws and did whatever they could to get by. True, Geldy's motives weren't exactly pure. He didn't do it to pay for heart medicine for his aging grandmother. He did it so he could maintain his bar-hopping, clothes-shopping lifestyle and pay for his expensive slim cigarettes. Still, how could I expect him to be the only honest man in Turkmenistan?

89

Although I understood why Geldy had done what he'd done, the whole affair just added to my growing bitterness, anger, and frustration with my situation, in general. At the dinner table, I would go on long rants about the situation while Olya listened sympathetically. "They invited me to come to Turkmenistan," I would fume. "They asked me to do this job. But everything I try to do, they shut me down. They would be happier if I just sat in my room and did nothing – but I won't do that. I didn't come all the way to Turkmenistan to sit and do nothing."

I began to wonder why Peace Corps was in Turkmenistan at all. I have never been able to figure it out. American foreign policy in Turkmenistan has always seemed a little bit confused and undirected. When the Soviet Union fell, the U.S.'s first concern was to deal with Russia and Eastern Europe. Relatively little thought was given to Central Asia except to send Peace Corps volunteers there in 1993. Then, in the mid-1990s, Clinton administration officials publicly outlined a policy for the region that focused on economic and political reform, conflict resolution, energy security, and enhancing commercial opportunities for US companies. By the end of the decade, US energy companies were scrambling for opportunities to get in on the production and distribution of Caspian Sea oil and gas and the Clinton administration was doing its best to help them.

Turkmenistan has some of the largest reserves of natural gas in the world. Energy companies tried to find ways to move the gas to major markets. The Clinton administration opposed north- and south-bound pipeline routes, hoping to curb the regional power of Russia (to the north) and Iran (to the south), by reducing their influence over Turkmen gas exports. That left east- and west-bound routes. Unocal considered a route (immortalized in Michael Moore's movie Fahrenheit 9/11) that would have gone southeast through Afghanistan to Pakistan and India. Other companies worked with the Clinton administration on plans for a pipeline underneath the Caspian Sea and across the Caucasus to Turkey. Meanwhile, the Niyazov regime's atrocious human rights record was more or less forgotten. After a few years of trying to balance financial considerations, logistical realities, US government policy priorities, and Niyazov's bizarre and capricious behavior, the big energy companies lost interest and more or less withdrew from Turkmenistan.

After George W. Bush took office and al-Qaeda struck New York and Washington, D.C., on Sept. 11, 2001, though, the US needed Niyazov's help. He was the relatively secular leader of a Muslim nation with a long border with Afghanistan, which the US was planning to invade. Faced with the Bush Administration's "you're either with us or against us" ultimatum, Niyazov decided he was with us. He allowed US forces to move humanitarian aid by land through Turkmenistan and into Afghanistan. He permitted US aircraft on humanitarian missions to refuel at the airport in Ashgabat. It has also been suggested that he disregarded Turkmenistan's official neutrality and allowed US combat forces to operate from within its borders.[43] Soon, though, the US began to need Niyazov less and less. The energy companies had given up for the moment, and the military had established major bases in Kyrgyzstan, Uzbekistan, and Afghanistan.

As US interests in Turkmenistan began to fade, the Bush administration started pushing Niyazov harder to improve its human rights policies and implement democratizing reforms. Perhaps this was part of the neocons' efforts to democratize the greater Middle East region. It could also have been in part the result of efforts by evangelical Christians, an important Bush constituency, pressuring the White House to do something about the mistreatment of Protestants in Central Asia in general, and in Turkmenistan in particular. Whatever the reason, Bush began to increase the pressure for human rights reforms. When Niyazov responded to an apparent attempted coup by cracking down on the political opposition and tightening restrictions on citizens even further, the gap between the US and Turkmenistan grew wider. The US sponsored resolutions at the U.N., "expressing concern about" the Niyazov government's human rights record, and downgraded trade relations slightly between the two countries.

Despite the chill, Peace Corps Volunteers remained in Turkmenistan, teaching English and health. Why would Niyazov allow a new group of Peace Corps Volunteers to enter his country every year? With his bizarre personality cult and atrocious human rights record, he might have felt that maintaining a Peace Corps presence in his country would give him an extra measure of legitimacy in the international community as a "normal" leader of a developing country. And tight restrictions on the Volunteers once they arrived could keep them from causing too much trouble. He was also concerned about making Turkmen citizens think he was seen on the international stage as a legitimate leader. When the Clinton Administration shunned him during a 1993 visit to Washington, he faked photos of himself at a White House meeting and disseminated them in Turkmenistan.[44] Also, while I was in Turkmenistan, the (government-controlled) newspapers often ran letters to Niyazov from world leaders – including Bush – wishing him well on holidays, though I don't know if they were genuine.

Why would the US want to maintain a Peace Corps presence in such a country? Didn't American officials worry that doing so would boost Niyazov's legitimacy at home and abroad? A US Embassy staffer in Turkmenistan told me that the Peace Corps presence was "a foot in the door," for the United States. US officials may also have decided that long-term positive effects would offset any short-term negative effects. Future relations between the two countries, after all, would surely be better if Turkmen leaders were people who had formed their opinions about Americans from first-hand experience with Peace Corps Volunteers rather than from the Niyazov regime's propaganda, the *Jerry Springer Show*, or the Moscow evening news. And better relations between the two countries could help the US secure Turkmen military and political cooperation when necessary, and move Turkmen natural gas and oil to its preferred markets.

Whatever the reason for my presence, one thing was becoming clear: I had not been brought to Turkmenistan to be a development worker, to try to improve the standard of living for the people in Abadan. The Turkmen government had no real interest in having me teach health classes – or do anything else productive. Neither, as far as I could tell, did the US government. I got the impression that both sides wanted me to do as little as possible. I was just a political symbol. Maybe that was an important role, but it was a frustrating one, too. I'd quit my job at the paper in Florida because I wanted to do something. I'd arrived in Turkmenistan to find that I was expected to do nothing.

14.
Merv

Fed up and frustrated with Aman, with Geldy, with everything, when I heard that some Peace Corps Volunteers were planning to go camping for the weekend among the ruins of the ancient Silk Road city of Merv, I jumped at the opportunity to take a vacation from my life. I packed a bag, took a *marshrutka* to Ashgabat, and found a shared taxi to Mary ("mah-REE"), about five hours east.

I sat in the back seat, squished between two sweating Turkmen men in suits. We stopped at checkpoint after checkpoint; I began to look forward to them. It was nice to have a few minutes to stretch my legs while the police copied my passport information into their logbook. We followed the railroad along the base of the Kopetdag range, skirting the southern edge of the Karakum desert. We passed through Dushak and Kahka, villages where the British had fought the Bolsheviks in 1918. East of Tejen, the mountains disappeared and the country began to change from desolate scrub desert into farmland. We were entering the vast Murgab oasis.

Like all of Turkmenistan's cities except Ashgabat, with its gleaming white marble core, Mary was nothing much to look at. More wide, deserted boulevards, more anonymous concrete apartment buildings, more statues and portraits of Niyazov. I was there for only a few minutes. The taxi driver dropped me at the bus station. I met the other Volunteers, boarded a *marshrutka*, and moved on. A half-hour later we arrived in Bayramali, the nondescript modern Turkmen town next to Merv. Well, not exactly next to. The two cities – the modern and the ancient – overlapped. Bits of medieval walls stood in the yards of modern apartment buildings. Taxis and *marshrutkas* waited for customers under ancient ramparts. We convinced a driver to drop us off at our campsite and pick us up the next morning.

On the way, he took us on a tour of the area. It looked to me like a vast swath of scrub desert – something I could have seen in Nevada – dotted with big mounds of dirt and tumbles of mud bricks. The grandeur of the ancient city can only be found in books these days. Merv was built in the oasis formed by the Murgab River, after it rushes down out of Afghanistan's Hindukush Mountains and onto Turkmenistan's scorched plains, spreading out into a broad delta in the desert. People have lived in this oasis since before the Egyptians built the pyramids of Giza. The oasis, however, has moved over time. About 5,000 years ago, people lived in a city within the oasis called Margush. They lived in fired-brick houses, made elaborate pottery, and built an underground water/sewer system.

As the glaciers melted and the river receded, the delta crept southward toward the river's source. Over the centuries, humans followed the oasis, abandoning Margush and a trail of other settlements to the desert. The youngest city in this chain is Bayramali. The ruins that are called ancient Merv are the overlapping remains of at least three different walled cities, from different time periods – the oldest of which was built in the sixth century B.C. – that spread for miles over the desert.[45]

We camped near an ancient wall, which rose some 40 feet above the desert floor. There was no real campsite. We just chose a patch of sand shaded by low, shaggy saksaul trees. The wall looked like a mound of earth. In one spot, though, the Soviets had bulldozed a cut through it, revealing that it was a brick fortification with a gallery walkway, arrow slits, and occasional towers. It had just been buried in dirt over the centuries.

We unpacked our belongings, unrolling carpets to cover the dusty ground, and unpacking the groceries for the night's feast. I helped other Volunteers gather saksaul branches for a fire. As night fell, I lounged on a carpet, drinking vodka, eating *shashlyk* and cucumber-and-tomato salad, and listening to two Volunteers play guitars. Abadan and all its frustrations were far away. My belly was full of good food. I was a little drunk, and more relaxed than I'd been since leaving the United States. I grabbed a blanket and climbed an ancient wall to find a place to sleep. On top, a cool wind kept the mosquitoes at bay. In the distance, I could see the walls of the ancient citadel of Erk Gala silhouetted against the starry sky.

Everyone from the ancient Persians to the ancient Romans

had written about this city. When Alexander the Great marched east from Macedonia, conquering Persia on the way, his army seized Erk Gala and the surrounding province of Margiana from the Persians and expanded it into a Greek-style metropolis. It was eventually named Antiochia Margiana, after king Antiochus I, who ruled the Seleucid Empire (which stretched from Turkmenistan to Syria) after Alexander's death. The new city was nearly square, with walls that measured more than a mile on each side.[46] It was one of those walls that I had chosen for my bed.

After the Seleucid Empire fell, Merv lived on as a part of successive Persian empires. After Arab armies conquered Merv in 652 A.D. and added it to the vast Islamic empire that sprawled across the Middle East, it became one of the empire's major eastern cities. A Chinese army officer named Du Huan, who was held at Merv in 751-752 A.D., described it: "[Merv] is enclosed from every direction, since all round is shifting sand ... The land is fertile; its people are clean. Residences are tall and solid; market quarters are level and neat. Wherever wood is used, it is carved and patterned and plasterwork is painted with designs." It was an agricultural center that produced grapes and melons, cattle and horses, cotton and silk.[47] From 811-818 A.D., it served as the residence of the leader of the Muslim world, Caliph al-Mamun, making it the *de facto* capital of the Islamic empire.[48]

The Oghuz, a tribe of Turkic-speaking nomads that the Turkmen claim as their ancestors, did not arrive in Merv until centuries later. They swept south from the vast Eurasian steppes, perhaps from somewhere near western Mongolia. In the ninth century, they appeared in what is now southern Turkmenistan, raiding the settlements of the area's largely Iranian and Arab inhabitants. An alliance led by an Oghuz family named the Seljuks conquered Merv in the eleventh century and extended its power south and west until it ruled huge swaths of Iran, Iraq and parts of Syria, the Caucasus, and Anatolia (modern Turkey). Merv served as one of the Seljuk Empire's regional capitals and it was during this period that the city reached its "greatest glory," when "scholars, including Omar Khayyam, flocked to live there, consult its libraries and study at its observatory."[49]

Under the Seljuks, the Turkmen, as they were beginning to

be called,[50] played an important role on the world stage. In 1058 A.D., the Seljuk leader Toghril and his troops came to the aid of the Caliph, who was ruling from Baghdad at the time and had gotten himself into a tricky spot. Toghril and his army marched into Baghdad and secured the city for the Caliph who, in return, named Toghril "Pillar of the State," "Partner of the Commander of the Faithful," and "King of the East and West." At least one scholar has argued that this incident launched the Islamic tradition of dividing power between a spiritual leader (the caliph) and a secular leader (the sultan).[51]

After this moment of glory, though, the Seljuk empire didn't last long. When the Syrian geographer Yaqut al-Hamawi visited Merv in 1219 A.D., one of the first things he saw was a great blue-tiled dome, "so high as to be visible a day's march away over the plain."[52] It was the mausoleum of Sultan Sanjar, the last of the Great Seljuk rulers, who had died about 60 years earlier. Yaqut lived in the city for three years, working in its libraries, collecting material for a book. The libraries "were very easy to access and I could borrow two hundred volumes without a deposit and take them to my house," he recalled. He left the city only when he heard Chinggis Khan's army was on the way.[53]

The Mongols reached Merv in 1221 A.D., destroyed the city, and torched its libraries, Yaqut recounted sadly.[54] "[They] ordered that, apart from four hundred artisans whom they specified … and some children, girls and boys, whom they bore off into captivity, the whole population, including women and children, should be killed…" The Arab historian Ibn al-Athir put the death toll at 700,000. The Mongols then destroyed the walls, the citadel, and the mosque, and burned the head imam.[55] By the end of the fourteenth century, the city had been more or less rebuilt and Timurlane liked to stay in one of its leafy suburbs when he wasn't busy conquering central and western Asia.[56] By that time, though, the Silk Road's importance was fading, and with it, Merv's fortunes.

Of all this history, little remained by the time I arrived. Most of the city walls had been buried under blowing sands. The ruins melded into the desert, the surrounding villages, and the city of Bayramali. People carried ancient bricks away from the ruins to build outhouses and sheds. The government maintained a small military facility within the ancient walls: a few one-story blockhouses secured with locks, barbed wire, guard dogs and patrolling soldiers. Shepherds grazed their sheep, goats, and camels among the ruins. Turkmen schoolchildren visited on field trips. An occasional busload of German or Japanese tourists meandered through.

There were still a few impressive monuments left, though. Perhaps the most striking were the *kushk*s, small castles that once served as residences for the city's elite. About 20 remained, in various stages of ruin.[57] The largest was Greater Gyz Kala, which covered more ground than a football field and had corrugated mud-brick walls that reached nearly 40 feet into the sky. The mausoleum of Sultan Sanjar had recently been restored and was still quite spectacular, though its dome no longer boasted the striking blue tiles that had attracted Yaqut's attention nearly 800 years earlier. Scattered among these buildings were assorted fragments of ice houses and cisterns.

Although Merv had been named a United Nations World Heritage site, it was not protected by walls, fences, or park rangers. Imagine if you could climb the wall of the Coliseum in Rome, lay out a blanket on top and go to sleep. That's the sort of thing I felt I'd done when I woke atop a 2,000-year-old wall. The sun was just beginning to rise over the desert. Merv's ruins stretched out around me for miles. I gathered my blanket and trudged down from my wall to help the others clean up the campsite. The *marshrutka* driver from the previous day picked us up and took us back to Bayramali. From there, we each found our own way home.

15.
A Wave of Revolutions

While I was exploring Merv, Uzbekistan was boiling over. The government had arrested 23 businessmen and charged them with being Islamic radicals. Their supporters in Andijan, insisting that the charges were trumped up, took to the streets in protest. Popular uprisings had deposed the leaders of three former Soviet states in the previous year and a half, and it looked for a while like Uzbek President Islam Karimov might be next.

In November 2003, Georgia's president had been forced from power in the Rose Revolution, though I'd been living in the US at the time and hadn't noticed. During the winter, I'd watched the Orange Revolution in the Ukraine bring opposition leader Viktor Yushchenko to power. In the spring, Kyrgyzstan's president had bowed to opposition pressure – in the Tulip Revolution – and resigned. It looked like a wave of popular revolution was sweeping the former Soviet Union.

As it developed, I'd been watching closely and thinking that maybe, just maybe, the wave would reach Turkmenistan and wash Niyazov's government away. Niyazov must have also considered this prospect. He closed the country's long northern border with Uzbekistan and suspended flights between Ashgabat to Uzbekistan. Turkmen TV stations carried no news about what was happening in Andijan. I kept my bag packed, just in case something happened and I got evacuated.

Wherever I went, people were talking about Andijan. They spoke in hushed tones, always worried about who was listening. They knew that saying the wrong thing in front of the wrong person could land them in prison. No one I met thought there was much chance that the spirit of revolution would spread to Turkmenistan.

"We're too lazy," Geldy told me. "And we've got no reason to have a revolution. We have food, drink, security. What more do we need? Things are okay."

"Everyone knows things are screwed up," said my friend

Ayjamal who had been a high school exchange student in the US for a year. "But they're all afraid to do anything."

While I was riding in a taxi with Sesili one day, the taxi driver started talking about what was happening in Uzbekistan and the chances that something similar would happen in Turkmenistan. He was a crusty old Turkmen man with skin that looked like a brown paper bag someone had crumpled into a ball and then tried to smooth out again. He was just too old to be scared anymore, I guess. Although it was just the three of us in the car, Sesili tried to hush him.

"Stop it," she pleaded. "We're all going to end up in jail."

He ignored her.

"Nothing like that will ever happen here," the taxi driver said. He told a story: Niyazov's son was gambling in Monaco and lost a million dollars. The loss didn't seem to bother him at all. The man sitting next to him asked him how he could be so nonchalant about losing so much money.

"It's nothing to me," Niyazov's son supposedly said. "My father owns 5 million sheep."

"That's us," the taxi driver said ruefully. "We're the sheep."

If there had been a wave of revolutions sweeping through the former Soviet republics, Karimov stopped it on May 13, 2005. That's the day his troops opened fire on protesters in Andijan, killing hundreds of unarmed civilians, and ending the uprising. The massacre was a warning to people across Central Asia who might have been thinking about rising up to take control of their governments. If anyone in Turkmenistan had ever had the inclination to take to the streets and oust Niyazov – and I never met anyone who admitted they did – the massacre at Andijan may well have convinced them to stay home.

16.
A Small Success

Summer arrived early, pushing temperatures into the 100s. The delicate carpet of grass that had covered the countryside wilted. The poppies and tulips dried out and died. The desert sun beat the springtime into submission and scorched the earth back to its usual monochrome brown. I no longer lived in a world of mud and slush; I lived in a world of dust and heat. After months of hoping that the clouds would part for just a few hours and let the sun shine through, I began wishing that a stray cloud – just one – would float across the bleached-out blue sky and block the sun for a few moments. When I walked home for lunch from Red Crescent, I would often stop for a few moments under one of the mulberry trees lining the road to eat a handful of sweet, black berries in the shade. I usually found children with purple-stained fingers and faces sitting in the branches, stuffing themselves.

There was no reason that I could think of for the sun to be so strong, so brutal. It was the same sun that had gently warmed my skin in the US. In Turkmenistan, though, it beat down on me, sapping my energy and baking my skin to a deep brown. During the 10-minute walk between Red Crescent and my house, my metal belt buckle would become painfully hot to the touch. The old white-bearded Turkmen men protected their heads from the sun with tall wooly hats called *telpeks*. I protected myself by staying inside as much as possible. The Red Crescent office was like a cave, dark and cool. The Plotnikovs had a single air conditioner that was just strong enough to keep the spot in front of the TV cool.

My life at home had become a bit lonely. Misha and Denis were both gone. Worried about the family finances, Olya had sent Misha to Russia to find work. He wasn't earning much with his carpentry business anyway, since he spent most of his time lying in front of the TV. We'd heard nothing from him since he'd left weeks earlier. Denis had shaved his head and left to serve his mandatory two years in the army. Olya and I didn't know where he'd be sent or what he'd be assigned to do. Turkmenistan was neutral and at peace, so most soldiers spent their two years picking cotton, guarding factories, staffing checkpoints, or planting trees in the desert as part of Niyazov's quixotic quest to reforest Turkmenistan. We figured that was the kind of thing Denis would be assigned to do, too.

Still, we were worried about him. Turkmen soldiers were often underfed and poorly treated. Some young conscripts had to beg in the streets for food. Others were beaten badly by their commanding officers. Denis, a Russian city boy with a disdain for all things Turkmen, was likely to have a hard time in an army dominated by Turkmen kids from the countryside. Olya had done her part to ensure that his first days would be difficult. On the day he left, she decided she hadn't packed him enough food. She chased after him, found his troop train and walked the aisles calling his name until she found him, at which point she gave him an extra package of *piroshkis*, some medicine for his snuffly nose, and, crying, a good luck kiss on the cheek.

With Misha and Denis gone, I often found myself home alone. I was going to have to get used to it. Sasha was leaving, too – going home to live with his mother. Olya planned to escort him on his trip home and spend a couple weeks in Russia while she was there. I'd be on my own for the first time since I'd arrived in Turkmenistan. I was sad my host family was disintegrating. I'd enjoyed living in a full house, despite Misha's binges, despite Denis's bitter sarcasm, despite Sasha's hyperactivity. Luckily, I had enough work to keep my mind off the changes at home. I was teaching English twice a week at School No. 1, I was giving health classes at various schools around town, and Geldy had commissioned me to create a coloring/activity book to teach middle school kids how to avoid getting HIV/AIDS. Also, I'd won a grant from the British Embassy to pay for my health mural project.

Actually, the mural project had morphed into a billboard project. The city owned all the apartment buildings in town and the new mayor had refused to let me paint anything on any of them. Instead, he'd suggested I paint a giant metal billboard, which he'd promised to hang at the town's main bus stop. So I'd tracked down a welder in Ashgabat who was willing to make me a billboard. His shop was in the construction supply district on the north edge of the city. Stores there sold everything from windows and toilets to hammers and nails, from paint and brushes to ladders and grout.

The welder was a wiry man who couldn't have been more than five feet tall. He worked in a roofless alleyway between two buildings, which was secured at both ends by tall metal gates that I'm sure he'd made himself. The alley was crowded with stacks of sheet metal, bits of ornate fence, and barred steel doors. I'd paid him half the money in advance and he'd promised to build the giant steel sign. It was to be nine feet tall and six feet wide, with special fittings so city workers could fasten it to a concrete wall.

Now it was time to pick up the steel canvas and haul it back to Abadan. When I arrived to pick it up, though, the bookkeeper was out to lunch. The welder was only in charge of fire and steel. He told me I'd have to wait until she came back from lunch to pay. While I waited, I wandered across the street to check out the horse track that dominated the neighborhood. When I'd worked as a newspaper reporter in West Virginia, I used to drive to the dog track outside the city after work with my editor Jody. We'd drink cheap beer and bet on horse races around the country via simulcast. A couple of times, we'd road-tripped out to Keeneland Park in Kentucky's white-fence horse country, a four-hour trip. The track's buildings were made from fieldstone and surrounded by shady trees and well-trimmed lawns. I stood by the rail while I lost my money, so I could feel the thunder of the horses as they passed me on the way to the finish line.

The track in Ashgabat, the *hippodrome*, was nothing like Keeneland. Surrounded by sprawling parking lots with pavement that'd been bleached light gray by the sun, it was a utilitarian concrete and steel complex. It was deserted. I climbed up into the bleachers and looked out over the track. It was an uneven dirt oval that looked smaller than Keeneland's, surrounding an overgrown, weedy infield where a massive Turkmen sheepdog (an *alibay*) roamed. His ribs were showing. Maybe he was searching for rabbits. On the other side of the track were the stables. I could see a few horses munching on hay in a paddock. I set out across the track to visit them, hands full of rocks. I didn't need the rocks; the dog kept its distance.

The horses, called Akhal Tekes, were sleek and delicate, with long, graceful necks and chestnut or golden coats. They wandered over to the paddock fence, where they nuzzled my hands and let me pat their haunches and scratch behind their ears. I'd read about them. They were said to have been favorites of Alexander the Great, and the ancestors of the English Thoroughbred.[58] They were national symbols, parts of the country's nomadic desert-warrior past. I'd seen them in the Independence Day parade and on TV. I'd visited a monument dedicated to them in a park in Ashgabat, near the monument to the *Rukhnama*. But I'd never seen one up close before. They had been nearly wiped out during the Soviet era and were still so rare and expensive that few Turkmen could afford them. In *Sacred Horses*, Jonathan Maslow's account of his obsession with Akhal Tekes, he explained why.

As the Soviets consolidated their control in the 1920s and worked to translate communism from theory into practice, horses – like almost everything else – became the business of the state. Private ownership of Akhal Tekes was banned and the government took over their care and breeding. Many soon died of disease, starvation, and neglect. To make things worse, the Soviets decided the wiry Akhal Tekes weren't sturdy enough to serve as military mounts and began to breed them with Russian Thoroughbreds.

Akhal Tekes as a breed faced extinction and many Turkmen were appalled. To protest the Soviet policy toward the Akhal Tekes, a group of Turkmen rode their horses from Ashgabat to Moscow in 1935. It took them 88 days to cross the Karakum Desert and the Kazakh steppe and arrive in the capital. It was a trek of nearly 2,500 miles, almost as far as from Los Angeles to New York. After they arrived, they entered their horses in a race around the city and won the first 16 places.

The trek and the race impressed the Soviet authorities and, for a time, the Akhal Tekes were held in high esteem in the USSR. When World War II ended, Marshall Georgi Zhukov led the victory parade in Red Square on a white Akhal Tekke. It seemed that the breed had been saved. But things began to go wrong again in the late 1950s and early 1960s. Nikita Khrushchev, then the leader of the USSR, was determined to mechanize agriculture in his country. This meant distributing tractors and getting rid of horses, which had been used to pull plows. "The Communist party began to treat horses as nothing more than a food product," Maslow wrote. "The state farms in Turkmenistan were issued quotas for horse-flesh."[59] A few old Turkmen, rather than see the graceful Akhal Tekes turned into steaks, began to lead some of them out into the desert and release them into the wild. Many Akhal Tekes, though, ended up on dinner tables.

When the Soviet Union fell, rich foreigners moved in to buy some of the finest remaining Akhal Tekes. Niyazov imposed tight restrictions on their sale and export. There weren't many left, after all, and Turkmenistan didn't want to lose the last few. By 1998, there were only about 2,000 Akhal Tekes remaining in the world. Niyazov dedicated a national holiday to them (April 27) and put one in the center of the new nation's official seal. He gave them as gifts to foreign dignitaries, including Bill Clinton.[60] Despite Niyazov's attention to the breed, its fate seemed uncertain. Few Akhal Tekes remained and those that I saw at the *hippodrome* were so skinny their ribs showed. A groom told me that was the way they were supposed to look, but it seemed more likely that at a time when many humans were struggling to get by, the horses weren't getting enough to eat.

After an hour or so with the Akhal Tekes, I wandered back across the track, through the parking lots, to the welder's alley. The bookkeeper had returned, a 16-year-old Turkmen girl with a calculator, a pen, and some scrap paper. She took my money, pocketed it, and wrote out a receipt. The welder and a couple guys from nearby shops helped me load my billboard onto a small green truck I'd hired. I climbed into the cab with my receipt, signed and stamped permission for the project, and passport in hand, ready for the inevitable checkpoints. We fought through the city traffic and out into the countryside, windows rolled down, elbows hanging out. It was late afternoon and we were headed west. The sun was coming straight at us through the windshield. The hot breeze blew up my sleeve and across my chest, drying some of my sweat.

"So where are you from?" asked the driver, a gray-haired Turkmen man with a beer gut.

"America."

"Ah, so what do you think of the Iraq war?"

I paused before answering to think of a careful response.

At a bar a few weeks earlier, a man with a bushy black

moustache who'd been sitting on the next stool had asked me the same question. I'd launched into a long riff about how George W. Bush was a bad man and a bad president and how his war in Iraq was a disaster. The man had drained his glass of vodka, smacked it down on the bar, and glared at me, swaying a little.

"Well fuck you. I love Bush. I'm a Kurd. He freed my people," he said and walked out of the bar.

I'd learned my lesson. This time, I mildly told the truck driver that I was against the war.

"But Saddam Hussein was a bad man," he said. "Aren't you glad he's gone?"

"Saddam Hussein might have been a bad man, but the US can't go around the world invading every country that has a bad leader. Why should American soldiers die because Iraq had a bad leader?"

"I don't care if American soldiers die," the driver said, looking straight ahead. "I'm Turkmen – who are they to me? I'm just glad Hussein is gone."

We rode the rest of the way in silence. I think we'd both decided that continuing the conversation would bring nothing but trouble. When we reached Red Crescent, he waited in the truck while I went inside and rounded up a group of teenaged boys who were breakdancing in the dining hall and made them unload the billboard and carry it inside. One of them, a 16-year-old named Maksat who was always nagging me to help him transcribe Eminem lyrics, was wearing his Osama bin Laden t-shirt again, even though he knew it pissed me off. I thanked the driver, paid him, shook his hand, and waved as he drove away. Then I went looking for Shokhrat.

* * *

Shokhrat was the 17-year-old Turkmen guy that Aman had hired to replace Geldy. He was a nice kid, but he wasn't cut out for the job. He was supposed to wrangle the groups of teenaged youth volunteers that hung out at Red Crescent, organizing them to teach health classes in schools, put on holiday events for orphans – all the stuff Geldy used to make them do. He wasn't assertive enough, though. He was about 5-foot-8, quiet, and shy. He wanted to be an interior designer or a painter. He hid from the youth volunteers, leaving them to do what they pleased. He was happier alone in the kitchen, painting educational health posters. Needless to say, he was excited when I told about the billboard. It would give him an excuse to avoid the youth volunteers for weeks.

Shokhrat and I got along well. We talked boxing and art. I'd spent nine or 10 months training at a boxing gym in Florida (I'd never fought, just sparred a few times). He'd spent two years training at the local sport center. We talked about Roy Jones Jr. and he lent me a videotape of the 1974 Muhammad Ali-George Foreman "Rumble in the Jungle." I'd done some painting and flirted with art school in Boston for a semester. Shokhrat's dad was a professional artist who was teaching him how to paint. He always promised to show me his work, but never got around to it. I think he was too shy.

One Saturday, Shokhrat convinced Aman to give him a morning off and took me to the new art museum in Ashgabat. He'd heard it had a real Rembrandt. The museum was built from white marble and reflective glass and topped by a turquoise and white dome – it was part of Niyazov's new Ashgabat city center. There were no other visitors, but the museum didn't feel empty because there were two docents loitering in every gallery.

I liked the modern Turkmen art on the first floor the best. The paintings' colors were bright, their lines strong, their subjects historical, and their tone martial. One showed a Turkmen mother in a *koynek* leading two strapping Turkmen lads into a Soviet recruiting office, to sign them up to go fight the Germans in World War II. Another showed the doomed Teke soldiers making their stand against the Russians at Geokdepe. There was also a painting of a company of Turkmen cavalrymen in full armor slaughtering Christians during the First Crusade.

Shokhrat wasn't interested in the first floor. He spent his morning with the European art on the second floor, wandering through the galleries, hands in his pockets, pausing in front of the pieces he liked. I joined him for a little while. The European works in the museum were nothing special. Most were attributed to "Unknown Artist." Plaques next to the paintings offered

106

descriptions in English, which were riddled with mistakes. A painting that showed a ship going down in a storm, for example, was labeled "Sheep Wheck." I later pointed out these mistakes to the museum staff and offered to help correct them. They said they'd call me but never did. They probably decided that there was no need, since there were no translation errors in Niyazov's Golden Age.

After our visit to the museum, Shokhrat and I spent three weeks painting the billboard. We worked from a design I'd drawn up months earlier and submitted to Aman, Abadan city hall, and the British Embassy. I'd chosen an anti-smoking theme because smoking was a widespread public health problem in Turkmenistan, but also for strategic reasons. In 1999, Niyazov had banned smoking in public "in name of the health of the nation." Violators were to be fined a month's salary.[61] This meant that smokers had to hide behind buildings and bushes so the police wouldn't catch them. It also meant that an anti-smoking project was likely to be approved. Geldy helped me insert a paragraph into my proposal about how the billboard would support the wise policies of "the Great Turkmenbashy" and, sure enough, I got permission.

The design showed a clean-cut Turkmen man stepping on an oversized pack of cigarettes. He was carrying a bag of groceries in one hand and a bag of clothing in the other. Turkmen text across the top of the billboard said: "Smoking a pack a day for a year will cost you 2,190,000 *manat* [about $88]. Don't you have better things to spend your money on?" More text across the bottom explained the health risks. Then, in big red letters in the middle, it said "Quit!" Shokhrat painted the man; I was in charge of the pack of cigarettes and the text. Some of the Red Crescent volunteers helped us with the background.

When we finished, Aman called city hall and told the mayor that the billboard was ready to be hung at the bus stop. Weeks passed and nothing happened so Aman called city hall again. This time the mayor said he needed to see the billboard – not a design, the actual billboard – before he could authorize city workers to hang it anywhere. So I tracked down my friend Omar, who managed landscaping crews for the city, and he assigned some of his men to help me. Eight of us carried the giant steel slab across town, sweating and cursing, and up the stairs to the second floor of city hall. We left it in the hallway outside the mayor's office.

Within a few days, it was hanging at the bus stop. Every morning, old Turkmen women in *koynek*s, young soldiers in fatigues, business men in suits, and children in their school uniforms, stood and stared at the billboard as they waited for their buses. There was nothing else like it in Abadan. My host family and friends congratulated me for finally managing to get something done. I made Geldy – who had insisted that the mayor would never, ever, hang the billboard – buy me a beer.

17.
This Is Not a Camp

I am a slow learner. When I applied for permission to run a five-day event in Abadan after school ended, I called it a "camp." I'd forgotten what Ovez had taught me: to avoid trouble, call it a "seminar," an "event," an anything – just not a camp. Being a plainspoken person, when I wrote a proposal for a week-long day-camp, I called it a week-long day-camp. Since I planned to invite 50 kids to meet me at the sports center every day to play soccer, volleyball, Frisbee, and kickball and then sit through short seminars on why it's good to play sports and eat well and how not to get AIDS or tuberculosis, I called it a sports/health camp. At first, my indiscretion seemed to go unnoticed.

I found 50 campers who wanted to attend. I also found funding. The costs were pretty low because the sport center's director had agreed to waive the entrance fee for our campers. Mostly, I just needed to pay for lunch for the campers and counselors every day. Geldy had managed to get a grant from Red Crescent Ashgabat because he worked in the AIDS program and the camp had something to do with AIDS education (I think he skimmed some money off the top to buy some new clothes). I contributed some money I'd earned from an article I'd written for an American newspaper about living in Turkmenistan.

Geldy, smooth talker that he was, took responsibility for getting permission for the camp from Abadan city hall. I was in charge of the Peace Corps-related paperwork. We both failed. Geldy didn't meet any resistance at city hall. He just couldn't get an answer. I got an answer, but it wasn't a good one. Two weeks before camp was supposed to start, someone at Peace Corps must have decided that it was too easy for Volunteers in Turkmenistan to run summer camps. So he or she started requiring signed permission slips from all campers' parents and signed "memorandums of understanding" from each organization involved with a camp. The parental permission slips were no problem, but there was no way I was going to get officials from

Red Crescent, Abadan city hall, and the sport center to all sign memorandums of understanding within two weeks. At best, it would take months of meetings, pleading, and frustration. More likely, they'd just refuse.

When I took a *marshrutka* to Ashgabat to tell my supervisors at Peace Corps that I was canceling my camp, I got an unexpectedly pragmatic and useful response from a friend there. He reminded me of the lesson Ovez had taught me.

"Sure," he said. "Cancel your *camp*. It sounds like a good *event*, though."

He winked.

The campers had already registered. We had the funding in hand and the venue reserved. Several other Peace Corps Volunteers had already made plans to travel to Abadan to work as counselors. So we decided to go ahead with it, even without permission. We figured that the worst thing that could happen was that the kids would get one good day at camp and then Peace Corps or city hall would catch on and shut us down. And one day was better than no days. So I continued with the preparations, making only one small concession to the American and Turkmen bureaucratic grinches. I'd been planning to divide the campers into four teams, which would compete for points on the sports fields and in the seminars throughout the week. I'd bought black, white, orange, and gray t-shirts to identify the teams. Now I took the shirts to a screen printer and had the words "This is Not a Camp," emblazoned in English across the front of each one.

This clever camouflage must have worked. A reporter and photographer from the state-run newspaper *Nitranyii Turkmenistan* came to do a story about the camp. The reporter interviewed me. The photographer separated the Turkmen girls in their ankle-length *koynek*s from the Russian girls wearing mini-skirts with g-strings showing above their waistlines. Then he spent an hour posing the Turkmen girls with some Turkmen boys so that they all looked like they were in mid-soccer game. In the end, the paper ran a snapshot I'd taken of the campers grinning in their "This is Not a Camp" t-shirts. I was sure someone at city hall would see the paper and catch on, but nothing happened. Then some of the staff from Peace Corps visited the camp. I was sure someone was going to ask for my memorandums of understanding, but nothing happened.

In fact, the camp went smoothly. Each morning, we met at the sport center and spent a few hours playing under the burning sun, in the 105-degree heat. When I was planning the camp, I'd forgotten to take the weather into account. Geldy had helped me with the planning but he didn't play sports. He'd assumed that anyone who was crazy enough to run around in circles for no reason would be just as happy doing it under the summer sun as at any other time. We all drank water by the liter and looked forward to our turns on the indoor volleyball court. Geldy sat in the shade chain-smoking, watching us sweat.

There was only one hitch during the whole camp. The campers were dominating the sport center every day. They used the volleyball court, the soccer field, and the two paved parking lots (for Frisbee and kickball). On the third day of camp, a fat Turkmen man with a three-day beard and a whistle around his neck pulled me aside. He looked like a coach, but he didn't introduce himself.

"You've used the sport center long enough," he said. "My team needs it. It's time for you to go."

I had no idea who he was. He could have been the coach of the Turkmen Olympic soccer team. All I knew was that he was rude and he wasn't the director of the sport center. So I decided to bluff him.

"Okay," I said. "I'd be glad to get out of your way. I just need the proper paperwork. You know how it is. You bring me your letter of permission to use the sport center and it's all yours."

He never came back.

* * *

After my sports camp was over, I packed my things and hit the road. I'd agreed to travel up to the northeastern city of Turkmenabat to work as a counselor at my friend Leo's English immersion camp. I'd also signed up to be a counselor at a Model United Nations camp at Chuli. After living at those overnight camps for about a month, I was planning to return to Abadan and spend a week commuting to an arts day-camp in a village near Ashgabat.

The first stretch was an eight-hour ride from Abadan to Turkmenabat. The taxi that took me from Ashgabat to Mary was not air-conditioned. The driver had lied to me, to all of us – there were four passengers packed into the little Lada. As we bumped along the by-now-familiar road through Anew, Dushak, Kahka, and Tejen, I sweated and dozed in the heat. It was 110 degrees out. Children sold cold drinks at checkpoints: water, soda, and *chal,* a mixture of camel's milk yogurt and soda water, which is sour and refreshing. I drank bottle after bottle of water. I felt sorry for the poor conscripts standing at the checkpoints in the burning heat. I kept my eye out for Denis.

In Mary, I changed taxis. This time I chose a roomy Toyota and made the driver prove to me that the air conditioner worked before we left the city. We rode north through the Karakum. It was remote country. For three and a half hours I saw almost nothing outside my window except for rolling sand dunes dotted with saksaul and camel thorn. The desert was pristine and beautiful, the sand fine and soft. I watched it slide by my window, wishing we could stop so I could get out and go for a walk. It looked so quiet, so peaceful, I thought.

When we reached Turkmenabat, I found that it was a ribbon of a city hugging the south bank of the Amudarya River. In length and character, the river was a lot like the Mississippi. It was capricious, though. It had always flowed northwest out of the Hindukush, past Turkmenabat, to the Khoresmian oasis, near the present day city of Dashagouz. Its course from there varied over the centuries. Sometimes it flowed north to the Aral Sea, providing that salty pool with the majority of its water. Other times, it turned southwest, leaving the Aral thirsty, filling a huge lake called Sarykamysh, and spilling over into a channel that led to the Caspian.[62]

When the Spanish ambassador Ruy Gonzalez de Clavijo visited the area in 1405 A.D., the river flowed into the Caspian and had done so for quite some time.[63] By the time Anthony Jenkinson, an English traveler, visited the area in 1558 A.D., the river had changed its mind and turned back toward the Aral Sea.[64] It may have been the natural wanderlust of a mighty river cutting a course through nothing more constraining than loose sand that caused it to turn south in the fourteenth century and head back north in the sixteenth century. It is also possible that when Chinggis Khan conquered Khoresm in the thirteenth century, his army's destruction of its dams and irrigation systems convinced the river to abandon the Aral for the Caspian and that the reconstruction of the waterworks corrected the river's course.

The city itself was once a stop on the Silk Road. The tenth-century Arab geographer Mohammed Abul-Kassem ibn Hawqal called it "a fertile and pleasant little town, of great importance by reason of constant passage of caravans."[65] It used to be called Amul, but after the Mongols destroyed it, it was rebuilt as Charjou. By the time I arrived, Niyazov had changed its name to Turkmenabat and it was just another provincial capital, just another Soviet-era, pre-fab concrete city.

The camp was held in a three-story brick boarding school in the middle of the city. It had been built in the 1970s and had aged well. It was shabby but clean. There were classrooms on the first floor and bunkrooms on the second and third floors. A high brick wall separated the school, some sports fields, and a dining hall from the surrounding neighborhoods. The 80 or so campers were divided into "cabins" named after American states. I was assigned to the Alabama cabin, along with an Alabaman Volunteer named Mike. We gave our kids temporary "camp names" related to their adoptive state (Martin Luther King Jr., Redneck, Blackeyed Pea, etc.) and taught them Alabama history and geography.

We woke our Alabamans each morning at 7 a.m. and drove them in a sleepy herd downstairs to join all the other campers at the morning assembly. Then they spent their mornings and early afternoons rotating through a series of classes: journalism, English, etiquette, yoga – whatever the counselors wanted to teach and the kids wanted to learn. The late afternoon, when the sun had cooled a little, was time for sports. In the evenings, the Volunteers organized elaborate group activities. Lights out was at 10 p.m.

The group activities were probably the most popular: a scavenger hunt, a quiz show, a live version of the reality TV show *Survivor*. My favorite was the carnival. We set up a midway on tables set up on a paved yard behind the school. Counselors wore costumes. I helped run a watermelon seed spitting contest from behind a table stacked with piles of sticky green and pink melon rinds. A group of girls ran a "kiss-o-gram" service, carrying pecks on the cheek (with plenty of red lipstick) from admirers to admirees.

During the days, I taught classes. In my journalism class, I staged a fake murder and had my students write articles about it. I picked one boy to pretend to be a celebrity he knew everything about (he chose Eminem) and had him sit in a creaky chair for a half-hour while the other students pelted him in questions so they could write profiles. At the end of the course, we used giant sheets of paper and magic markers to publish a single newspaper, which we hung in the hallway for the whole camp to read.

I also taught a class about the American political system. In the section on participation in government, I had the kids brainstorm about what they'd like to change about their camp. They decided that they wanted a later bedtime. I had them collect campers' signatures on a petition and present it to Leo, one of the camp's directors. Leo, who had a slightly cruel sense of humor, told them to stop disrupting classes by gathering signatures or he'd throw them out of camp. They were terrified. On the last day of camp, though, he pushed bedtime back to 11 p.m.

Keeping one step ahead of 80 teenagers every day for two weeks was exhausting. We had to be up a little bit earlier than them every morning, wake them up, make sure they were doing what they were supposed to be doing all day long, send them to bed, and make sure they didn't sneak out in the middle of the night. They were teenagers, after all. Turn your back on them for a moment and they'd be climbing in each other's windows carrying bottles of vodka. If the day-to-day work of running the camp weren't enough, we had to cope with two mutinies, an epidemic, and an earthquake, too.

The first mutiny came early in the camp. In addition to Peace Corps Volunteers, there were local teachers working as counselors. (Helping to run the Alabama cabin with Mike and I, for example, was a 35-year-old English teacher named Berdi, who was obsessed with Dire Straits front man Mark Knopfler). One of them had apparently come to the camp just to get some time off from work and away from home. She refused to do anything useful, so the camp directors, who were Peace Corps Volunteers, told her to

114

go home. Some of her colleagues were indignant when they found out. They brought it up at a counselors' meeting after the campers had gone to bed one night.

"You give us all this big talk about democracy and then you didn't consult us when you kicked her out," one said.

"This is not a democracy," Leo replied. I couldn't tell if he meant the camp or Turkmenistan.

A couple of the angry teachers left the camp the next day in protest. We distributed the extra work and went on without them.

We had another rebellion when a well-liked but unruly Jewish kid with the camp name "Redneck" got sent home for repeatedly breaking the rule against speaking Russian (it was an English immersion camp, after all). Other campers made posters to protest the decision: "Counselors, Human Rights, One [More] Chance for Red Neck! [signed] From All Campers." Teaching civil disobedience has its downside.

The epidemic struck at night. I woke to find Black Eyed Pea leaving the cabin and most of the other campers already gone.

"Where are they all?" I asked him.

"In the bathroom," he said, rushing out the door.

I looked out my third-floor window at the whitewashed outhouse building behind the school. There were kids lined up five and six deep for a turn on the squatters. The boys' lines moved much more quickly and several times I saw a girl who just couldn't wait anymore run around to the boys' side and push her way to the front of the line and into one of the stalls. Most of the camp had food poisoning. I was up for hours, forcing kids to drink water and re-hydration solution.

The earthquake hit at night, too. My Alabama boys were in bed and I was at the nightly counselors' meeting. I was lying on the floor, waiting for it to end. I hate meetings; they're usually a waste of time. Then the windows started to rattle and the floor trembled. My first thought was that there'd been a powerful thunder clap. Then someone yelled "earthquake" and everyone started running for the exits. With a few other counselors, I ran upstairs, rousted the kids out of bed, and led them out of the building. We spent the next two hours sitting on the playground waiting to see whether the old school would fall down, whether there would be an aftershock, trying to figure out what to do.

115

Kids in their pajamas stood in tight circles on the crumbly old basketball court, sleepy but excited, all talking at once. At first, my Alabama boys sat in a row on a bench. The earthquake had knocked out the power and they spent a while arguing about whether all the planes in the area would crash without help from the ground-based navigation systems that had been disabled. Pretty soon, though, they noticed that everyone else was standing except them. They had a conference and decided to give up their seats. They chose the prettiest girls in the area and offered them the bench. They'd been taking the etiquette class and, apparently, paying attention. The school didn't fall down and there were no aftershocks, so eventually we all went back to bed.

* * *

A few days later, the camp ended. I said goodbye to the campers, stuffed my clothes into my backpack and hit the road again. I rode back across the Karakum and changed taxis in Mary. On the road to Ashgabat, my taxi stopped at a gas station. (Gas, which was subsidized by the government, cost about 4 cents a gallon). I got out to stretch my legs as the attendant filled the tank. The station was at the corner of the highway and a side road that led to Kahka.

I'd heard there was a beautiful old mosque in Kahka, but I also knew that it was in a restricted zone on the Iranian border and that I didn't have the right documents to go there. I peered down the side road. There wasn't a checkpoint or uniform in sight. I paid my taxi fare, retrieved my backpack from the trunk, and started walking. I don't know why I did it. I knew I was breaking the rules, but I just didn't care.

The road was lined with trees and led straight toward the towering Kopetdag Mountains. Kahka, which looked much smaller than Abadan, was probably less than a mile off the highway. I stopped the first person I saw and asked for directions to the old mosque. In a few minutes I was standing at a tiny, one-room mosque that seemed to belong in New Mexico or Mali. It looked like it was made from adobe, with the ends of support poles poking out of the mud. It was crowned with an adobe dome pierced by a single window, and decorated with an intricately carved double door. The caretaker said it was 150 years old but didn't know anything else about it. He told me there were even better things to see in Kahka and flagged down a taxi to take me on a tour. Across the highway from Kahka was an old fortress with sand-covered walls, a miniature version of Merv's ruins. A few miles west along the highway were the remains Abiverd, a once-prosperous stop on the Silk Road. The ground around its ruined houses and fortress was sprinkled with glazed shards of pottery.

When I'd finished seeing the sights at Kahka, I went to the bazaar, found a taxi to Ashgabat, and continued on my way. My illicit sightseeing jaunt had gone well. No one seemed to have noticed that I'd violated the government's ridiculous travel rules, just as no one seemed to have noticed my illegal sports/health camp. I was beginning to suspect that the Turkmen government was not as omniscient and vindictive as I'd been led to believe.

I was half-disappointed. I assumed that if I got into enough trouble, I'd get kicked out of Turkmenistan. After all my troubles in Abadan, I was pretty fed up with the country and wouldn't have minded. Whatever the consequences, though, it felt good to stop living like a prisoner in an invisible cage, to abandon my paranoia and anxiety. I decided to see what else I could get away with. Before reporting to camp at Chuli, I rode a *marshrutka* to Darvaza to look for the pit of fire. At first I thought I'd gotten away with that trip, too. But when Geldy showed up at the Chuli drunk a few days later, he told me the KNB had been to my home and to Red Crescent asking questions about my travels. Heading home from Chuli after camp, I felt ambivalent: half hoping I was about to get kicked out of the country, half fearing it.

18.
Robbed

While I'd been away for the summer, Olya had gone to Russia to bring Sasha home to his mother. She'd also tracked down Misha and dragged him back to Turkmenistan. When I got home from camp in Chuli at mid-day, he was sitting at the kitchen table drunk, watching TV and chain-smoking. From the overflowing ashtray, it looked like he'd been there for a while. He probably hadn't been sober since he'd left Abadan in the spring. I dropped my backpack in my bedroom and sat down at the table with him to drink a cup of tea. He looked up at me, eyes glazed.

"They've been looking for you," he slurred. "Called me into their office. Asked me how many tape recorders and cameras you have."

"They?"

"The KNB."

"Well, tell them whatever you want."

"I'm not telling those whores anything. Call me into the office. Order me around. Fuck them."

"I'm just saying. I've got no secrets. Don't bother lying for me."

"Fuck them. Gimme 5,000 *manat*, will you?"

I gave it to him. He walked down the hallway with his hand on the wall for balance and out the front door. Off to get another bottle. I wouldn't see him for the rest of the day.

Olya came home from work in the evening. She looked tired and worn – more than usual. We puttered around the kitchen making dinner. I sliced onions, she thawed some frozen chicken legs, and we traded stories about our summers. It turned out that before she'd gone to Russia she'd visited Denis. He was posted in a town called Garragula in a restricted area on the Iranian border. She'd spent weeks getting permission to make the trip. When she'd arrived, she'd found Denis was doing well. His commander had assigned him to be a troubleshooter for the base's computers, a cushy job.

While in Garragula, Olya had been shocked to run into her

former secretary from the paint factory – the one who had disappeared. She was an attractive, 18-year-old girl from Ashgabat named Orazgul, half Tajik and half Turkmen. She'd simply stopped coming to work one day. When Olya had called her parents, they'd said they hadn't seen her, either, but had refused to call the police. Olya had been puzzled by Orazgul's parents' reaction, but there'd been nothing she could do except wonder what happened to Orazgul. In Garragula, she'd found out.

Orazgul had arranged to cruise around town with another woman from the paint factory after work one day, just for fun. The woman's brother had agreed to drive. When they'd stopped at a checkpoint, the woman had jumped out and slammed the door. The brother had sped away with Orazgul still in the car, taken her to Garragula, and told her that she was going to marry him. It had been a bride kidnapping, a traditional practice in some parts of Central Asia. Banned in Soviet days, it had made a modest comeback after independence, though it was still rare in Turkmenistan. Orazgul had contacted her parents, but found them unhelpful (she'd suspected that they were complicit in the kidnapping). So she'd decided to make the best of her situation; she'd refused when Olya offered to help her escape.

When Olya finished telling me Orazgul's story and I finished telling her about the earthquake in Turkmenabat, there was a long silence. The chicken legs sizzled in a pot on the stove, the TV blared, the fan whirred.

"Sam, I want you to forgive me."

"For what?"

"Forgive me first, and then I'll tell you what I did."

"Okay ... I forgive you. What did you do?"

"Well, when I saw my daughter in Russia, she was very sick. She needed an operation. So when I got back I went into your room and ... well, I went into your room and I took $200 and sent it to her."

We stood there in the kitchen, sweating, watching the chicken cook. I was angry, but I didn't know what to say. She'd stolen a lot of money from me. I got about $80 a month from Peace Corps and it was enough to cover my rent, food, clothing, and incidental expenses. She'd taken more than two months' salary

119

from me. It hadn't been hard for her to steal it. I'd left the $500 of just-in-case cash that I'd brought with me from the US hidden among the books on the shelf in my room. I never bothered to lock my door, since Olya had a key anyway. So she'd just walked in, searched through my room, and taken what she needed.

"I wish you'd waited until I got home. I would have given you the money."

"It was an emergency."

I stalked down the hall to my room.

"You said you would forgive me," she called as I closed my door.

We never sat down and talked about the money. We were busy, and avoiding each other. We had words about it as we passed each other in the mornings, on the way to work, in the evenings on the way to bed.

In the apartment building's stairwell:

"When can you pay the money back?"

"I don't know. Misha's not working. Look, I'm late to work."

In the kitchen doorway:

"What if you pay me a little every month?"

"Do you want tea?"

After a while, I realized she wasn't going to pay me back. When I confronted her, she admitted as much. I was furious. I'd lived with her for nearly a year. I'd thought she was my friend. I'd trusted her. And she'd robbed me. I yelled at her, calling her a thief, telling her she was a bad person. When I ran out of cruel words in Russian, I switched to English and kept going. I told her I was moving out. She stood in the doorway to my room, watching as I crashed around, throwing my belongings into bags. I cut my still-incomplete carpet off of the loom and stuffed it into a backpack. I couldn't carry the loom by myself and I had no one to help me.

"You don't have to go," she said, looking at the floor.

"Don't have to go!? You robbed me."

"I'm not a thief."

"You took $200 from my room without asking. You're a thief!"

I didn't have anywhere to go, but I wanted to get out of the Plotnikovs' house as soon as possible. When I'd arrived, the house had been full and happy. We had family dinners every night, went for walks in the evenings, helped each other out, cheered each other up. Somehow, without my noticing, it had all slipped away. I'd ended up living with a bitter alcoholic and a worn out thief. I had no where to go, so Ana and Sesili offered to let me stay with them for a couple weeks while I looked for something more permanent.

I told the Peace Corps security officer in Ashgabat that Olya had robbed me. He was a kind, middle-aged Turkmen man named Aman with glasses and a paunch who, coincidentally, lived in Abadan and knew Olya. He had a talk with her and a few days later, she showed up at Ana and Sesili's. We stood in the front hall. I didn't invite her in.

"Aman came to see me," she said. "Here."

She handed me the same pair of hundred dollar bills – they had the same tears and stray markings – that had gone missing from my room. She'd never sent the money to her daughter in Russia. Maybe her daughter had never even been sick. Then she pushed a handwritten document at me. I read it. It said that I acknowledged that she'd paid me back.

"He said I had to bring him this."

I signed it and gave it back to her. I never spoke to her again. I only saw her once more, on the street near the bazaar. We both looked away and kept walking. I never figured out why Olya had robbed me. Maybe she had just needed the cash. Maybe she'd thought I owed it to her. Maybe she'd wanted me to leave, but hadn't been able to bring herself to ask me to move out, so she'd taken the money to drive me out. Whatever her reason, I wish she hadn't done it.

* * *

Living with the Burjanadzes turned out to be even more hectic than living with the Plotnikovs had been, back when we'd all been together, when everything had still been good. There was a constant stream of women knocking on the door, pleading with Ana to ask her cards for answers to their questions: Is my husband cheating on me with the neighbor? Where's the wedding ring I lost last week while I was cheating on my husband with my co-worker?

Will my husband ever get off the couch and get a job? Will my next child be a boy or a girl? Ana griped and grumbled but obliged every one of them. They usually paid her for her time, after all. As she sat at the kitchen table telling fortunes, there was almost always a small herd of cats and kittens circling her chair, begging for scraps and attention, and a meal cooking on the stove.

The apartment's walls and ceilings were stained, streaked and peeling. A plumbing problem somewhere upstairs had caused a flood the year before and Ana didn't have the money to repair the damage. There was no air conditioner, so the place was stifling. There was no phone; to make a call we had to walk down to the post office. There was no hot water. I had to heat tap water on the stove in a metal bucket, carry it to the *banya*, mix it with some cold water to get the right temperature, and pour it over myself with a ladle. I slept in the back bedroom and Ana and Sesili slept on a couch and a bed in the living room, under a huge photograph of a waterfall.

Ana usually went to bed in the early hours of the morning and didn't rise until midday. She couldn't get any time to herself during the day because of all her visitors, she explained, so she stayed up late reading, thinking, and planning. Before I moved in and started paying rent, the Burjanadzes had scraped out a living in bits and pieces. The previous winter they'd sold salads at the bazaar, but when the summer had arrived, the salads began to spoil in the heat before they could sell them. So they had to make do with Ana's fortune-telling money and whatever they could make from the socks, shawls and scarves they knitted and sold at Tolkuchka. I think Ana's brother, who lived across town, also helped them out when he could.

While the Plotnikovs' few friends and acquaintances were Russians, the Burjanadzes welcomed Turkmen, Russians, Koreans, Uzbeks, and Georgians into their home. Ana just wanted smart and interesting people to talk to and didn't care who they were or where they were from. At the Plotnikovs, I'd spent a lot of time reading, which suited me fine. People tire me out. Ana was never alone and couldn't understand why anyone would ever want to be. She talked to me nonstop, often carrying on conversations with me even as she read fortunes.

She told me stories about working in the carpet factory in the Soviet days, when all the mechanical looms were up and running and the factory floor was packed with 1,800 people. (When she took me to visit the factory, there were only a few dozen employees and a handful of looms working; the rest of the shop floor was dark and covered in dust). She told me how her father had come to Turkmenistan from Georgia after the 1948 earthquake with a construction crew assigned to help rebuild Ashgabat and had never left. She told me about the men she knew in town who had been on one of the many teams sent from across the Soviet Union to help clean up the mess in Chernobyl, Ukraine, after the nuclear reactor there melted down in 1986, and how some had came back sterile and others had later had deformed babies.

She was a great storyteller, animated and ironic. I loved listening to her, but at first, before I had built up my endurance, she gave me a headache. My brain just couldn't handle three- and four-hour stretches of conversation in Russian. I'd plead fatigue and try to go hide in my room and read, but Ana would just follow me and keep talking. Eventually, I learned to be direct. "Ana," I'd tell her. "You're hurting my head. Stop talking to me for a while." She would turn to Sesili or whoever else was in the apartment and continue her story without missing a breath.

***

With the summer ending and my summer camps over, it was time for met to get back to work at Red Crescent. The weather had cooled a little and the sun had lost its burning edge. The temperatures were still in the 90s, but when I was outside I no longer felt like the sun was boring a hole in the top of my head. At the back of the bazaar, old men sat on carpets in the shade and played chess or backgammon or checkers. The gardens outside my new apartment building were lush and full. Crinkly orange squash flowers bloomed, heavy purple-black eggplants gleamed, red peppers ripened, bees swarmed around bunches of grapes. I could see why Olya had been so enchanted by Turkmenistan when she had visited from Siberia back in the 1960s. In late summer, at least, it really was a land of plenty.

123

At Red Crescent, nothing had changed. When I arrived one morning at 8 a.m., I found Aman lounging at his desk, reading his newspaper. He grunted a greeting at me and told me I needed to write a new work plan. Vera, Aynabat, and Shokhrat, who were sitting in the kitchen drinking tea, asked me about my summer travels. We sat and chatted for a while and then they went back to work. It took me a few days to get my bearings. I visited Geldy in Ashgabat and Ovez at the school district headquarters. I made some phone calls to embassies and nongovernmental organizations to check on my various pending grant applications. Eventually, I got an idea of what my fall was going to look like. There was some bad news and there was some good news.

The bad news was that, with the school-heating project dead, Ovez had rescinded my permission to teach at the schools. That meant I had very little to do. I couldn't resume my English classes at School No. 1, my weekly meetings with the Quartet, or my health classes. The good news was that it looked like I might soon have something else to occupy my time. Before I'd hit the road for camp season, the American Embassy had approved the grant I'd written with Geldy to fund an Internet center at Red Crescent in Abadan. I'd submitted the grant and the letter of approval to the Ministry of Justice. Now the ministry had approved the project and it was time to pick up the money and get to work.

I met Geldy at his Red Crescent office in Ashgabat one afternoon and we went to the American Embassy to pick up the cash. The building was fenced in and guarded by irritable men who were always blowing whistles at loitering pedestrians and lingering drivers. It was not a welcoming place. The first time Geldy and I had gone to meet with the grants officer, she'd greeted us in the guardhouse, next to the metal detector, and refused to allow Geldy into the building. A bulletin board on the outside of the fence informed passersby that American embassies in Central Asia were targets for terrorism and that, therefore, standing near one put the reader at risk. This time, though, they allowed us inside. We passed through security, entered the building, and picked up $2,050 in cash. As we left the building, Geldy handed it to me.

"Hold onto this. You know me, I'd just spend it," he said. "I'd go to Thailand for vacation or something. And then I'd have to fake the grant report and you'd be angry at me and I'd feel bad."

We both knew he was right. I pocketed the money.

To spend it, I had to change it into *manat*, so I did what Peace Corps Volunteers typically did when they had large amounts of dollars they needed to change (amounts too large for the bazaar ladies): I called George. He met me outside the Peace Corps office in a nice new Toyota sedan. He was a middle-aged guy with a mask of dark stubble, wearing an earplug in one ear, which was attached to a cell phone in a hip holster. He had a leather briefcase on his lap. He looked straight out the windshield as he spoke.

"How much do you want to change?" he asked.

"Two thousand," I said, a little nervous. "And fifty … two thousand and fifty."

He clicked open his briefcase and looked at the stacked bundles of 10,000-*manat* bills inside. Although 10,000-*manat* bills were the largest denomination available, they were only worth about 40 cents each.

"We're gonna have to go to the trunk," he said.

We got out and walked around behind the car. George popped the trunk. Inside were bundles of 10,000-*manat* bills stacked like firewood. He grabbed handfuls of the bundles, counting them as he dropped them into the bag I'd brought along. When he was done, we shook hands and I walked away with a grocery bag that looked like it was stuffed with a jumbo-sized bag of tortilla chips. I took it home and hid it under my desk, knowing it was a bad idea to keep that much money in the house. After all, my previous host family had robbed me.

I didn't have many choices, though. There were safes available at the Peace Corps office, but they were meant for short-term use only. I didn't know how long it would take me to spend the grant money, but it would probably be months. And I couldn't take the money to a bank, since banks were completely unreliable.

Peace Corps wired my salary to the bank in Abadan every month and picking it up was often a hassle. Sometimes the bank was closed for no apparent reason. Other times the teller asked me to come back on another day because the bank was "out of money." Since I was a foreigner, my withdrawals required the bank manager's approval and, once, he had flatly refused to release my money. I returned every day for a week to try again, but the guard at the barred front entrance refused to let me in. Finally, I ran out of cash and just got fed up. I stood outside the door, holding onto the bars and yelling for the manager to come down and give me my money – which he did. All that was over $80; I wasn't about to entrust the bank with $2,050. So I left it under my desk.

The first thing I had to do was fix up the Red Crescent "youth center," which Aman had agreed to let me use for my Internet center. It was a three-room basement apartment in an anonymous concrete apartment building across the street from the main Red Crescent office, where I usually worked. It had no windows, no paint, no furniture, no heat, no air conditioning, and no lights. All it had was a strong smell of sewage, which emanated from a pipe in a hole in the concrete floor.

Aman had twice received funds from Red Crescent in Ashgabat to renovate the apartment so the youth volunteers who were always breakdancing and gossiping in the main office could use it, instead. Each time, he had pocketed the cash and sent a report to Ashgabat about all the wonderful progress he'd made and how much the youth volunteers appreciated it. Once, a monitoring team had come to see the results. Aman claimed to have forgotten the key to the youth center at home. They never returned.

Geldy and I drew up a plan for the renovations. We would install two new locks on the front door. Inside, the first two rooms would become a real youth center. We would fix the lights, paint the walls, hang some pictures, and put in some furniture. The third room would be the Internet center. It would have a separate door, with a separate lock. We would install two computers, each with its own desk and chair. The phone company, Turkmen Telecom, promised to install Internet service as soon as we bought the computers and connected them to phone lines.

Geldy would handle the accounting, paperwork, permits, and applications. I would teach the classes on how to use computers and the Internet. Together, we would start a debate league for teenagers. The kids would use the Internet to research the debate topics, which would improve their Internet research skills, their ability to critically consume information, their public speaking skills, and their knowledge of a variety of subjects. It was going to be.

126

19.
My Three-Part Plan

In the United States it would have taken me a week to put together an Internet center. One day driving around strip malls, shopping at hardware, electronics and second-hand furniture stores, and I would have had all the materials I needed. A few minutes with a telephone and the yellow pages and I could have arranged everything with a locksmith, a carpenter, the phone company, and an Internet service provider. But with no phone, no car, no yellow pages, and a first-grader's grasp of the local language, shopping was a challenge. It took me weeks to arrange everything, little by little, step by frustrating step.

I spent my mornings at Red Crescent or running errands for the Internet center. I spent my afternoons at home. Although I'd planned to live with the Burjanadzes for only a couple weeks while I looked for someplace permanent, we'd gotten along so well that they'd invited me to stay. One of my household chores was to bring home a loaf of fresh *chorek* every day for dinner. As summer ended and fall began, this became difficult because of a flour shortage, which brought high prices, long lines, and empty shelves at the bakeries. So after work, I would go from bakery to bakery, searching for bread.

At home, I'd hide the bread in a giant Tupperware so the cats couldn't eat it (they loved fresh *chorek*) and sit down for a cup of coffee with Ana. Once the sun was low and the day's heat had passed, I would change into my sweatpants, lace up my shoes and go running. The neighbor kids, who were always playing soccer in the street, would abandon their game and follow me, pelting me with questions as we ran.

"Do you have PlayStation in America? How much does it cost to play for an hour?"

"Do Snickers bars have more peanuts in America?"

"Why can't you speak Russian right?"

"Have you ever seen a black person?"

"Do you own a car? What kind is it? How much did it cost?"

"Where are you going?"

At the edge of town, only a few blocks from Ana's apartment building, they would usually turn back. I would continue on through a wasteland of sterile soil, crushed concrete, twisted bits of rebar, and piles of garbage. It was as if a whole concrete neighborhood had been demolished and the remains had been run over with a giant steamroller again and again until they were nothing but gravel.

Further on, the farm fields began. The cotton was ready: white puffs dripping from green bushes. There were no fences, hedgerows, or trees to divide the fields. The cotton stretched unbroken to the horizons. I ran on dirt roads, leaping irrigation ditches and dodging the occasional tractor. To my left, a sign on a barbed-wire fence warned: "Restricted Area." A series of empty guard towers watched over what looked to me like just more farm fields. On hot days, I'd take off my shirt and drop it next to the road. I knew no one was going to steal it.

It usually took me 45 minutes to reach the base of the mountains. There were a half-dozen low blockhouses there, with rusty steel doors and no windows. The barbed wire surrounding them was slack and tangled and rusty, the guard towers vacant and rotting. The complex had once been an arsenal, I'd been told. It looked like it had been abandoned but I stayed away anyway – better not to be seen snooping around old Soviet military installations.

I would follow a path that turned right, skirted the arsenal, and climbed up into the dusty, treeless hills. Even this path was not entirely innocent, though. It kept its distance from the blockhouses and barbed wire, but snuck right up close to a group of bunkers dug into the hillsides. They were arched like Quonset huts and made from concrete, of course (the Soviets had apparently disdained all other building materials as bourgeois). Their doors were big enough to drive trucks through. Inside, there was only the usual debris found in hidden places at the edges of towns all over the world: empty liquor bottles, used condoms, and the remains of campfires.

On the hillside above the bunkers, I'd sit in the dirt and sweat and try to catch my breath. The countryside stretched out below me, forbidding and desolate. There were no shady forests or rushing streams. There were no meadows or ponds. There was just the strip of irrigated cotton fields and towns at the foot of the mountains and beyond that, open desert. Abadan was a clutch of dreary miniature buildings surrounding the red-and-white striped smokestacks of the electrical plant. It was so threatening and overwhelming when I was down there in it. From up on the mountainside, though, it looked fragile – a huddled settlement of crumbly concrete and dusty roads, dwarfed by the enormous emptiness of the landscape. It was easier to think up there on the hillside where I didn't feel so outnumbered, so crowded, so followed, so watched.

During the previous winter's school-heating debacle, I'd decided that trying to teach basic health classes to kids in Abadan was futile. Their real problem was not a lack of knowledge, but a combination of unemployment and bad government. When I'd taught lessons on tuberculosis the previous winter, for example, I'd found that the kids already knew what they needed to know: they knew what they should do to avoid contracting the disease; they knew the signs and symptoms; they knew that if they caught it, they should go to a hospital and get tested and treated. But it was unclear how much that knowledge would help them.

Niyazov had announced that he was going to close every hospital outside the capital. "If people are ill, they can come to Ashkhabad [sic]," he explained.[66] Luckily, he didn't follow through, but many of the kids I taught would not have gone to the hospital, anyway. Their parents were unemployed, underemployed, or underpaid; they avoided hospitals except in emergencies. I could teach lessons about tuberculosis all I wanted, but -- even if the kids learned something new -- it wasn't going to do much to improve the public health situation. Going to Turkmenistan to teach kids basic health lessons was like going to a plane crash with a box of Band-Aids. What people in Abadan needed were more jobs and a new government.

I suspected that the Turkmen government would never get much less oppressive, even if Niyazov were somehow replaced as president. The country's gas and oil wealth provided a huge incentive for elites to keep tight control of the government. If they allowed the country to become more democratic, they might have to share the profits from gas and oil exports with the people instead

129

of keeping it for themselves. The gas and oil wealth also provided the means for the elite to hold onto power. With it, they could buy supporters and pay the KNB to intimidate opponents, all without having to rely on tax money from their citizens or aid money from the international community. Until Turkmenistan's gas and oil reserves were depleted, or the West lost its taste for fossil fuels, fundamental change was unlikely. Still, incremental change is always possible – and I had to do *something*.

I spent a lot of time sitting on that hillside above Abadan, looking out over the countryside, thinking about what I could do that might be more useful than teaching health classes. My options were limited by Peace Corps' requirement that I stay out of politics and by the KNB's interference with even my most innocent projects. Neither government wanted me to rock the boat. Gradually, after several visits to that hillside, I pieced together what I came to think of as my Three-Part Plan. I would: 1) try to help people make money in the private sector, to reduce the Niyazov regime's ability to intimidate people by threatening to blackball them from government work; 2) teach people to use the Internet to make money and to gather and distribute uncensored information; 3) hold classes on critical thinking, democracy, and human rights to get people thinking about alternatives to their current political system.

After sitting on the hillside for a while, plotting, scheming, and catching my breath, I'd get up, stretch a little, wipe the dirt off my butt, and start running back. If I'd left my shirt on the side of the road, I would pick it up along the way. Back at the apartment, I would pick a bunch of grapes from the vine in the garden, pour myself a big glass of cool water from the tap, and sit down at the table with Ana.

"How far did you go?" she'd ask me, taking a drag off her cigarette or a sip from her cup of coffee.

"Out to the mountains again."

"You're crazy. It's bad for your heart to run that far. Why can't you just go down to the sport center and run a few laps?"

"It's beautiful out there."

"What, the garbage and the cotton fields? You're just going out there to look at those restricted areas. You *are* a spy, aren't

130

you?" she would tease me. People often asked me if I was a spy. I wasn't, but I couldn't convince them of that. They didn't believe that I had left a good job in America to come to Turkmenistan and teach kids for $80 a month. They assumed that either I had an ulterior motive or I was nuts.

20.
Picking Cotton

Though Ana was puzzled by my running habit, she was even more puzzled by my attempts to find a way to spend a day picking cotton. The previous autumn, I'd tried and failed. The government required teachers to pick cotton, so I'd pestered the teachers I knew to take me with them. They'd thought I was kidding. They'd been forced to pick cotton all their lives and couldn't imagine why I would want to do it on purpose. This autumn, I was more successful. The quartet of teachers at School No. 8 had known me for a year and they'd come to realize that I wasn't kidding, I was just weird. So in mid-September, one of the two Natalyas agreed to take me with her to the fields. I was just curious. Cotton growing was such a big part of life in the country, I wanted to check it out, see what it was all about.

Nearly half the employed population worked in agriculture and half the farm fields in the country were planted with cotton.[67] Picked, packed, and shipped across the borders each fall, it was the country's second most important export after fossil fuel-related products.[68] It hadn't always been that way. For centuries, small amounts of cotton had been grown in Central Asia, but it was gray and coarse and there was little demand for it outside of the region. Then in the late nineteenth century, the American Civil War began and American cotton exports plunged, creating a global shortage. A group of Moscow merchants, afraid the shortage would hurt their businesses, asked the tsar to help them find a new source of cotton. The ruler's desire to plant cotton in sunny Central Asia was one of the reasons for the Russian conquest of Turkmenistan. The Russians replaced the local variety with better quality American "upland" cotton. As World War I approached, the Russian empire – thanks to Central Asia – had become one of the world's leading cotton producers.[69]

This might have been good for Russia, but it was bad for Central Asia. As more land was set aside to grow cotton, less was available for growing food. Orchards were uprooted and wheat fields converted. Turkmenistan became increasingly dependent on Russia as a market for cotton and a supplier of food. So, when World War I and the Russian Revolution struck in quick succession, Turkmenistan sank into poverty and famine. In addition to ending Turkmenistan's food independence, cotton monoculture also sucked up prodigious amounts of water and degraded the soil. Nevertheless, as soon as they had consolidated their control, the Soviets moved to expand cotton production, aiming to end the USSR's need to import cotton.[70]

After the fall of the Soviet Union, Niyazov continued to demand that Turkmen farmers grow cotton and the new nation produced more cotton per capita than any other country in the world.[71] He also started building textile mills. Rather than sending their raw cotton to Russia for processing, Turkmen farmers began to send it to these new, local textile factories, which produced clothing for Western companies.

One of these factories, which made jeans, was near Abadan. Young women who worked there sometimes ended up in Abadan's hospital, coughing up blue goop. I visited a few and offered to get them masks to wear over their mouths while they worked. They refused, saying they were scared their boss would fire them for wearing the masks.

The keys to Turkmenistan's cotton industry are an extensive irrigation system, an abundant supply of sunshine, and cheap labor. For years, Niyazov's government forced teachers and students to skip classes for several weeks each autumn to pick cotton. This meant that students spent an average of only 150 days a year in school, well below the international standard of 180 days a year.[72] Under pressure from the international community, Niyazov had publicly denounced child labor. Even after he banned it in 2002, though, his government "strongly encouraged children to help in the cotton harvest; families of children who did not help could experience harassment by the government," according to the US Department of State.[73] When this "encouragement" didn't provide enough labor, traffic police reportedly took to stopping motorists, demanding they pay impossibly high fines, and then – when they couldn't pay – suspending their licenses until they spent 10 days in the cotton fields.[74]

Since I'd arrived in Turkmenistan, Niyazov had again banned child labor in the cotton fields. Few of my Turkmen friends believed the ban would be enforced; they'd heard it all before. Natalya told me, however, that this time it was for real. At least in Abadan, city hall had declared that neither teachers nor students were allowed to pick cotton on school days. On Sundays, students were allowed to pick and teachers were required to, the result being that most teachers paid students 25,000 *manat* (about a $1) to go in their places. Natalya, however, said she liked to go do it herself sometimes. In mid-September, I arranged to go with her.

She banged on my door about 7:30 a.m. and woke me. My friend Alei (a Peace Corps Volunteer) was visiting and we'd been up late drinking and talking. She waited by the door while we got ready, warning us we were going to miss the bus. We hurried across town and joined a crowd on the street near Dom Pionerov, where men with clipboards and lists of names were loading buses with teachers and students. Natalya had a few quiet words with one of the men, who studied his clipboard, crossed off three names, and told us to climb onto an ancient, orange crank-start bus. Once the bus was full, it bumped slowly along the road to a farm outside Geokdepe, hugging the shoulder, cars whizzing by.

The cotton plants were waist high, lush and green. We piled out of the bus and waded in among them. Our group was half teachers and half students, half men and half women. The youngest was Rahat, a serious 12-year-old boy with short black hair. We all spread out and started picking. There was no shade, but it wasn't too hot – probably just in the high 80s. I stripped off my shirt and picked with the sun on my back. Each tuft of pure white cotton was partially hidden inside a tough, spiky pod. I had to be careful not to jab my fingers. Soon, though, I got the hang of it, and started moving down the rows, picking with both hands, stuffing my apron full of white gold.

The work wasn't hard. It was just boring. I spent a lot of time chatting with people across the rows. I talked to several people – adults and children – about the new law banning children from picking cotton. They were all against it, arguing that parents should be allowed to decide whether their children went to the fields. Sometimes families needed money badly enough to pull their little ones out of school and send them to pick cotton; it was none of the government's business, they all told me. For a long time, I talked to a physics professor from School No. 8, a bookish man with salt-and-pepper hair. He wanted me to explain why the American women's soccer team was so much stronger than the American men's soccer team. I couldn't help him. He also wanted to talk about the US government response to Hurricane Katrina. He was astonished that "the most powerful country in the world" couldn't manage to help its own people clean up after a rainstorm.

About noon, Alei, Natalya, and I took a break for lunch. We sat among the rows on our cotton sacks, which were mostly full and made excellent cushions. We'd brought a picnic: hard-boiled eggs, baked potatoes, dried sausage, bread, and sweet rolls. After eating, we lounged in the sun and rested for a few minutes. Then we picked some more.

Instead of choosing a row and picking it from end to end, people jumped from place to place, searching for the bushes that were heaviest with cotton. There were no quotas or supervisors. Most people picked at a leisurely pace. A few older people, though – either because they needed the money more or because they had retained a work ethic from an earlier age – picked furiously, filling sack after sack.

When the day ended, we hauled our bags over to the boss, who weighed them on a hanging fish scale and then had some boys dump their contents into a shallow trailer. The scores: Natalya, 15 kilograms; me, 12 kilograms; Alei, 5 kilograms. The boss, a sun-browned Turkmen man of about 30, wearing a light-blue button-down shirt, paid me 5,000 *manat* for my day's work – about 20 cents.

After everyone else took their turn weighing in and getting paid, we all settled down to wait for the bus. Three boys lounged in the mountainous, white pile of cotton on the trailer. The adults mostly sat cross-legged in the shade underneath. A group of teenaged girls spent their time making each other pass out. One would press on the sides of another's neck with her hands, cutting off the blood flow. After a few minutes she would collapse into a pile in the dust and then spring back up, laughing. Pretty soon, a teacher caught on and scolded them, so they went to the other side of the trailer and continued their game.

On the way home, I spent my day's salary: We stopped at one of the ubiquitous *gazly suw* stands, where a girl mixed carbonated water with flavored syrups to make Alei and I two cold, homemade sodas. When we were done, she rinsed the glasses and put them back on the counter for the next customers. Then we went to the bakery and bought two loaves of *chorek* for dinner. And that was it. After a whole day's work, that was all I could buy. No wonder the government had to force people to pick cotton.

21.
Korean Salads

Nearly everyone in Turkmenistan dreamed of secure government jobs, like the ones they'd had in the Soviet days: teacher, doctor, nurse, bureaucrat, postal clerk, factory worker, street sweeper, policeman. There weren't nearly enough of these "real" jobs to go around, though, and most people had to find other ways of making a living. They were often entrepreneurial and occasionally ingenious. A fairly common scheme was to fly to Dubai, buy a used car, ship it across the Straights of Hormuz to Iran, drive it through Iran to Turkmenistan, and switch the steering wheel from the right side to the left side in a friend's garage. Bringing the car to market cost around $2,000 and selling it brought about $3,000. Then there were the taxi drivers, the moneychangers, the subsistence farmers, the prostitutes, the wedding planners, the smugglers, the scribes, the drug dealers, the free-lance welders, the laundresses, the seamstresses, and the cooks.

Perhaps the most common line of work, however, was selling goods at the bazaar. That's how Ana had made her living during the previous fall and winter, and with cold weather on the way, she wanted to restart her salad selling-business. Over the summer, though, she'd spent all her savings, so she didn't have any startup capital. After some negotiations at the kitchen table, I agreed to lend her a million *manat* (about $40). I figured it fit well with my Three-Part Plan. She spent the next week gathering the materials she needed, traveling from bazaar to bazaar to find the best prices for sacks of carrots, cabbages, and beets. She bought graters and washtubs, spices and salt, bottles of oil and vinegar. Then we started washing and peeling and grating and mixing and tasting. For a week, we ate nothing but salads, taste-testing recipe after recipe to find just the right combination of sugar, oil, vinegar, coriander, salt, and red pepper to flavor the grated carrots and cabbage.

The salads Ana was going to sell were called "Korean salads." They were common items in bazaars all over the country, but their origin was a mystery. Allen, the Korean-American Peace Corps Volunteer, insisted that there was no such thing as a Korean salad and, indeed, the dishes that Ana sold did not resemble anything I'd ever seen in a Korean restaurant or cookbook. My best guess about why they were called Korean salads was that they were made and sold mainly by Koreans (Ana being an exception). Thanks to Stalin, Turkmenistan had a small but significant Korean population, concentrated in urban areas.

Koreans started migrating to the Russian Far East in the 1860s, fleeing drought and famine. In 1937, Stalin ordered them all moved to other parts of the Soviet Union. He might have done it because he was worried about a nationalist uprising or because he thought that war with Japan was on the way and doubted the Koreans' loyalty.[75] Whatever the reason, Soviets officials loaded at least 175,000 Koreans onto trains and scattered them across Central Asia. Years later, a Kazakh witness recalled the arrival of one group: "They brought Koreans in trucks, leaving them among the withered bushes of camel thorn and tamarisk. Deprived of any amenities or self-respect, the people in white gowns and grey padded jackets clutched the drivers' and policemen's boots, begging to be taken to inhabited places, for in the cold and wind, with neither hearth nor roof, young children and the elderly would die, and even teenagers would hardly last."[76]

Either Ana didn't know this story or she didn't want to talk about it. When I asked her how all the Koreans and their salads had ended up in Turkmenistan, she just held out a spoonful of marinated, roasted eggplant.

"Taste this," she said.

Once Ana had perfected her recipes, Sesili rented a booth at one of the Abadan bazaars. Every night, Ana would mix, taste, and pour. She would fill buckets and washbasins with four or five kinds of salad. Every morning, Sesili would wake at dawn, haul the salads to the bazaar, and spend the day selling them by the sandwich bag-full. At first, Sesili would come home with only a pocketful of change, but as she built a loyal clientele, the money started rolling in. She'd come home with a stack of bills and a few treats – three pomegranates or a bottle of name-brand soda. She'd hand the money to Ana, who would sit at the kitchen table, count it, and then hide it in a closet or a book.

"My favorite daughter," Ana would say, giving Sesili a kiss on the cheek.

"I'm your *only* daughter," Sesili would reply, dryly.

22.
Isolated and Smothered

As autumn deepened, I was slowly transforming Red Crescent's extra apartment from a sewage-scented concrete dungeon into an inhabitable space. It was well on its way to becoming the Internet center I'd been planning for so many months. I'd hired a metal worker to install two new locks to secure its steel front door and I'd put in a heating and cooling unit. I'd laid new linoleum on the floor. Using a half-can of brown paint he'd found in a closet, Shokhrat had painted the walls to look like they were made from rough-hewn stone. The youth volunteers had borrowed tables and chairs from the Red Crescent dining hall across the street. Someone had scrounged some secondhand bookshelves and an old stereo.

One cool afternoon, I sat outside the front door waiting for an electrician, a friend of Vera's named Alexander. I needed him to wire the heating and cooling unit and install some extra lights to brighten the place up a bit. Alexander turned out to be a wiry 50-year-old who covered his short, graying hair with a baseball cap. I followed him inside and held a flashlight while he worked. He asked me questions about myself: where I was from, why I'd come to Turkmenistan, the usual. Then the conversation took an interesting turn.

"Do you believe in God?" he asked.

"No."

"Neither did I, until my son died three years ago. He was 17. The doctors couldn't figure out what was wrong with him. He just died."

"I'm sorry."

"At the hospital, I met a man who was a Jehovah's Witness and he told me about God's plan. I started going to meetings and began to understand. Have you read the Bible?"

Alexander spent more time trying to convert me than working. He didn't know that it was futile. My parents hadn't taken me to church when I was a kid and I hadn't found my way there as an adult, either. In fact, I'd only been twice – once in high school when my coach forced the whole football team to go before a big game, and once for my grandmother's funeral – and I didn't plan to go again any time soon. Still, I didn't mind listening to Alexander. I wasn't paying him by the hour and I'm always curious to hear what people have to say. Besides, I was impressed by his courage.

Alexander was taking a big risk. It was one thing for a Jehovah's Witness to go door-to-door hawking the Watchtower in the US. It was another for him to proselytize in Turkmenistan where there was no freedom of religion. Only Sunni Muslims and Orthodox Christians were allowed to practice their religions in Turkmenistan and only under state supervision. Members of other faiths were "arrested, detained (with allegations of torture and other ill-treatment), imprisoned, deported, harassed, fined, and have had their services disrupted, congregations dispersed, religious literature confiscated, and places of worship destroyed. Members of some religious minority groups in Turkmenistan have been forced to renounce their faith publicly, swearing an oath on a copy of *Rukhnama*," according to a report from the US Commission on International Religious Freedom.[77] I asked Alexander if he was scared.

"Whatever happens, happens," he said, "but I have to do what I believe."

Once Alexander had finished the electrical work, the next thing on my list was to install a door separating the first two rooms, which would become the new youth center, from the third room, which was going to be the Internet center. The door was meant to separate rowdy teenage delinquents from expensive computer equipment. Vera had asked another friend to hang the door, but she'd made the mistake of giving him the money before he'd done the work. Whenever I called, he promised he'd do it the next day. Weeks passed and he still hadn't shown up. I ran out of patience. I went to his apartment one morning and knocked until his wife answered the door.

"Is Berdy home?" I asked.

"No, but I'll tell him you came by," she said.

"I'll just wait for him, if that's okay."

140

Unfortunately for Berdy, his wife had excellent manners. She let me in and set me up in front of the TV with a pot of tea and a plate of cookies. I sat there watching music videos until Berdy appeared out of the back bedroom, where he'd been sleeping. He seemed more annoyed than surprised when he saw me.

"Good morning," I said.

"Hmm," he said.

We sat and watched TV and drank our tea for a while. Once he'd had a chance to wake up a bit, I tried again to talk to him.

"You said you were going to install the door today. I came to help you carry it up to Red Crescent," I told him.

"My friend's going to help me install it. I have to find him. You go up to Red Crescent and we'll meet you there," he said.

"I'm in no hurry, I can wait with you until your friend gets here," I said, smiling.

He looked angry, but he couldn't quite bring himself to throw me out of his house, so he called his friend Maksat, who soon showed up on an ancient motorcycle with a sidecar. The two men hauled an unpainted pine door out of the apartment building's basement and loaded it into the dented green sidecar. Maksat drove the door up to Red Crescent on the motorcycle and Berdy and I followed him on foot.

Berdy and Maksat were grizzled, middle-aged Turkmen guys. Their clothes were stained with what looked like engine grease, their hands were calloused and scarred. They didn't appreciate me sitting and watching them work for six hours, but every time I left them alone – even if I just went to the bathroom – they'd stop working to sit around smoking cigarettes and cracking jokes. Berdy alternately called me Michael, George, or Smith. He said all American names sounded the same to him.

"Hey Smith, what are you doing sitting there? Why don't you go back to your own country? You don't see me going to America do you?"

The two guys heckled me all day as I sat and watched them work. It took them forever because they were installing a rectangular wooden door into an irregularly shaped concrete doorway. It didn't help that they were lazy and only marginally competent. If I'd had tools and a door, I could have done the same shoddy job in a quarter the time. By evening, Berdy and Maksat never wanted to see me again, but the door was hanging on its hinges and the youth center was ready for its computers.

I met Geldy at his office in Ashgabat one afternoon and we walked together to the electronics store to pick out two computers. It was a sleek, modern, air-conditioned store. Geldy flirted with the pretty young clerk, who was wearing a black mini-skirt. After a few minutes talking monitors, mice, and modems, we agreed on a price. I pulled several packets of 10,000-*manat* bills from the shopping bag I was carrying and stacked them on the counter. The clerk ran my money through a counting machine (a necessity for stores selling big-ticket items) and wrote me a receipt. Then one of the store's stock boys loaded my purchases into his car and drove me out to Abadan.

At Red Crescent, I unloaded all the white boxes full of computer components at the youth center, and spent an hour cutting them open, and setting up the computers. Aynabat and Vera and all the youth volunteers came over to watch. Even Aman stopped by to order me around a little bit. He was more full of himself than usual. All of a sudden he was a big man, in charge of an office with *three* computers.

Aman, Geldy, and Turkmen Telecom had all promised me that hooking up the Internet service would be simple and quick once the center was ready and the computers were installed. That turned out not to be true. Aman called his friend at the telephone company to get a new phone line installed for the Internet center, only to learn it was impossible. He was told that the system in Abadan was already at capacity; no more phone lines were available. The best Aman's friend could do was to run an extra cable from Aman's office, across the street to the Internet center, so we could all share a single party-line. Any time Aman wanted to make a call or anyone called Red Crescent, the computers would get kicked off the Internet.

When Geldy called Turkmen Telecom and told them we were ready to hook up the Internet, they told him he needed to fill out some more paperwork. They wanted a letter from Red Crescent, pledging to cover the cost of the Internet service if I didn't make the payments. So Geldy got started drawing up the papers and trying to talk Red Crescent officials into signing them. We began to realize that what we'd thought would take a few days, was going to take weeks or months.

**

I had nothing to do while Geldy fought through red tape, so I found other ways to occupy myself. Aman had hired a new "assistant," a pretty 18-year-old girl named Shemshat who wore her hair pulled back tight and her eyebrows plucked into razor-thin arches. She didn't have any actual duties in the office – Aman didn't need any assistance reading the newspaper or staring at the wall – so every morning I would give her computer lessons. I showed her how to turn the machines on and off, type, and use a mouse. Then we started on software: Microsoft Word, Excel, etc. Most mornings, at about 10 a.m., Aman would lumber over, end the lessons, and take Shemshat away in his car for a couple hours. One day I asked her where they went together. She turned bright red and told me it was none of my business.

Though I still wasn't allowed in the local schools, I now had my own classroom. The Internet center didn't have Internet, but at least it was a clean, quiet, well-lit room with a conference table and chairs. One day, browsing through a thin book that a Peace Corps Volunteer named Ray had published, the result of a poetry club he'd organized for in Ashgabat his English students, I found a poem about a zoo by a student named Trina Asadi: "Observe the effect of captivity/ In the sad eyes of a hawk and an owl/ In the timid faces of a fox and a jackal/ In the sorrowful groan of a lion and a bear/ You cannot make them happy in a golden cage/ They live and die for freedom/ So value their free nature and their freedom/ Look at the always chewing mouth of a camel and a goat/ And avoid living just to chew." I decided to start my own poetry club and publish a second volume of Turkmen students' English language poetry.

I rarely read poetry and never wrote it, but I didn't see that as an obstacle. Ray had published a handbook on how to start poetry clubs for English students. With a copy in hand, I convinced my friend Sasha, an Abadan girl who had just returned from a year abroad, to help me find some interested students and get started.

The poetry club usually had only three or four students, young teenagers from School No. 8. We'd sit around the table in the windowless Internet center, the door closed to block out Eminem or Usher or whatever the Red Crescent youth volunteers were playing on the stereo, and work together on cinquains, pantoums, haiku, alphabet poems, and acrostics. The kids struggled to rhyme foreign words, stretched their brains to find synonyms, and often broke into giggling fits at the resulting group poems: "My best friend is my dog/ It barks from day to night/ We call him crazy frog/ He is always in a fight."

On days when I wasn't working with my poetry club or teaching my bosses' mistress how to use a computer, I taught basic English lessons. My class had three students and when we started, none of them knew more than "hello" and "okay." We worked slowly, building vocabulary, learning basic grammar. One day we were standing in a circle practicing the words for clothing.

"Shirt," I would say, and everyone would point to a shirt.

"Dress," I would say, and everyone would point to a dress.

About 10 a.m., Aman swung the door open and beckoned for Shemshat.

"Ah, here's a good example," I said in English, gesturing toward Aman. "He's wearing a 'suit,' a '*costum.*' Everybody say suit."

Aman looked confused for a second and then really, really angry.

"I'm a *suka*?" he yelled in Russian, using the word for bitch. "Fuck you, you're a *suka*!"

He stormed out with Shemshat in tow. Everyone else in the room had heard the difference between 'suit' and *suka*. When Aman slammed the door, they looked at each other for a second, stunned. Then they started laughing. Aman didn't talk to me for a week, even after Aynabat took him aside and explained what had happened.

***

In addition to the classes I was teaching at the youth center,

I started teaching classes in Ashgabat. I wanted to put my Three-Part Plan into effect, and figured I'd have a better chance of escaping notice in the big city, where no one knew me, than in Abadan, where I was under surveillance. Also, my plan required Internet access, which was available to English students in Ashgabat but not, of course, in Abadan.

With help from another Peace Corps Volunteer, I taught classes at Internet centers in Ashgabat on how to use the eBay to sell Turkmen crafts to Western consumers. I gave talks on how to use Web sites to attract tourists and their dollars to home-stays and tours of local attractions. I took a road trip to a tiny village called Yerbent, a few hours into the desert from Ashgabat, and tried to convince the residents that they could make some extra money offering home-stays and camel rides (they thought I was insane and wanted nothing to do with me). I began working with a woman named Mehri, who'd spent a year in high school in the US, to organize a nationwide debate tournament for English students. We wrote a debate team coach's handbook, used it to teach about a dozen Peace Corps Volunteers how to start debate teams, and then sent them back to their cities and towns to organize teams and start preparing them for the tournament.

My most successful venture during this period was a class I called "Global Citizenship." I'd chosen a vague name to avoid attracting unwanted attention. My friend Maral, an overeducated 20-something from Ashgabat, agreed to help me teach it. Few students signed up, probably because they had no idea what the class was going to be about. On the first day, we had only five teenagers.

We taught our students about democracy in the US and invited them to draw comparisons with Turkmenistan's system, which Niyazov insisted was also "democracy." The size of the class tripled. We talked about the importance of participation in civic organizations and local government. We talked about the concept of human rights and about which rights were included in the U.N.'s Universal Declaration of Human Rights (UDHR). I pointed out the passages in the *Rukhnama* where Niyazov had guaranteed Turkmen citizens many of the rights from the UDHR and suggested they ought to hold him to his promises. Maral taught a session on what the Quran said about women's rights.

About half way through the 10-week class, I was at the Peace Corps office checking my mail, when one of my supervisors appeared beside me. She told me she'd heard about my class and reminded me that as a Peace Corps Volunteer, I was supposed to be politically neutral.

"Your class is exactly the kind of thing that Peace Corps Volunteers can get sent home for," she warned me. "Be careful."

Although I'd long been half-hoping to get thrown out of the country, when the opportunity presented itself, I balked. I tracked down Maral and told her I was going to cancel the class.

"They're going to send me back to the States if I don't," I told her.

She looked at me for a long moment.

"Do you know what could happen to *me* for teaching that class?" she asked me, and then walked away, leaving me to think about the answer.

Shamed, I decided to continue the class.

Even though I wasn't allowed to teach in the schools, I managed to keep myself busy throughout the fall with my various classes in Abadan and Ashgabat. I was excited and energized in a way I hadn't been since Ovez had asked me to try to fix School No. 8's heating system. I felt like I was making myself useful, addressing the real problems that the country was facing (albeit in small ways). I began to feel like I'd outsmarted the government. They had tried to shut me down. They'd probably thought they'd succeeded. But I'd just gone underground.

***

I soon found out, though – yet again – how naïve and arrogant I was. The KNB had, of course, noticed what I was doing. They began to send me messages. First, a KNB man called one afternoon and told Aman to make sure I would be at Red Crescent the next morning. He said he needed to talk to me. I waited all morning in Aman's office but the man never showed up. So I went on with my classes as usual. That happened twice more.

Then, one evening about 9:30 p.m., Ana knocked on my

door to tell me someone had come to see me. I'd been lying in bed in my plaid pajama pants and a t-shirt, reading. I put on some flip-flops and shuffled out to the garden gate where a 30-something Russian man in a suit was waiting for me, flanked by two pimply Turkmen conscripts in uniforms. The Russian said he needed to check to make sure my visa and registration stamps were all in order. He refused to come inside, preferring to wait on the sidewalk while I fetched my passport. He paged through it again and again, examining each word and each stamp. I stood there in my t-shirt in the late fall chill, shivering. After about 20 minutes he thanked me for my time, told me to call him if I needed anything (he'd never introduced himself), and left. I went on with my classes as usual.

After a few more weeks, one of Catherine's students came to find me in my Internet-less Internet center. Although I'd been unable to work with Catherine at School No. 8 all fall, I'd still visited her regularly. She always seemed happy to chat with me, make me tea, and try to feed me. That had to end, her student told me. "They" had told Catherine to stop associating with me, or risk losing her job. I went on with my classes as usual, but it was starting to dawn on me that I must have pissed someone off.

I had imagined that if I ever went too far, an angry policeman in a uniform would show up, slap me in handcuffs, and either beat the shit out of me our take me to jail. It would be unpleasant for a while, but when it was all over, it'd be something to brag about. And what could they do to me? I was an American. It never occurred to me that the KNB might take a more subtle approach. (Though it should have – in most situations confrontation is much less acceptable in Turkmenistan than in the US) As autumn turned to winter, my circle of friends and acquaintances slowly, mysteriously shrank. Soon, the only people in Abadan that I had any contact with were at home and at Red Crescent. The more my world closed in around me, the more isolated I got, the more frustrated and paranoid I became.

"What the fuck is wrong with this country?" I asked Ana one evening at the dinner table.

"I told you not to curse. Put 1,000 *manat* in the jar."

"Why don't you people do something?"

147

"You see what happens when *you* try, and *you're* an American. Nothing will ever change around here."

"Nothing will ever change as long as no one stands up and does anything."

"Oh, listen to you. You talk big but the worst thing that could happen to you is that you'd get sent home to America. That's no punishment. I'd love to get sent to America."

23.
It All Comes Crashing Down

Aynabat hurried over from Aman's office to the Internet center to tell me I had a phone call from the Red Crescent office in Ashgabat. I walked back across the street with her and picked up the receiver, which was lying next to the phone on Aman's desk. He lounged in his chair, reading the paper. He ignored me as I stood next to him and talked on the phone to a woman named Bahar whom I'd never met.

"Can you come to Ashgabat today?" she asked. "I need to talk to you."

"Of course," I told her. "I'll be there in an hour."

I couldn't imagine what she wanted to talk to me about, but I wasn't surprised that she didn't want to tell me over the phone. People were often skittish about talking on the phone, since they assumed someone was listening.

I took a *marshrutka* into the city and found Geldy hiding in some bushes behind the white marble Red Crescent building, smoking a cigarette. Bahar had asked him to come to the meeting, too. He had no idea why, but he wasn't concerned. He was always getting yelled at for something; I think he was used to it.

When Geldy finished his cigarette, we filed into Bahar's immaculate office and stood in front of her desk with our hands in our pockets, looking at the ground, like high school students waiting to be disciplined by the vice principal. She was a petite woman in her early 40s with short black hair.

"The Ministry of Justice called me," she said. "They chose your Internet center grant for a random audit. They said you never deposited the money in a bank. If you'll just give me the deposit slip, I'll pass it on to them and we can clear all this up."

Silence.

Geldy and I looked at each other and then back at her.

"We don't have a deposit slip," Geldy said. "We never brought the money to the bank. We just changed it and started spending it."

149

Bahar knew this would be the answer.

Almost no one deposits money in Turkmen banks if they can help it. As I'd learned first-hand, sometimes the banks were reluctant to give the money back. Besides, depositing dollars in a Turkmen bank meant that they'd be converted to *manat* at the official exchange rate of 5,000 *manat* to the dollar instead of the bazaar rate of 25,000 *manat* to the dollar. So, depositing a dollar in the bank meant, in effect, losing 80 percent of its value when you withdrew it later in *manat* (the only option). True, it was technically illegal to change money at the bazaar, but it was like speeding – everyone did it and only a few people got caught.

Unfortunately, we'd gotten caught.

Geldy was facing two years in prison, Bahar said. She didn't know what the consequences might be for me. Everything could be put right if we would just return the money to the US Embassy, start again, and – this time – obey the letter of the law, she said.

This was complicated, since we'd already spent a lot of the money to open the computer center in Abadan. But after several weeks of phone calls and meetings with people from Red Crescent, the Ministry of Justice, and the US Embassy, it was agreed that we could return the money that remained. After that, the embassy could decide whether or not to grant the same money to us again, properly, through the bank. This deal kept Geldy out of prison (which made us happy) and effectively killed the Internet center project (which presumably made the Ministry happy).

"No more grants, Sam. No more projects," Geldy told me afterward. "Enough."

It was clear to me that the audit had not been random. It had been meant to send me a message to me: shut up and sit still. When it was all over I was angry, but I was also relieved. I'd been ready to suffer the consequences of my actions, but it had scared me when it had looked like someone else might be punished for what I'd done. Whoever decided to threaten Geldy with two years behind bars had surely thought of this; the government had outmaneuvered me again.

I thought that once the Internet center was dead, the incident was over, but the fallout continued. Aman, that greasy vulture, saw his opportunity, took one of the computers from the Internet center, where I'd been using it to teach basic computer skills to Shemshat and the youth volunteers, and set it up on his desk. He didn't bother to plug it in, since he didn't know how to use it anyway.

"You don't need both computers," he told me, grinning. "You don't even have Internet access."

The next morning, I was typing up my students' handwritten poems (I'd promised them I would publish them as a booklet) on the remaining computer in the youth center. With no windows, dim lighting and walls painted to look like they were made from rough-hewn stones, the place felt like a dungeon. Shemshat breezed in, took off her jacket, and laid her purse on a chair. Her eyebrows were plucked almost out of existence and she was wearing a *koynek* that was appropriately ankle-length, but way too tight to have been called modest.

"You can go now," she told me.

"I'm a little busy here," I said, without looking up.

"No, Aman says that I'll be working here in the mornings now – not you."

I turned away from the computer and looked at her for along moment. Then I understood. I was furious, but I was also not surprised. I shut down the computer, just to be mean. Shemshat wasn't terribly bright and I hoped she'd forgotten how to turn it back on. I packed my things and left. I'd been kicked out of the youth center I'd built – by the boss's mistress.

There was nothing I could do. Geldy was in Ashgabat so he couldn't help me and, besides, he was trying to lay low. I could complain to Aman's superiors in Ashgabat, but that probably wouldn't do much good since they were still upset with me for bringing the Ministry of Justice down on them. Six months earlier, I would have stormed into Aman's office and told him off in my broken Russian. I was tired, though – worn down. I just left the office and never went back.

I moped around the house, reading, writing bitter letters home, practicing my guitar, and driving Ana and Sesili crazy. I'd refused to follow the rules and the system had targeted me and shut me down. The worst part was, there was no one to fight back against. No police squad had burst through my door and dragged me off to sit in jail or be deported. The state bureaucracy had simply wrapped around me like a boa constrictor and squeezed until I was isolated, ineffective, and demoralized. Flailing around wouldn't loosen the boa's grip; it would just wear me out.

I couldn't teach in the schools because Ovez wouldn't grant me permission. I couldn't run classes or projects outside the schools because the KNB discretely visited anyone who wanted to work with me and told them not to. I couldn't visit my former colleagues from School No. 8 because they'd been forbidden to associate with me. My job at Red Crescent had imploded thanks to the Ministry's "random" audit. My life in Abadan had been squeezed down into Ana's four-room apartment and back yard. The only work I had left were the courses I taught in Ashgabat, which had somehow gone unnoticed by the authorities.

* * *

Without my job at Red Crescent Abadan, it was unclear what would happen to me. After all, I couldn't just sit around Ana's apartment until it was time for me to return to the US. Sachly, my supervisor at Peace Corps, offered to try to smooth things over with Red Crescent, to get me back to work there somehow. I refused. I'd had all I could take of Aman and the government in Abadan. I asked for a different job. Over time, I'd become increasingly ambivalent about staying in Turkmenistan – and now I was truly torn. On one hand, I felt I wasn't wanted and was deeply frustrated and furious that while I'd been trying to help Turkmenistan, officials of the government that had supposedly invited me had been doing everything they could to make my life difficult and make sure I didn't accomplish anything. Each time I was at a breaking point, though, ready to get on a plane home – thinking "To hell with Turkmenistan," since it clearly didn't want my help – I would have some small success that would encourage me to stay. And then everything would go wrong for months and I'd be ready to leave again. I thought maybe things would be better in a different place, at a different job. While Sachly and her boss considered what to do with me, I stayed home and sulked.

After a few days, Ana got fed up with me. After all, she'd lived her entire life in Turkmenistan. She wasn't sympathetic: I'd showed up, ignored her advice that I should stop making waves and was now complaining about suffering what she'd told me all along would be the consequences. She was sitting at her kitchen table, sucking down a cigarette and a cup of coffee and listening to a sobbing, elegantly dressed Turkmen woman confess that she'd cheated on her husband and plead with Ana to ask the cards whether she was going to get caught.

"Sam, you're never going to change anything," Ana said, dealing the cards. "I hate to see you driving yourself crazy, banging your head against the wall. Why don't you just go home?"

"Thanks Ana," I said. "Thanks for your encouragement."

"Just trying to help," she said.

My apathy soon wore off – even if my bitterness didn't – and I started looking around for something to do. There was nowhere left for me to work in Abadan and I only had classes to teach in Ashgabat a couple afternoons a week. I was bored and restless. When I asked Ana what I could do around the house, she told me to fix the light in the *banya*. We'd been washing in the dark for two weeks. Why not? I thought.

I traced the wires from the light bulb in the *banya* out into the hallway and the problem became obvious. They were charred and melted. I cut out the damaged sections, spliced the wires back together and, *voila*, there was light. I was so impressed with my electrical skills that I decided to fix the electrical socket next to my bed, too, so I could plug a space heater into it. The problem was, there was no way to turn off the current. So, as I was working with the live wires, I electrocuted myself.

I yelped.

"What happened? You just electrocuted yourself didn't you?" Ana called from the kitchen. "Cut that out. You don't know what you're doing. You're going to hurt yourself."

"I'm fine. I just dropped the screwdriver," I lied.

I tried again and zapped myself again. With the current running through me, I couldn't hear anything. But apparently I yelped again.

"Sam, I told you …!" Ana yelled.

153

"Ana, everything's okay. Don't worry," I called through clenched teeth, my whole arm tingling.

The third time I shocked myself, sparks shot out of the socket, landed on the bed, and set the blanket on fire. As I discretely smothered it, hoping Ana wouldn't smell anything from the kitchen, I looked up to find her standing in the doorway. She marched over, yanked the screwdriver and pliers from my hands, pushed all the wires back into the concrete wall where I'd found them, and went back to the kitchen. That was the end of my career as an electrician.

Still looking for ways to occupy my time, I was sitting on the porch one afternoon, playing my guitar, surrounded by giant sacks of carrots and piles of green cabbages that Ana had bought to make salads, when I got an idea. I leaned my guitar against some cabbages and walked the four blocks to the bazaar. I found a sturdy-looking, long-handled hoe, paid a few thousand *manat* for it, slung it over my shoulder, and carried it back to Ana's apartment.

The back yard was overgrown with weeds and wildflowers, strewn with trash that passing kids had thrown over the fence. For the next two days, I gathered the debris and hauled it, little by little, to the eternally smoldering trash pile at the end of the street. The weather was cool, crisp, and sunny – perfect for working outside. I was stabbed by burs, stung by nettles, and bitten by bugs, but I didn't mind.

When I finished, I had a bare dirt lot, about 20 feet wide by 30 feet long. Grape vines climbed the fences on the left and right. A hedge grew along the fence that separated the garden from the sidewalk. I used my hoe to turn the yard into a garden like the ones I'd seen in our neighbors' back yards, with high planting beds rising from a shallow depression. I turned the hose on and filled the moat with water and the planting beds stayed dry, like long, skinny islands.

When I showed Ana what I'd done and asked her what she'd like me to plant in her new garden, I thought she'd be excited. She wasn't.

"It's December, Sam. Nothing's going to grow," she said.

"It might be winter, but it's still warm and sunny," I said.

"People don't plant gardens in the winter."

154

"I do."

"*You're* crazy."

Even though she thought sowing seeds in December was a bad idea, she fished out an old tin can stuffed with seed packets made from scraps of newspaper, labeled in pencil. We spread them out on the table and picked parsley, cilantro, chick peas, peppers, and onions. From then on, I spent several hours each day in the garden. I picked up the leaves that had fallen from the grape vines. I filled the garden with water, weeded it, and used my hoe to re-shape the planting beds so they were straight and even. Sometimes I'd just sit out there and wait for the seeds to sprout. Anna came out to the back porch one afternoon and stood among the sacks of carrots, looking down on me in the garden.

"You're going to be waiting a long time," she said, and went back inside.

* * *

When I heard back from Sachly, I learned that Peace Corps and Red Crescent had divorced; they wouldn't be working together anymore. I needed to choose another place to work, she said. I told her I'd go anywhere she sent me – I just wanted a fresh start. If possible, though, I'd rather live in the country than in the city, I said. She chose a tiny little town named Nurana for me. It was about an hour south of Mary, which was about five hours east of Ashgabat, which was about a half-hour east of Abadan. Plenty far away.

I was supposed to move in January. I had only about six months left in Turkmenistan. I considered getting on a plane and going home to the US instead of moving to Nurana. I had nothing in particular to do in America, though, and I was hoping to salvage something from my time in Central Asia. I didn't want to go home angry and bitter. Besides, I thought I might finally get to live my original Peace Corps dream. Maybe my host father in Nurana would be a shepherd. Maybe we'd live in a yurt. Maybe I would get to commute to work on a camel.

I started preparing for the move. I handed over my poetry class to Sasha. I told my Global Citizenship students I was leaving and would have to cut the course a couple weeks short. I asked Phoebe, a Peace Corps Volunteer posted in Ashgabat, to help Mehri with the debate tournament. I didn't have many goodbyes to say in Abadan. I couldn't talk to Catherine. I didn't want to talk to the Plotnikovs. I had a farewell dinner with Tanya, told the youth volunteers at Red Crescent goodbye and good luck, and went out and got drunk in Ashgabat with Geldy.

By this time, it was almost New Year's. Ana and Sesili had been looking forward to the holiday for weeks, buying groceries little by little and storing them away. I didn't want to ruin the event with regretful goodbyes, so I tried to keep my mouth shut about my move. They kept talking about what we would all do together in the new year, though, and I kept vaguely saying that, hopefully, yes, we would all do that. Eventually, Ana figured out that something wasn't right and I confessed.

"You're just sick of living with me," she said sadly. She seemed deflated. "I know, I know, I talk too much."

"No, Peace Corps is sending me – it's not my choice," I lied.

"Oh," she said, knowingly. "They're sending you to *ssilka* [exile]."

She'd seen it before. That's what used to happen to troublemakers in the Soviet Union. They'd been sent to Siberia or some other faraway place so they couldn't make trouble anymore.

* * *

Ana was too busy to dwell on my exile for long because it was high season for her Korean salad business. (Or maybe she was glad to be rid of me. Given my troubles with the government, I'm sure having me around made even tough-as-nails Ana nervous). We stayed up late most evenings, grating carrots into four-inch-long strands, marinating baby eggplants, and seasoning cotton-seed oil. Sesili woke before dawn every morning, bundled herself up in so many layers she could barely move, called a taxi, and went to the bazaar. She stood there in the cold all day, selling the salads by the sandwich bag-full. Each night, she came home with fistfuls of cash.

"Ah, my favorite daughter!" Ana would sing out as Sesili arrived home in the evening, exhausted. "What did you bring me today?"

Sesili, worn out, would produce a few tangerines and ruby pomegranates, and maybe, if it was a really good day, a bottle of soda. And then we would sit at the kitchen table and count the money, piling the worn out, crumpled 10,000-*manat* bills into stacks of 10, the cats milling around our feet. We'd eat dinner and gossip about our days and then it was back to cooking, preparing the salads for the next day.

After months of unemployment, the money was rolling in for Ana and Sesili. They were so busy they had to hire a neighbor to help them. Sesili bought a cell phone. Ana paid back the loan I'd given her, insisted on taking me to the Tolkuchka Bazaar to buy me a new winter jacket as interest on the loan, and told me to stop paying rent (I refused).

It was a bittersweet time. We were all excited for the holiday. Things were going well for Ana and Sesili. I was relieved to be leaving Abadan and excited about going to Nurana. But I was also sad to be leaving Ana, Sesili, Tanya, Natalya, and my other friends. Almost everyone in Abadan had been welcoming and kind to me. Even the government officials and KNB men had been polite and respectful; they were just doing their jobs. The only people who had really done me wrong were Olya and Aman. As for the rest, I'd certainly caused them more trouble than they'd caused me.

Matt, who had lived with Ana and Sesili during training, came to visit for New Year's. We all spent the afternoon cooking. The table was loaded with stuffed grape leaves; stuffed peppers; chicken legs; lamb stewed with eggplant, tomatoes and potatoes; six different Korean salads; bowls of fruit; and bottles of wine and vodka. That night, Sesili brought home 4 million *manat*—twice my monthly salary, four times the salad business's startup cost. About 10 p.m., we sat down to eat. Visitors dropped by now and then to eat a little and make toasts. We watched Russian variety shows and Putin's holiday speech. It was a cozy night; I was content. I went to bed around 4 a.m. and, before falling asleep, I lay in the dark for a while thinking about how much I would miss Ana and Sesili.

The next day, we slept until noon and then had leftovers with wine and vodka for brunch. As dinnertime approached, we took a *marshrutka* across town to Ana's brother Andrei's house for a second New Year's celebration. It was chilly out. Matt, Ana, Sesili and I were wrapped in jackets and hats and gloves and scarves, and packed into the minivan with a half-dozen other passengers. The windows were half-fogged as we rolled past the bazaar. I wiped mine clean and looked outside. We passed the main bus stop. On the wall, there was a big blank space.

My billboard was gone. It had been ripped off its fasteners, leaving nothing but four scars in the building's concrete hide.

"They tore my billboard down," I said.

"Well what did you expect?" Ana asked.

"Are you gonna go postal?" Matt asked.

24.
Accused of Kidnapping

After New Year's, there was still one last thing I had to do before I could move to Nurana. Months earlier, I'd promised to teach at an English immersion camp during winter break. An Ashgabat English teacher named Yelena, a friend of Catherine's, had organized it. She was a round, soft-spoken woman in her forties, relentlessly polite and optimistic. She'd found funding, picked the campers, organized the logistics, and recruited me and five other Peace Corps Volunteers to be counselors. I was impressed. She seemed to have thought of everything.

The camp was supposed to be at Chuli, but the government had demolished almost everything there, planning to replace the old campsites and hotels with a gleaming new, white-marble resort. For some reason this involved not just tearing down the structures at Chuli, but also razing whole villages along the Ashgabat-Chuli road. Riding to Chuli in a taxi one day, I'd seen bulldozers flattening several dozen houses while the residents sat in the streets with all their belongings, looking shocked and disoriented.

"They'll get nothing," the taxi driver said. "We live like dogs in this country."

Since we couldn't hold the camp at Chuli, Yelena went looking for another site that fit her budget. She discovered that flying the two dozen campers to a hotel in Avaza, a Caspian Sea resort town just outside the city of Turkmenbashy, would be cheaper than holding the camp at a hotel in Ashgabat. Hotel rates were low in Avaza, since no one wanted to vacation on the beach in January; tickets on Turkmen Airlines' new Boeings were subsidized – only $1 for a flight anywhere in the country (for Turkmen citizens and Peace Corps Volunteers).

Two days after New Year's I boarded a plane at the Ashgabat airport at 7 a.m., with the other Peace Corps Volunteers. The campers would follow the next day. The plane took off and headed west. A portrait of Niyazov in a powder blue suit hung on the bulkhead, keeping watch over the cabin. An anti-evil eye charm hung near the door to the cockpit. The flight took an hour. Below the plane, the Turkmen landscape was all brown-and-gray sand dunes and half-evaporated lakes and mysterious trenches and dirt tracks.

As we approached Turkmenbashy (formerly Krasnovodsk), the tired, tree-less Balkan Mountains rose up out of the desert. And then there was the Caspian, a pool of water about the size of Montana, and about a third as salty as most seawater – calm and blue. It is a remnant of the massive Tethys Sea, which had covered Central Asia millions of years ago and then mostly dried up, leaving the Caspian and Aral seas behind. Underneath are substantial reserves of oil, which the surrounding countries pump and sell.

Our campsite in Avaza was a short walk from the shoreline, where waves crashed onto the rocks, filling tide pools with frigid seawater. It was a small hotel: about 10 two-story cabins and a dining hall arranged around a small park, protected by a fence. Surrounding our hotel were dozens of *dachas* (vacation houses). Young conscripts in uniforms were busily tearing them down and loading their remains onto trucks. Like Chuli, Avaza was to become a shiny new resort, whether its residents liked it or not.

The campers, teenagers from Ashgabat and Abadan, bunked in two-bedroom apartments in the cabins for the week. The Peace Corps Volunteers taught them dance, origami, English, astronomy, and a course based on Joshua Piven's "Worst Case Scenario Survival Guide." We played soccer with them in the park and took them on long runs through the desert. One evening we walked them down to the seashore and had a campfire. Three boys had formed a band and, dressed in black, wearing heavy eyeliner, performed a few songs. Those were the highlights. Most of the camp was a disaster.

One afternoon, the kids living in the apartment above the counselors' locked the door and left for their classes, forgetting that they'd left the tap open in their kitchen. To be fair, the water wasn't working so it was hard for them to tell. While they were gone, the water started working again, overflowed the sink, collected about four inches deep on the apartment floor, and started dripping through the ceiling into the apartment below.

Two counselors, returning to their apartment, discovered the disaster, and called for help. With buckets, brooms and dustpans we all bailed the water out of the upstairs apartment onto the balcony, where it froze and formed long delicate icicles as it dripped off the edge. Inside the apartment downstairs, we arranged teacups, trashcans, and Frisbees to catch the drips, and sat on the couch, watching the ceiling rain.

Meanwhile, Yelena was getting nervous because city officials kept showing up at the camp, demanding to know why there were six Americans and two dozen Turkmen students at a condemned beach resort in January. On Friday, angry school officials from the Ashgabat area started calling us on the emergency Peace Corps cell phone we had with us and asking the same sorts of questions. How they got the number was a mystery because only Peace Corps staff had it.

One principal called six or seven times, demanding to know whether we'd "kidnapped" any of *her* students, and insisting we give her a list of the kids who were at the camp. Government ministries started calling Peace Corps, asking questions; Peace Corps staff started calling us. Some of the campers had relatives who lived in the Turkmenbashy area and stopped by the campsite to see if everything was okay. It turned out Yelena had neglected to get government permission to move the camp to Avaza.

The situation just kept getting worse until Saturday. Then, for whatever reason – maybe all the government officials went home for the weekend – the phone stopped ringing, officials from city hall left us alone, and the KNB stopped visiting. On Monday, the camp ended and the kids went home. When they returned to school, the kids from Abadan who had attended the camp were forced to write essays on why they'd gone to the camp. Several wrote that Catherine (from Abadan's School No. 8) had inspired them to do whatever they could to improve their English skills, so they always attended camps and special events in English. As punishment for inspiring her students, Catherine was forced to retire. I don't know what happened to Yelena.

* * *

After the campers went home, I stayed in Turkmenbashy with my friend Alei. We had a plan: we were going to search the western Karakum Desert for the ruins of an ancient city named Dekhistan.

I'd heard it was southeast of Turkmenbashy, so we took a taxi to the biggest city in that area, an oil town called Balkanabat. We went to the nearest *marshrutka* stand and started asking questions. At first, no one had any idea what we were talking about. It took us about an hour to discover that the locals called the city Mashad-i Misirian and that we needed a four-wheel drive vehicle to get there.

We did our best to convince one of the five taxi drivers who were standing around near their cars, drinking tea, to take us. They weren't interested. Mashad-i Misirian was a long way down a dirt road and the day was all but gone, they told us. It looked like it was going to rain.

"You'd rather stand here talking to each other for the rest of the day than make some money?" I asked.

"Yes," one of the men said.

"Come on, we've got food and vodka," Alei tried. "It won't be like work – you'll just be partying with Americans."

They laughed, but still refused to take us.

They did, however, point out the road that led toward Mashad-i Misirian. We walked over to it and flagged down a car headed our way. It took us to a grimy little town called Gumdag. At the taxi stand there, we found a wiry man with a bushy mustache named Rahat who agreed to take us to the ancient city in his Toyota sedan for the right price, dirt road or no dirt road, end of the day or not. As we were about to leave, Rahat's friend Navod jumped into the car, explaining that he was going the same direction as us. He needed to pick up a sheep for the big Kurban Bayram holiday meal he was hosting the next day at his house.

We drove south through the desert along a nice paved road. This wasn't graceful sand dune desert like I'd seen near Darvaza. It wasn't rolling scrub desert like I'd seen between Mary and Turkmenabat. It was wasteland. Flat, yellow-orange sand as far as I could see, with almost nothing growing. Now and then, we passed a herd of bobbing oil wells, spread out across the barren plain. We overtook several tanker trucks with Iranian plates that appeared to be carrying oil. After about an hour of driving, we cleared a

162

checkpoint and stopped at a roadside stand to pick up a half-dozen *somsa*s filled with onions and chopped mutton fat. I ate a couple in the back seat, staring out the window, content to be on the road.

A little while later, the highway ended and we turned off onto a dirt road that led out across the desert. We passed herds of camels dressed in winter sweaters with holes cut out to accommodate their humps, tended by shepherds on ancient motorcycles. Though there were no villages in sight, the dirt tracks were busy with cars, trucks, and motorcycles. When the road ended, Rahat drove into the open desert, heading for two minarets on the horizon. The landscape had changed. The sand was now dotted with bushes, which made it seem less forbidding.

We roared along at 40 miles an hour across the open desert, dodging holes and bushes and ditches. When we got to within a quarter-mile of the minarets, Rahat stopped the car. Piles of bricks – the remains of houses – blocked our way. We got out and walked, passing a desiccated camel carcass, ribs bleached by the sun, fur clinging to its face. The ground was littered with pottery shards, beautifully glazed bits of turquoise, cobalt blue, black, white, and green. Some were decorated with patterns or Arabic script. Beyond the ruined houses was a moat and then a dirt-covered city wall with brickwork showing through in places – like the ones I'd seen at Merv but much smaller. Towering over it all were three structures: two minarets and a partially ruined *pishtaq* (mosque entrance). We combed through the pottery shards and circled the walls.

Rahat and Navod couldn't tell us much about the city. It wasn't their fault, though. Mashad-i Misirian's history was lost for centuries. When the British spy Arthur Conolly passed its ruins during the Great Game, he complained that, "Of Meshed -e Misraeun [sic] we could obtain no satisfactory accounts. From what the Toorkmuns [sic] said, it was evident that they knew nothing about [it]."[78] Since Conolly's time, though, archaeologists have uncovered bits and pieces of the city's past.

Dekhistan area was inhabited for thousands of years. It was once a flourishing agricultural district, watered by the Atrek River. The tenth century Arab geographer Mohammed Abul-Kassem ibn Hawqal wrote that Dekhistan was located near the Caspian Sea. It was on a bay was filled with boats and many of its residents made their livings by fishing.[79] Caravans passed through on the way across the Karakum from Persia to the Khoresmian oasis.

Over time, the Atrek River wandered south, away from Dekhistan. Residents built canals 30-40 miles long to bring water from the Atrek to their city. It's unclear why the city was eventually abandoned – perhaps because of continuing environmental change, perhaps because of Chinggis Khan's invasion – but by the time the Soviets arrived, it was nothing but a pile of ruins. Red Army gunners used the minarets for target practice and hit one, leaving a gaping hole.[80]

Alei and I climbed the minaret and I peered through the hole, out over the barren landscape. The sun was setting and a light rain had begun to fall. Rahat and Navod, who were waiting with the car, yelled that it was time for us to go. Alei and I made our way back across the ruins to the car and we all set off through the darkening desert. A few minutes after Rahat had miraculously managed to get us back to the paved road alive, we came to the village where Navod's brother-in-law lived. We stopped and Navod went inside to buy his sheep.

It was supposed to be a quick stop. Turkmen hospitality being what it is, though, Navod's brother-in-law insisted on treating us to dinner. Before we knew it, the *klionka* on the floor was loaded with meat and bread, vodka and soda. Alei produced the picnic he'd tried to tempt the taxi drivers in Balkanabat with – Korean salads he'd bought in Turkmenbashy – and added it to the feast. By 11 p.m., none of us could eat or drink any more. Our host invited us to stay the night, but, Alei, Rahat, Navod, and I decided we should leave.

Outside, the wind was whipping across the desert. It was pitch black and the sky was sprinkled with glitter. Navod and I went out behind the house to a pen where a single sheep was pacing. Navod grabbed it and threw it on its side. I held it down while he bound three of its legs and tossed it in the trunk of the car. "If I tie all four of its legs, it'll die before we get there," he explained.

And then we were off. We didn't get far, though. The soldiers at the checkpoint wouldn't let us through. Rahat and

Navod negotiated with them for a while but got nowhere. The guards wanted a big bribe and Rahat didn't want to pay it. We sat in the car waiting for them to give in; they sat in their guardhouse, waiting for us to pay up. After a half-hour, Alei went over to the guardhouse and banged on the window.

"Are you kidding?" he yelled through the window. "You've got to be kidding. You're kidding, right? This is a joke?"

"Get back in the car," the soldier said.

Eventually, Rahat worked it out. I don't know how. I was dozing in the back seat, full of too much vodka and dinner, worn out from camp and from the day's travels. We got back to Alei's apartment about 3 a.m. and went to sleep. The next day, I dragged myself off the couch, cleared my head with some coffee and aspirin, and said goodbye. I caught a taxi to the airport, where I went to the nearest café for more coffee. On the plane, I fell asleep under the benevolent gaze of Niyazov's portrait and slept all the way back to Ashgabat.

Part III: I Find an Oasis

25.
Nurana

Ana and Sesili helped me load my bags into a taxi, hugged me goodbye, and told me to be careful. They were worried about me. From their perspective, I was going to live at the end of the world, among a bunch of hicks. It was as if I was leaving a Manhattan family to go live in a small town in eastern Kentucky.

I promised to visit when I could and to call them now and then on their new cell phone. Ana gave me a package of food: jars of spicy eggplant chutney, sweet pickled red peppers, and caramelized garlic spread. I sat in the taxi's front seat and watched Abadan roll by my window. I was more hopeful and relieved than sad. I knew I would miss Ana and Sesili and Tanya and my students, but I was glad to be leaving Abadan. I knew I would miss Geldy, but I was also aware that he was trouble and I was better off far away from him.

The plane from Ashgabat landed at the Mary airport about 7 a.m. and I took a taxi to Murgab, a 30-minute drive. It was about half the size of Abadan and had a completely different character. While Abadan had been an industrial satellite of the capital, Murgab was the county seat in a farming county. There were no factories and few of the concrete apartment buildings I was so used to seeing. Most people lived in one-story family compounds, with a house or two, a kitchen building, a *banya*, an outhouse, and a courtyard garden – all surrounded by high walls.

Shops, restaurants, a post office, a pool hall, a hardware store, and a photo developing shop lined Murgab's main street. There was also a small bazaar with a mud floor, which was sheltered by a patchwork of canvas tarps. Since there wasn't enough room in the bazaar, merchants spilled out onto the street, piling their tomatoes or cucumbers on cloths laid on the pavement. In contrast to Abadan's cosmopolitan mix of Russians, Caucasians, and Turkmen, Murgab was almost entirely Turkmen. There were no Russian bottle-blonds in miniskirts and high heels browsing the shops. The women shopping at Murgab's bazaar wore long clothes

169

and covered their hair. The men wore dark slacks, button down shirts, and sometimes suit coats.

I met my new host family at the hospital in Murgab. Jeren, my host mother, was in her early 30s. She worked at the hospital and wore a white coat and a tall white hat. Her personality was so big that it took me a while to notice how physically small she was. She had thick black eyebrows and long black hair, which she kept covered with a colorful kerchief. She wore modest clothes: ankle-length dresses or skirts, and wrist-length blouses. Her husband, Döwlet was about the same age. He worked in an electronics store in Murgab, selling televisions and satellite dishes. He was tall and gangly with an overgrown crew cut and the manner of a football player trying really hard in calculus class. Thankfully, both Döwlet and Jeren spoke Russian.

"We're going to have to teach you to speak Turkmen," Dowlet said, smiling.

In his rattley old Soviet car, he drove us to Nurana: his home, my new home. We rode along paved country roads, through a handful of villages and endless farm fields. The sky was low and drizzly. The mountains that had loomed over my life in Abadan were gone. The landscape reminded me of Ohio in the winter: flat brown farm fields separated by rows of leafless trees. After 20 minutes, the fields ended and we entered the village: a few dirt roads flanked by low houses surrounded by gardens and vineyards. We passed three convenience stores, crossed a bridge over the Murgab River, turned onto a dusty road, and stopped in the driveway of a whitewashed house.

The house had four rooms and few furnishings other than the carpets that covered its floors. Its entrance faced the backyard, which was as big as a football field and contained a garden, a vineyard, a kitchen building, a *banya*, an outhouse, a *tamdur*, a small orchard, and a giant satellite dish. Döwlet helped me unload my bags and carry them to my room. It was big and bright, with a window that opened onto the back yard. The walls were painted sky blue, the floor was covered in carpets. This was going to be a different life, I thought, looking around. There was room to breathe, room to move, room to live.

Jeren had laid out a *klionka* on the living room floor and set out a pot of tea and some sweets, a loaf of *chorek* and some butter. The room was cozy, heated by an iron box the size of a sleeping puppy, which burned government-provided natural gas. There was a television in the corner and no other furniture. Döwlet and Jeren's two daughters, who had been playing at a neighbors' house, joined us. Kümüsh was three, a little imp with short hair and a frilly white dress. Altyn was prissy, perfect and seven. The girls sat near Jeren and stared at me, ignoring their tea. Döwlet and I shared family photos and talked.

Jeren, it turned out, was from Murgab. She considered herself a city girl. Döwlet, on the other hand, had lived in the same house in Nurana his whole life. He was raised in the country and had spent much of his life working as a farmhand. Until Döwlet reached his late teens, Nurana had been a Soviet *kolkhoz*, a collective farm where all the residents worked together to tend all the fields and harvest all the crops. It had been created in the 1930s when the new Soviet government was remaking the USSR's countryside, replacing small, privately owned farms with *kolhoz*es and other types of large-scale communist farms – a process called collectivization.

Soviet officials descended on the Turkmen countryside, forcing Turkmen peasant farmers and nomadic stockbreeders to give up their land and livestock to the state, join *kolkhoz*es, stop producing food, and grow cotton. In response, thousands of Turkmen families packed their belongings and fled to Iran and Afghanistan.[81] Thousands more, in cities all over Turkmenistan, took to the streets to protest. In the spring of 1930, things began to turn violent. When 500 people (mostly women) marched on the city of Dashagouz, they destroyed the school and beat up several Soviet officials.[82] As the months passed and the Soviets refused to significantly change their policies, the protests gave way to armed rebellion. Insurgents on horseback began to appear out of the desert to attack Soviet officials, and loot and burn collective farms.[83]

This uprising was not new. It was a revival of a resistance movement that had been active more or less since 1917. The Soviets, upon taking control in Moscow, had outlawed Muslim religious schools, closed Islamic courts, and nationalized lands held by the Islamic religious establishment. Muslims across

171

Central Asia saw this as an assault on their way of life and took up arms. Loosely organized as the *Basmachi* or Freemen's Movement, by 1919 they had 20,000 fighters and controlled much of Central Asia.[84] There was even talk of secession from the USSR. But by 1924 or so, the Soviets managed to put down the *Basmachi* revolt. They granted political concessions, re-legalized religious organizations, returned religious lands, and eased restrictions on religious courts. They also sent in more troops.

Things were relatively quiet until the collectivization drive reignited the *Basmachi* uprising in Turkmenistan. The *Basmachi* knew the land. Much of the populace supported them. They were very effective. In 1931, they seized Krasnavodsk, an important port on the Caspian, and the Soviets had to send 20,000 troops to retake it. In the end, Moscow had to grant some political concessions to restore order, returning livestock to their owners, and ending calls for the sedentarization and collectivization of all the area's nomads.[85] Once peace had been restored, the Soviets were able to impose their secularization and collectivization policies, gradually, over many years.

This was not ancient history. It was recent enough to still be part of family lore, in the same way that the Great Depression is still ingrained in the histories of many American families. Döwlet's grandfather could have been among the nomads who were forced to settle on *kolkhoz*es. Perhaps he fought with the *Basmachi*. Döwlet, however, was no rebel. He'd grown up on the *kolkhoz* and loved it. He told me Nurana had been a rich *kolkhoz*, with frequent good harvests, and once, an end-of-the-year bonus big enough for his family to buy a car – the car he was still driving. Those had been the good years.

Since independence, though, things had gotten harder. After the Soviet Union fell, the new government renamed the *kolkhoz*es *dayhan berleshigi* (farmers' associations). It divided the communal fields into 2.5-acre sections and put these sections under the care of individual farmers, telling them that – if they worked hard and met certain benchmarks – the land would eventually be theirs. As of 2001, the state still owned all Turkmenistan's farmland. The government supplied the seed to the farmers, told them what to grow (cotton or wheat, in Nurana), and bought crops at prices well below those available on world markets.[86]

Döwlet couldn't make a living off his plot. Even with his full-time job at the electronics store and Jeren's part-time job at the hospital, money was tight. And things were even harder because the Soviet social safety net had been torn apart after independence. Döwlet didn't talk much about politics. He was more interested in being a dad and a husband. But he was nostalgic for the Soviet days.

After tea, Döwlet and I drove to Mary to fill out paperwork. I had to register with the local government, let them know where I lived, who I lived with, what my job was, and how I could be reached. The bureaucrat in the suit behind the desk warned me that if I ever wanted to leave Nurana for any reason, I was to call him and let him know where I was going and why. I assured him I would, he wished me well, and Döwlet and I drove back to Nurana.

As we bumped along the country road in the dark, the radio glowed green on the dashboard. Outside my window, the stars winked and danced.

"I'm very glad to meet you and to have you in my home," Döwlet told me earnestly.

"I'm very glad to be here," I said.

* * *

There was a bed in my room, but it was too short for me so I put the mattress on the floor and slept there. My room was warm and clean and comfortable and I slept well. I didn't dream. When I woke the next morning, the sky was just getting light. I stumbled sleepy-eyed out of my room, slipped on some flip-flops, and walked out past the vineyard, across a plank bridge over an irrigation canal, past a grove of fruit trees, to the outhouse. It was just a wood-plank shack with a hole in the floor and some torn up newspapers in a box hanging on the wall. When I was done, I walked back across the bridge and across the yard to the *banya*.

At the Plotnikovs' apartment, the *banya* had been tiny and crowded, the bathtub often filled with Misha's fish. I had to risk blowing myself up every time I lit the hot water heater. At the Burjanadzes, the *banya* had been even smaller – I could stand in the middle and touch all the walls – and before I could wash, I had to clear the dirty salad-making dishes out of the tub. I heated my bathwater in a metal bucket on the stove and rationed it carefully. This new *banya* was luxurious.

There were two rooms. The first had pegs on the walls to hang clothes and towels and a small, high window to let in the sunlight. In the inner room, a tank of hot water simmered day and night on a gas burner and a tank of cold water sat in a corner under another high window. The room was always as hot as a sauna. To take a bath, I stood on wooden slats laid over the concrete floor, mixed hot and cold water in a pitcher and poured it over myself. I stayed in the *banya* for 20 minutes, taking a long, hot bath while looking out the window at the sleet and mud. It was glorious.

Breakfast in the living room was tea, bread, butter, honey, and jam. The girls were dressed in their school clothes, hair combed and held in place with colorful barrettes. Jeren ironed Döwlet's shirt on a towel on the floor. Döwlet sat at the *klionka*, eating and watching TV. I made myself coffee and ate bread with butter and thick, crystalline honey. After breakfast Döwlet, Jeren, and the girls piled into the old Lada and headed for Murgab, where half of them would spend the day at work and the other half in kindergarten or school.

Once they were gone, I left for work, too. I walked out the front gate, waited for some cows and camels to amble by, crossed the street, passed a tiny brick mosque, and there I was – standing outside the health clinic where I was to spend my final six months in Turkmenistan. It was a one-story yellow-brick building with blue trim. Inside, the floors were made from creaky wooden planks and everything smelled like disinfectant. I had a desk and a chair in a shared office. Unlike Red Crescent, the clinic had heat, light, and running water. My boss was a stout, round-faced Turkmen woman in her 40s named Oraztach. She was serious, efficient, and hard-working. She was my new counterpart, my new Geldy, though any comparison between the two seemed absurd.

It soon became apparent that my new life in Nurana had only one drawback. Döwlet and Jeren were kind and friendly and interesting. Their girls were adorable. Their house was spacious and clean and comfortable. My new colleagues were welcoming. But I had virtually nothing to do. The first week, Oraztach put me to work drawing a health poster about anemia. Then she told me I had to write a three-month work plan. So I spent another week doing that. Geldy had taught me well. I didn't agonize over it. I just wrote up a wish-list of things I'd like to do in Nurana and gave it to her so she could pass it on to her boss in Murgab.

Then I ran out of things to do. I could only draw so many posters: the only places to hang them were on the walls inside the clinic – and it was a small clinic. So one day I walked across the empty lot that separated the clinic from the village school and called on the principal. He was a skinny, 50-something Turkmen man, and wore a furry Russian hat. I asked him whether he could put me to work and he said he'd love to have me teach English. He was supposed to have two English teachers but he had none, he explained. We agreed on a schedule and he said that if I taught English four days a week, I could teach health on the fifth to please my boss at Peace Corps who wanted me to be a health teacher.

The principal drew up a proposal and sent it to the superintendent for a signature and a stamp. For a week, I sat at my desk in the clinic, writing letters, studying Turkmen vocabulary, drawing a poster about dental hygiene, and waiting. When the principal sent a student over to the clinic to fetch me (there was no phone), I was excited for good news. In his office, though, he fidgeted and seemed embarrassed. The superintendent, it turned out, had decided that, since I was posted at the clinic I should stay in the clinic – and out of the school. When I told Oraztach what had happened, she thought for only a moment before settling on a solution.

"I'll give you one of the rooms in the clinic for a classroom," she said. "The principal can just send the students over from the school when it's time for their lessons."

Oraztach drew up a proposal and forwarded it to her boss in Murgab for a signature and a stamp. Again, I waited. Again, the answer was negative. If I wanted to do any teaching, I could teach the clinic's dozen or so doctors and nurses, Oraztach's boss had decided. Other than that, I was to be hard at work at my desk all day, every day, he said. (He didn't explain what I should be hard at work doing). The message was clear: sit still and shut up.

"If they're going to be like that, just don't teach anyone anything," Jeren told me, disgusted with the whole affair.

175

I'd like to say that I resisted, that I fought for permission to do something useful and important because I hadn't come all the way to Turkmenistan to sit still and shut up and the country was really fucked up and something had to be done and it might as well start with me. But I didn't. I'd tried that for a year and a half and it had done no good for anyone. I'd driven myself half-crazy, gotten my friends into trouble, and disappointed my few supporters. Instead, I decided to spend my remaining time hanging out with my host family, drawing a few health posters, and letting someone else fix the country – if it wanted to be fixed.

26.
Working in the Vineyard

Nurana was peaceful. There were no KNB men, no surprise audits, no crises. That stuff all spread like a disease from Ashgabat's white-marble palaces and (unlike Abadan) Nurana was a long, long way from Ashgabat. There weren't even any police in the village. A month before I'd arrived, Döwlet told me, a man had been caught stealing. A bunch of guys had stripped off his clothes, tied him to a telephone pole in the village center, and left him there to be tut-tutted by passing grandmas.

Nurana was the kind of place where the postman knew everyone in town and their schedules, and would bring their mail to them whether they were at work, at home, or out shopping. It was the kind of place where gaggles of children jumbled through neighborhoods, bursting through one unlocked door after another, looking for a softhearted mom to feed them cookies and tea instead of chasing them away. It was the kind of place where, if you were walking home late at night from a party and found yourself too drunk to make it the whole way, you could knock on the nearest door and be sure you'd be offered a place to sleep.

Everyone was kind and polite and friendly – and curious about me. People would come to my house and to the clinic just to look at me. They would direct their questions to the nurses or Döwlet, because they assumed I couldn't speak Russian.

"So that's the American, huh? How old is he?"

"Twenty-nine? And he's not married? What's wrong with him?"

"He looks skinny. I thought Americans were fat. Are you feeding him enough?"

I usually worked at the clinic until lunchtime and then went home to heat up some leftovers and eat them while watching American movies dubbed into Russian. I was supposed to spend my afternoons finding projects around the community that I could work on. I made a few attempts. I tried to start an Ultimate Frisbee club, for example, on the premise that exercise is healthy for kids. I invited some kids I'd seen around town to join and they all promised to come, but didn't show up. So I spent an hour every afternoon for a week throwing my Frisbee from one end of a dirt soccer field to the other by myself, hoping some kids would see me and get curious enough to come over and ask what I was doing. None did. I gave up.

After lunch, I'd often go for a run. It was winter so I liked to go when the sun was high enough in the sky to warm me a little. In a sweater and sweat-pants, I'd run out the front gate and follow the dusty streets for two or three minutes to the edge of the village. Then I'd follow the hard-packed dirt and gravel road out through the farm fields. The first time I went out, I turned left at the fork and found myself at the old brick factory. A dog came tearing out at me, barking and snapping. I scooped up a couple rocks. As I raised my hand to throw the first one, the dog skidded to a stop, tucked its tail between its legs, and slunk away, whining.

The brick factory was just a massive trench, big enough to fit a short parade of Land Rovers lined up two by two. Over the trench was a crane. I climbed up to take a look and found two guys drinking vodka in the shack at the crane's base. They hadn't had much yet and seemed sober and friendly, if a bit grimy. One stood up, introduced himself, and shook my hand. I asked him which road I should follow. The one I'd taken snaked past the brick factory and out to the graveyard, he told me. It would be better to retrace my steps and take a different road, one that led out into the farm fields, he said. I followed his advice, jogging along the dusty roads that bordered the bare cotton and wheat fields, hopping over irrigation canals and ducking to avoid the branches of the mulberry trees that lined the roads in places. When I was tired, I used the crane as a landmark to find my way home. The run took 45 minutes and became my standard route.

I usually got home from running at about 1:30, just about the time Jeren and the girls came home from Murgab. Then I'd play with Kümüsh and Altyn and help Jeren around the house a little bit. What she wanted, I think, was company, not help; we did a lot more talking than working. She wanted to know about my life in America, about the books I was reading, about anything and everything outside Nurana. Sometimes we looked at my photographs of Turkey, Thailand, Cambodia, the US.

"When I see pictures of such beautiful places, I don't want to live because I know I'll never go there," she said one day. "You're so lucky."

"Yes," I said, feeling guilty. "I *am* lucky."

* * *

Spring comes early in Turkmenistan. By mid-February, the weather had already warmed and Jeren and I started working in the yard. In the afternoons, we'd go outside with teardrop-shaped spades and turn the earth under the grape vines and in the gardens.

"You know. When I married Döwlet, I set two conditions: I don't pick cotton; and I don't work in the garden," she laughed.

The vineyard was laid out like the garden I'd made in Ana's back yard, with raised planting beds surrounded by irrigation ditches. The planting beds were long and skinny, two or three paces wide, and about 30 paces long. The ditches were waist-deep and almost always dry. When it was time to water the garden, Döwlet would dig a cut into the side of the village irrigation canal that separated our yard from the neighbor's. The water would creep through the labyrinth of ditches in our yard, filling them two feet deep, and over several hours, the planting beds would sop it up until all but the top layer of soil was moist and soft. Then he would throw shovelfuls of dirt back into the cut until the water stopped flowing.

On our first afternoon out in the garden, Jeren and I each picked a skinny strip of vineyard and began working from one end to the other. An irrigation ditch divided us. A white *alabay* puppy wandered over from the neighbor's yard, tumbling into an irrigation ditch and struggling to climb up onto the planting bed where I was standing. Its ears and tail had been pruned, according to custom, and were still raw. At first it was terrified when I tried to pat it. But once it got used to me, it wouldn't leave me alone. It started attacking my ankles as I worked, biting my pants cuffs, pulling and growling.

"No fair, you've got a helper," Jeren said.

"He's helping you a lot more than he's helping me," I said.

A neighbor stopped by with a plate of curly strips of fried

dough, sprinkled with sugar. I stopped to squat on my heels, eat a little, and drink from a bucket of cool water I'd pulled from our cistern. (There's a trick to getting water from a cistern: drop a tin bucket on a rope in and it'll just float; it takes a special flick of the wrist to make it fill with water). Altyn came over, a skinny little thing in a long dress, hair pulled back in a lacy, white scrunchy. She squatted next to me and watched her mother work. When she said something in Turkmen, Jeren started laughing.

"What did she say?" I asked.

"She said: 'Mom if you win, I'll buy you a really nice birthday present,'" Jeren told me.

When I was done with my snack, I went back to work. My soft, city boy hands were starting to blister and my back ached, but as the sun began to sink, I was a few feet ahead. I wasn't about to give up.

"Aren't you thirsty?" Jeren asked. "Take another break and have some more water."

"I think I smell dinner burning," I said. "Maybe you better take a break and check on it."

When the sun set fat and orange behind the house and the muezzin called the evening prayer over the loudspeaker attached to the mosque, we both quit. We lay our spades behind the cookhouse and squatted on our heels next to the vineyard, sharing a dipper of water from the bucket. I'd won by several yards. I gloated.

"Of course you won," Jeren said. "You're a man. It would have been embarrassing for you if you hadn't won."

"If you knew I was going to win, why'd you race me?"

"Because you're an American. I didn't think Americans knew how to do this kind of thing."

From that day on, we worked in the yard most afternoons until sunset. Jeren would take breaks to get dinner simmering and steaming on the stove in the cookhouse. When it got dark, I'd lay out the *klionka* on the living room floor in the main house and help her fetch the meal from the cookhouse across the yard. That's about when Döwlet's car would clatter into the driveway. The girls would run outside to meet their daddy and a few seconds later, he would appear in the doorway, grinning. Some nights, he'd come alone. We'd have a quiet family dinner sitting cross-legged at the *klionka*, gas stove burning to keep the room cozy and warm. After eating, I'd often give Döwlet an English lesson.

"In school, I wanted to learn English so badly, but my teacher was terrible and I didn't learn much," he'd told me. "I think a person who knows a lot of languages and has seen a lot of beautiful places is the richest kind of person."

On the nights when the power was out, we'd sit in the pitch-black living room (candles were expensive), backs against the walls, talking. When we ran out of things to say, I'd fetch my guitar and play a little bit. I'd had the thing for a year and a half, but I still wasn't any good. Jeren would always tease me for not being able to sing and play at the same time – "half a bird," she'd call me.

On the nights when Döwlet brought guests home, we'd sit for hours with them, talking and eating. It was often a surprise. We didn't have a phone, so he couldn't call ahead to warn us. Jeren was a great cook. She'd make *plov* (lamb pilaf with carrots and onions), or *manty* (steamed ravioli-like dumplings filled with lamb, squash, and onions), or salty lamb stew, or fresh-baked spinach *somsas*. And there was always *chorek*, which she baked twice a week in the *tamdur* in the yard. The guests often brought vodka or beer. Döwlet didn't touch alcohol because liver problems ran in his family and Jeren didn't drink because it was an unseemly thing for a good Turkmen woman to do. They didn't mind if their guests drank, though.

Döwlet's best friend Azat visited often. They were the same age but, while Döwlet looked 40, with a creased face and deep-set eyes, Azat was boyish and could have passed for 20 except for the sprinkling of gray in the black hair at his temples. They had always been neighbors, had gone to school together, and now worked together. While Döwlet was a simple, good man, Azat was a hustler. He always had some shady business deal going and a couple mistresses in Murgab.

Azat barely spoke any Russian, so he and Döwlet would talk in Turkmen and I'd do my best to keep up with the gist of the conversation. But when Jeren left the room, Azat would often mock Döwlet for being too much of a wimp too get a woman on the side – and he'd switch to broken Russian to make sure I understood. Döwlet would laugh bashfully and insist that he wasn't scared, he just didn't want to do it. I'd tell Azat he was a jerk and that he should leave Döwlet alone.

Gaigasyz, a retired English teacher from Murgab, also visited now and then. He was in his mid-60s and had a big belly and bristly gray hair, which he covered with a fedora. He spoke excellent English with an archaic touch (using "shall" instead of "will," for example). He'd been an English teacher for a few years before climbing his way into the ranks of the local branch of the Communist Party. He'd spent most of his working life overseeing Party admissions and expulsions, he told me, and had always loved his job. He was still loyal to the Party.

"Gorbachev was a traitor," he said one night. "He sold out the Party."

Gaigasyz struck an imperious, worldly attitude with Döwlet, Azat, and the other country boys from Nurana. They deferred to him, calling him Gaigasyz Aga as a sign of respect, and listening attentively to whatever he said. While he was holding court in Russian or Turkmen, he'd try to make me feel included with English-language asides that only he and I understood.

"These fools think Turkmenistan is paradise because they've never been anywhere else," he said once. "If they only knew."

One night while both Gaigasyz and Azat were over for dinner, after several rounds of vodka, Azat started going on about his new mistress. She'd given him a watch and he passed it around the *klionka*, showing it off.

"Azat you better be using condoms with these girls," I said.

"I don't even know how to use a condom," Azat said. "I've never tried."

"I used to use them, but now that I've gotten older, I can't anymore – it doesn't work," Gaigasyz said. "But you should be using them, Azat. You're still young."

Döwlet just listened and looked embarrassed.

"Azat, I need a favor," Gaigasyz said. "Can you find me a nice woman in Murgab to keep? She should be about 45 years old and very respectable – I have a family, you know."

Azat thought about it.

"My wife can't even walk anymore. The only time she stands up is to go out to the bathroom," Gaigasyz said to me.

"That's very sad," I said.

"Yes it is. She doesn't have sex with me. I may be old, but I still want sex. Not a lot. Maybe once a week," he said. "They have that Viagra from India at the bazaar now. It works pretty well."

"I think I know a woman for you," Azat said. "I'll introduce you to her."

27.
Conversations With a KGB Agent

My life in Nurana had a rhythm. Each day was nearly the same as the next. The events that defined my weeks were finishing a health poster at work, getting a letter from home, or Jeren cooking *plov*, my favorite. I thought I would hate the monotony of such a quiet life. Jeren did. She suffered from a nagging dissatisfaction. She was always saying things like, "I want something, but I just don't know what it is." Maybe it was because I'd had enough excitement in Abadan to last me for a while, but for some reason, I found the routine comforting. As the weeks passed, my anger, bitterness, and frustration faded away.

My journal entries from my time in Abadan were filled with cryptic references. I'd feared the KNB would send someone to read my journal. (After all, they read my mail and clumsily resealed it before forwarding it to me). The entries were filled with screaming capital letters, furious exclamation points, and sarcastic asides. They focused on my frustrations at work, the wrongs done to me, the country's flaws. In Nurana, I wrote my entries in neat, even letters. I didn't use any cryptic entries because I wasn't doing anything worth hiding. I recorded my little adventures, small discoveries, and tiny triumphs:

Kümüsh, my little imp, my sweet little demon sister, stopped being shy around me. It took a while because I was an alien; I spoke only a few words of her language. One evening, while we were all lounging around the living room in front of the television, she walked over me in her frilly white dress, all lace and taffeta and bows in her hair, sat down and started talking to me. When she realized that I still didn't understand Turkmen, she stopped trying to explain and just took my wrist and tied a white string around it, a makeshift *alaja*, a charm against the evil eye. Then she kissed me on the cheek. I was charmed – hers forever. From then on, when Jeren went to a neighbor's house after dinner, Kümüsh would curl up next to me on the living room floor. I'd sing her nonsense lullabies until she fell asleep and then lie there reading my book with her snuggled up in my armpit until Jeren came home and put her to bed.

While I was watching a Russian satellite TV station with Jeren one evening, waiting for Döwlet to get home from work, a furniture commercial came on. "Buy this furniture set now and we'll give you 20 percent off," and that sort of thing. It showed dining room sets and couches, four-poster beds and bookshelves. Jeren was nearly drooling with desire. "Look at the bed," she said. "And the table..." I'd been told during my Peace Corps training that Turkmen ate and slept on their carpeted floors for cultural reasons, because for generations they'd been nomads and so that's the way they'd always lived. I told Jeren that and she laughed at me. "It's not cultural. It's just because we're too poor to buy furniture," she said.

Döwlet and Azat decided I needed to "try" a Turkmen girl. They were offended that I'd spent a year and a half in the country and hadn't already done so. Azat said he knew a girl in Murgab whom he thought I could afford. I thanked him but demurred, telling him that, as a rule, I didn't pay for sex. He was shocked – it was an idea that apparently had not occurred to him. One night Döwlet asked me to help him install a satellite dish in Murgab, something he often did for extra cash. When we arrived, Azat was there, with a mischievous grin and a gorgeous Turkmen girl, with long black hair, dark eyes, and a delicate homemade dress, which, although it covered her from wrist to ankle, left little to the imagination. I chatted with her while I helped Döwlet install the dish, but I declined to go inside with her. Azat, frustrated, got in his car and roared off.

* * *

As winter turned to spring, my routine changed in two ways. One was completely unexpected. I was sitting at my desk in the clinic one morning, working on a poster about anemia, drawing foods that were high in iron. Through the window, I could see three boys standing outside. They'd been whispering to each other and pointing at each other and looking nervously at me for about 15 minutes. Finally, two of them pushed the third toward the door. He

185

was maybe 12 years old, and looked like a miniature Döwlet, with deep-set eyes, dark skin, and bristly black hair. He shuffled in, hands in his pockets, looking at the floor. I put down my colored pencil.

"Hello," I said.

"Will you teach us English because we really want to learn but there's no teacher at school so we don't know what to do and we were thinking you might teach us because we heard you can speak English," he blurted out.

"I'm sorry, but I can't. I'm not allowed in the school and I'm not allowed to teach you here," I said.

"Oh," he said, looking disappointed.

He walked back outside and conferred with his friends for a few moments. They sent him back in to talk to me again.

"Hi," I said.

"You could teach us at your house," he said and stood there looking at me.

I thought about it. I was bored sitting in my office and coloring pictures of spinach, liver, and beans all the time, but I'd resolved to avoid trouble, and government officials had already made it clear to me that they didn't want me teaching English in Nurana. So I put the boys off, thinking they'd lose interest.

"Come back tomorrow," I said. "I'll think about it."

The boys came back the next day – and the day after that and the day after that. They were telling me two important things: first, how they wanted me to help them; and second, how to get around the obstacles to doing it. It took about a week, but I finally heard them. It turned into one of my most pleasant, most satisfying, most productive projects in Turkmenistan and it never caused any trouble with the local authorities.

* * *

At first, I had only three students. They'd meet me at my house at lunch time three days a week and we would sit cross-legged in the living room, the heater making us all sweat, since winter's chill was gone. We started with the alphabet and numbers. I made up games and songs. I drew posters. I invented dialogues.

186

And little by little, my class grew. "We have a friend who really wants to learn English. He's a good student. He won't be any trouble," the boys would plead. "Okay, but this is the last one," I'd say.

Soon I was teaching two or three classes a day, six days a week. I split the kids into beginner and advanced classes (those who knew the alphabet and those who didn't) and divided them into boys' and girls' sections (trying to teach them together led to too much pigtail pulling and giggling). Village fathers and mothers started showing up at my door, asking me to let their sons or daughters into my classes. The two basic classes, which met three times a week, grew to 25 students each. I was having a wonderful time.

Two of my students knew some Russian. The vast majority, however, spoke only Turkmen. That was fine at first. I knew more Turkmen than they knew English – I knew my alphabet, my numbers, my greetings, my colors, how to give directions, and a few simple sentence constructions. I studied in the evenings, adding to my vocabulary, but it soon became clear that my students were learning English faster than I was learning Turkmen and that I was going to have trouble teaching them if I didn't do something drastic. So I started looking for a Turkmen tutor.

When the principal sent a student messenger to the clinic to fetch me, I thought he'd gotten permission for me to teach at his school. Having my kids seated at desks would have cut down on poking and fidgeting. Having a chalkboard would have been easier than drawing a new poster every day. When I arrived in his office, though, it turned out he'd heard I was looking for a tutor. He, like everyone else in Nurana, was eager for me to learn his native language, so he'd convinced one of his teachers to take me on.

That's how I met Maksat. He was a short, stocky middle-aged man with bushy black eyebrows – gruff but friendly. He lived on the far side of the village from me. Two nights a week, after dinner, I'd cross the bridge over the Murgab River, pass the three shops that made up Nurana's downtown, and then follow dirt roads to Maksat's house. It was a large compound, covering about two acres. A yellow-brick wall wrapped around a main house, a cookhouse, and a *banya*. There were also brick houses for his chickens and sheep, a big garden, and an orchard. He had three nearly grown sons and a daughter. His wife was a teacher.

At first, Maksat was wary of me. He mixed pro-government propaganda into his lessons, teaching me words like *Rukhnama*, democracy, independence, and neutrality, which were commonly used in Niyazov's slogans. We sat side by side in easy chairs in his living room, with a coffee table between us. His daughter would bring us a thermos of tea and a plate of hard candies. We would study Turkmen for an hour, until my brain was full, and then sit and talk in Russian for a few minutes before I started home along the unlit streets.

After a few weeks, I learned why Maksat was uncomfortable. In the Soviet era, he'd earned a degree in Marxist-Leninist ideology and then applied to join the KGB. When the recruiter had asked him about his motivation, he recalled, he'd told them: "During the Great Patriotic War the fascists tried to destroy the Soviet Union and my father went to the frontlines to face them. Now, the fascists have been defeated and the capitalist imperialists are trying to destroy the Soviet Union by sending their spies to infiltrate it and spread lies. I want to fight on this new, internal front line, to defend my country." He'd been accepted. Although he'd tried to adjust to the post-Soviet reality, it was still hard for him to have an American sitting in his house. For most of his life, Americans had been enemies, saboteurs, and spies.

One day, Maksat and I were sitting in our twin easy chairs sipping tea when he put his cup down on the table, looked at me, and cleared his throat. He paused and reached down to fiddle with his cup, turning it in circles.

"Sam, you were brought up and educated in a capitalist system and I was brought up and educated in a socialist system. Do you see a big difference? Do we disagree a lot?" he asked me.

"No, I think we mostly agree," I said.

"Me, too," he said. "I think you're not that different from me."

From then on, our Turkmen lessons got shorter and our Russian conversations got longer. We talked about history, politics, economics, religion, and culture. He was well-read and curious. Each of us was fascinated with the other's experiences and ideas. We talked for hours at a time. Maksat was careful not to criticize Niyazov's government. He talked about the country's problems, but like Geldy, insisted that Niyazov was doing as good a job as anyone could, given the circumstances.

"My country is still young," he said. "They didn't build Moscow in a decade. First it was wood and brick, then concrete, then marble. It took time. It'll take time here, too. It's all well and fine to have lots of gas, but if you can't sell it at a good price, it doesn't do you any good."

He told me how, after the Soviet Union fell, he'd lost his savings. He'd had 3,000 rubles in the bank, which was enough at that time to buy two or three new cars or four or five good bulls, he said. When Turkmenistan switched from the *ruble* to the *manat*, inflation wiped out his savings.

"I haven't been back to the bank since then. I ask my friends sometimes whether the building is still there," he said. "I keep hoping that the government will give me some kind of compensation."

Since independence, Turkmenistan had moved toward a democratic political system and a capitalist economy. Like most middle-aged Turkmen I'd met, Maksat believed that democracy was equivalent to chaos and that capitalism was a brutal, Hobbesian system, a lot like the law of the jungle. He saw it as the opposite of the humane communist system he'd grown up with. Still, he had come to believe that capitalism probably worked better in the long-run.

"Capitalism is when the strong succeed and the weak fail, when the hard workers prosper and the lazy ones don't," he said. "I agree with that. That is the way the world works. That's okay. But you have to let it work. Right now there are too many obstacles."

Niyazov had abolished communism and moved toward capitalism. But his constant meddling, regulating, and restricting meant that Turkmenistan still didn't really have capitalism, Maksat said. Instead, it had the worst of both worlds: captialism's brutality and uncertainty and communism's poverty and government interference. People were poor and desperate, he said.

"In the old days, you didn't need to lock your door. You would just put a brick in front of it to keep the wind from blowing it open. Now there are poor people so there are thieves. People are building gates and walls and locking their doors," he said.

"People don't do their jobs well anymore because they

189

aren't thinking about their jobs. They are worrying about how to make more money, how to make a living, how to feed their families. Usually the salary from one job isn't enough to do that. Take me, for example. It would be good if I could just teach my students. I want to teach them. But I can't do good work when I have so much to worry about."

"Why do you think so many people are having problems with blood pressure, strokes, and paralysis since independence? Our diet is the same. Our genetics are the same. I think it's the stress. When the USSR was around, we didn't have to worry about anything. Everything was provided for us: jobs, food, everything. Now we worry all the time."

"I'm raising three boys. I don't have enough money to send them to university. There are no jobs for them. I need to find 60 million *manat* (about $2,400) for bride prices and weddings to marry each of them. I lie awake at night worrying: Where am I going to get the money? What's going to happen to my sons?"

"I guess I won't have to worry for long. I'm 50 and the life expectancy for Turkmen men is only about 60. Most of the time we don't even live that long," he said grimly.[87] "Folk wisdom says that women live longer because they cry themselves clean. Men keep everything bottled up inside and it eventually kills them."

"Every generation here has had its challenge," he said. "My grandparents went through collectivization and the revolution. My parents faced World War II, when there was nothing to eat, no clothes to wear, nothing. I have seen the end of the USSR and the Golden Age of Turkmenbashy. During World War II, there was always hope, at least. They knew the war would end. But now? There is no end in sight. What can we hope for? When will things get better? No one knows."

"I don't know why we put up with it," he said. "The people in Kyrgyzstan, Georgia, Uzbekistan and Ukraine all stood up. Either we are just quiet and obedient like sheep or the future will show that we are wise. I like to think that we are wise."

One of the subjects he returned to week after week was his fear that Turkmenistan was somehow inferior to the rest of the world. He saw Russia, Europe, and America on TV and wondered why those places were so much more developed than Turkmenistan.

"Do you think the intellectual development of people in Turkmenistan is equal to that in America?" he asked me one evening. "During the Industrial Revolution in Europe and America, Turkmen people were still nomads in the desert. Development here is stunted for some reason."

"In China they make televisions," he said. "I have a Chinese television and I can't even work all the different functions, much less make one myself."

As the weeks passed, our post-lesson conversations got darker and darker.

"People here, when they are young, often ask why they were born here," he said on one particularly black day. "'Why not somewhere else, like America? People live well in America,' they say. When they get older, they stop asking. There's no use."

28.
A City Inside a Mountain

After two months in Nurana, I was starting to feel like I was running out of time. I'd applied to graduate schools the previous fall, while my life in Abadan was spiraling out of control and Ana was urging me to go home before I drove myself and everyone around me crazy. To attend, I'd have to leave Turkmenistan early – serving only 22 months of the full, 27-month Peace Corps term.

That was part of the plan, of course. It was an excuse to leave Turkmenistan early without having to admit that I was quitting. Since I'd moved to Nurana, I was no longer so eager to leave Turkmenistan, but I'd organized my life around a June 30 departure date. The wheels were in motion. I was going early whether I liked it or not. That meant that I had only four months left to see everything I wanted to see.

At the top of my list were: Margush, Merv's abandoned Bronze Age ancestor; Yekedeshik, a city-within-a-mountain near the Afghan border; and the Kugitang Nature Reserve, which had petrified dinosaur footprints and good hiking. I decided to start with Margush, since it was an established tourist site in an unrestricted area. It was easy. I just hired a guide and a *marshrutka* and invited my friends Leo and Heidi to come down from Charjou and join me. Döwlet agreed to come, too.

The ruins of the city of Margush lay in the heart of the desert, several hours north of Mary. Called Gonur by archaeologists, it was probably the capital of a kingdom that had thrived in the Murghab delta during the Bronze Age, some 5,000 years ago.[88] The river had receded to the south, though, leaving what had once been a network of perhaps eight major oases thirsty, stranded in the sands of the Karakum. The winter wind kicked up dust and cut through our coats. The ruins were desolately beautiful and our guide brought them to life, conjuring stories from the brick foundations.

The city's residents had been mostly and the guide showed us the remains of one of their massive temples. It was surrounded by little booths set aside for the preparation of a narcotic ceremonial beverage, he said. Inside, there was a vast basin that he said had been a swimming pool, where worshippers in white gowns had ritually bathed (presumably while high).

Lying discarded in the midst of these Bronze Age ruins, we found a four-inch piece of what looked like thick bronze wire. It was green and crusty with corrosion. The guide said that thousands of years ago a woman had probably used it to apply her eyeliner. I held it in the palm of my hand and looked around, trying to imagine all the bricks and broken pottery as a thriving city filled with people not so different from me.

After the tour was over, on the ride home, I asked Döwlet what he'd thought.

"It was boring," he said.

* * *

Visiting Yekedeshik was more complicated because it was in a restricted zone along the Afghan border. Kelly and I decided to try it anyway. We met at the bus stop in Mary early one morning and browsed the shared taxis idling there. They had signs in their windows indicating their destinations. We walked down the row: Yolotan, Murgab, Bayramali, Tagtabazaar.

We asked the driver of the Toyota with the cracked windshield and the Tagtabazaar sign how much he was charging and how long the trip would take. Only 50,000 *manat* (about $2), he said. Only three and a half hours. We decided to give it a try. Worst-case scenario, we decided, we would hit the first checkpoint, the soldiers would tell us we couldn't go any further, and we'd have to get out of the taxi and find our way to Mary. We'd be out maybe $3 and a few hours. We squeezed into taxi's back seat and rode south along the highway, passing through towns and villages, farm fields and pastures.

The middle-aged man sitting next to me in the back seat was from Tagtabazaar, so the stamps in his passport showed that he lived there and was allowed to come and go even though it was in a restricted zone. The old woman in the front seat had a chunk of flesh missing from her nose, a common ailment for people in the Mary area, which I'd been told was caused by some kind of bug bite. She was visiting a relative in Tagtabazaar and had had to apply at a government office for permission and get a sort of visa, almost as if she were traveling to another country.

When we reached the first checkpoint, about an hour and a half south of Mary, we expected to be sent back home. It was a sleepy little place, a booth next to the highway, staffed by two policemen. The driver parked the car and we got out and presented our passports, trying to look nonchalant. The two officers were helpful and friendly, writing down our information in a log book and wishing us a safe journey. They didn't seem at all surprised or troubled by our presence.

We followed the Murgab River south. The flat farmland gave way to barren plains. Then the plains started to wrinkle and rise into hills. The river, which further north had flowed free, winding and curving as it pleased, began to straighten out now that it was trapped in a valley. As we drove, the earth's desolate winter brown gave way to a delicate green. The hillsides were covered in new, spring grass. Flowers sprouted here and there: pink tulips and red poppies. At the next checkpoint, we again braced for rejection. Again, the guards pleasantly sent us along our way. The other passengers and the taxi driver, Berdy, were as surprised as we were.

The landscape was all rolling green hills, treeless but very much alive. We were following the river valley roughly from its delta in the desert near Merv, toward its source in Afghanistan's Hindukush Mountains. It was a route that people had been traveling for millennia: merchants and pilgrims, scholars and migrants. The flow of people continued into the beginning of the twentieth century, when hundreds of Baloch families moved down the valley from Afghanistan into Turkmenistan, settling in towns from Tagtabazaar, to Yolotan, to Bayramali.[89] They looked more Indian than Central Asian and spoke their own language. When the Soviets took power, they closed the border, severing the ancient route.

It felt like the taxi was driving me right out of winter and into spring. The further south we traveled, the greener the countryside became. On the left, a mosque stood on the grassy slope below the road, near the river. It was a square brick thing topped with an onion-shaped turquoise dome. It looked like a Disney mosque, plopped down on a vast swath of Astroturf.

194

At the next checkpoint, the soldiers were more serious. They wore woolen greatcoats and had ornamental daggers tucked into their waistbands. They examined our passports for a long time inside their little booth. I was in a good mood, though, undaunted. Winter was behind me. Everything was going to be fine. I pulled two tomatoes from my jacket pockets, went over to the booth, and offered them to the soldiers. Looking puzzled, they declined. I put one back in my pocket and ate the other one like an apple, pacing next to the road. The wind blowing down the valley was cold, but it didn't have winter's sharp edge. The soldiers waved us on.

Tagtabazaar was like any other medium-sized Turkmen town, except that it wasn't in the desert. It was on the wide valley floor next to a placid stretch of the Murgab River. There was a bank, a bazaar, a city hall, and a taxi stand. The town was surrounded by *kolkhoz*es. It reminded me of Murgab: a county seat in farm country. We dropped the middle-aged man and the woman with the ruined nose at their destinations and Berdy invited us to lunch at his house, promising to take us to Yekedeshik after we'd eaten.

He lived on a *kolkhoz* outside town, in a ramshackle family compound. He'd worked at a natural gas plant until two weeks earlier, when he'd been laid off. Jobless, he was trying to support his wife and three children with the 50,000 *manat* per person that he earned hauling people between Tagtabazaar and Mary. He must have been worried about money, but he still got his teenaged daughter Dunya to fill the table with fried eggs and tomato sauce, tomato-and-cucumber salad, fresh yogurt, and *chorek*.

When we were finished eating, he drove us through Tagtabazaar to a low, treeless mountain – more of a high hill, really – with a hole in its side. We followed narrow access road to a parking lot near the top, got out, and walked down some stairs to the hole. It was reinforced with brick, and secured by a steel door. There was a caretaker sitting on a chair inside the door. He charged us 11,000 *manat* (about 40 cents) and took us on a tour.

The caves had been carved out of the mountain's sandstone heart centuries earlier. They were not rough-hewn caveman caves. The walls met at 90-degree angles. The ceilings were vaulted and, in some places, decorated with raised bands of stone. On the level we were on, there were about two dozen rooms, connected by

195

doors, stairwells, and passageways. The caretaker said there were four additional levels, above and below us. They were filled with sand, though – inaccessible. He showed us a passageway that led out into the dark, further than my keychain flashlight could reach.

"That one leads through the mountain to another cave complex like this one," he said. "But it's full of sand."

Yekedeshik was probably built as a Buddhist monastery sometime around the third century A.D., as Buddhism spread northwest from India into Central Asia. And it was probably abandoned around the ninth century, when Arab armies arrived, pushing Buddhism out of the area, and replacing it with Islam.

The first European to report its existence was a certain Captain F. de Laessoe. It was 1885. The Great Game was in full swing. The Russians had recently taken Merv and had their eye on Tagtabazaar, which was then called Panjdeh and nominally belonged to Afghanistan. The British, worried the Russians were planning to march right through Panjdeh, into Afghanistan, and perhaps on to British India, had pledged to support Afghanistan if Russia tried to seize the town.[90]

As the Russian troops crept south down the Murgab valley from Merv toward Panjdeh – along the same route I'd taken – the British readied two army corps in India to send to Afghanistan's defense. They also convinced the Afghans to reinforce Panjdeh and they sent some British officers to the area to observe. De Laessoe was probably among these.

As the two great empires moved closer and closer to war during February and March of 1885, de Laessoe busied himself with archaeology. A local man led him to Yekedeshik and he quickly hired a crew to dig the sand from its passageways and rooms.[91] But before de Laessoe could finish his excavations, the Russians descended on Panjdeh, killing 800 Afghan soldiers, and seizing the town. De Laessoe was forced to flee, leaving behind the artifacts he'd gathered. The *New York Times* ran a story headlined "England and Russia to Fight," which began: "It is war."[92]

Fortunately, the *Times* was wrong. The ensuing crisis convinced the Russians to stop their southward advance, but they kept Panjdeh. The caves at Yekedeshik had received little attention since that time. "The archaeologists are more interested in Merv and Margush," the caretaker explained.

After exploring the caves for a half hour or so, Kelly and I had seen enough. We climbed back out into the daylight. We found Berdy sitting on a carpet on the grassy hillside above the entrance with two other men, enjoying a picnic. They invited us to join them. I pulled the last tomato from my pocket and added it to the feast of stewed meat and *chorek*. We talked a little about Yekedeshik's history. The Murgab valley spread out below us, the town of Tagtabazaar (once Panjdeh) just a messy concrete blotch on its perfect curves. I looked south, hoping for a glimpse of Afghanistan's mountains, but the gray clouds were hanging too low.

It was getting late and we had a long drive ahead of us so we thanked our hosts, drank a vodka toast, and left. A few minutes north of town we hit the checkpoint with the serious, dagger-wearing soldiers, the ones who'd refused my tomatoes.

"Where have you been?" one of the soldiers asked.

"To Tagtabazaar, to see Yekedeshik," I said.

"How do I know that's where you really went?"

The soldier was bored, I realized. I was in trouble.

"You don't believe me?" I asked.

"If you really went to Tagtabazaar, then what color was the door?"

"I don't remember. Maybe green?" I said, my first mistake.

"It was blue," he said and turned to his partner: "I think we have a problem."

That was when I made my second mistake.

"I have proof that I was there," I said. "I took pictures."

I pulled out my little point-and-shoot digital camera, turned it on, flipped to a photo of Yekedeshik's entrance, and handed it to one of the soldiers. He looked at the photo without commenting and then began to examine the rest of my pictures, one by one. The camera's memory card held more than 500 photos. Fifteen minutes passed. Kelly and Berdy went back to the car. The soldier browsed my pictures of Ashgabat, Abadan, Dekhistan, Anew, Kahka, Darvaza, Turkmenbashy, Avaza, Turkmenabat, Mary, Murgab, Merv, and Margush. The more photos he saw, the more suspicious he got.

"Something's not right here," he said. "Something's definitely not right. You were in all these places? Why did you take so many pictures?"

197

"To show my friends when I get home," I said, starting to get annoyed. "Don't you take pictures when you go on vacation?"

"Why did you take this picture of frozen laundry hanging on a line?"

"Because it's beautiful."

"No it's not. It's stupid."

"What are you, an art critic now? Look, we have to go."

"You'll go when I give you permission to go. I am the police," he said. "They'll do this at the airport when you leave the country, too, you know. It's no big deal."

I was getting impatient. I was sick of being pushed around. I started tapping my fingers on the wall and getting surlier and surlier with my responses to the soldier's questions. None of this seemed to have any effect, though, so I tried the direct approach.

"Look, what's your problem?" I snapped at him. "What do you want?"

He seemed a little taken aback.

"Nothing," he said. "Take it easy."

He looked at a few more pictures and then handed back my camera.

"I was just checking your photos," he said. "Relax."

As we pulled away from the checkpoint, Berdy started yelling at me.

"What's wrong with you!? Why did you give him the camera!? From now on, at checkpoints, don't talk! Hand over your passport and stand there with your mouth shut!"

I sat silently on the lumpy front seat for the next couple hours, chastened. The old Toyota hauled us out of spring and back into winter. We left Kelly in slushy, gray-brown Yolotan so she could find another taxi to take her north up another road to her home in Turkmengala. Berdy and I continued up the highway to Murgab. We passed the former Communist Party headquarters and the World War II memorial and then he pulled over to the curb in front of Döwlet's store, let me out, and headed to Mary to find some more customers.

The store's windows were fogged and its floor was slick with slush and mud. Döwlet and Azat were drinking tea from bowls at a low table set up among all the televisions and refrigerators.

Döwlet poured me a bowl and pushed a plate of hard candies toward me.

"Hello Sam," he said, practicing his English. "What did you do today?"

"I went to Tagtabazaar," I told him, with a self-satisfied grin.

"You went to Tagtabazaar?" he said, switching to Russian. "*We* can't even go to Tagtabazaar. We need permits."

I hooked up my camera to one of the televisions and showed him my photos. He looked at them all twice, asking questions all the while. After another cup of tea, I took a taxi back to Nurana and ate a delicious dinner of potato and mutton-fat soup by candlelight with Jeren and the girls. As we lounged around the living room in the flickering light, talking about our days, Kümüsh curled up next to me, giving me her cutest puppy dog eyes, hoping I would let her have just one more chocolate-covered cookie even though her mother had already cut her off for the night. I did, of course. Who could resist? Jeren scowled at me, but Kümüsh beamed, leaning against me and munching on it, spilling crumbs everywhere. I went to bed that night tired and content.

29.
Reminders

All winter, Nurana was brown and gray, dust and mud. Tree branches were bare, fields were empty, the river was slate. Then one day the naked trees in the village woke from their winter naps and, bashful, draped themselves in gauzy blankets of delicate pink and white blossoms. The village was in an oasis. People had lived there for millennia. There wasn't a square foot of earth that hadn't been turned by human hands, or a single tree that hadn't been planted for a purpose. The modest beauties in their spring petal-shawls were apricot, apple, and plum trees. When the desert wind whipped through the village at night, it shook their branches, pulled at their delicate flowers, and tossed stray petals like confetti onto the ground.

Soon the trees donned leaves to go with their blossoms, the earth sprouted grass, and the village, which had been sterile and dead only weeks before, was lush with life. The children, cooped up all winter, tumbled into the streets to play. Six yellow and brown ducklings took up residence with their parents in the irrigation canal at the edge of my yard. Clumsy lambs appeared in the flocks of sheep that passed my house on the way to pasture each morning. The neighbor's camel gave birth to a gangly baby with long black eyelashes. Birds began to appear from nowhere and ants started building their hills.

I sat in the clinic and watched the spring arrive. The neighbor's camel and her awkward baby grazed outside my window. The seedlings the nurses had planted along the irrigation ditch during the winter sprouted tiny leaves. I was coloring in the letters of one of 10 signs Oraztach had asked for, warning Nurana residents to drink only boiled water. It was a futile task. No one in the village boiled their water unless they were making tea. Posting a few signs wasn't going to change anything. I didn't mind, though. After the long winter, I felt a little drunk from all the color and life of spring.

I shared my office with a doctor and a nurse. The doctor,

Islam, had bad teeth and squinted constantly. He'd stayed out late the night before so he was sleeping face down on his desk next to his abacus. The nurse, Maral, was a half-deaf old battleaxe two months from retirement. As I colored and Islam slept, she swabbed the entire office with a rag soaked in bleach water, as she did each morning. She sterilized the doorstep and the windowsill, the picture frames and the chair legs, the desktops and the walls. When she was done, she sat her heavy backside down on her chair with a sigh and started shuffling through the papers on her desk.

Gözel, the new doctor, walked by our window. She was in her twenties, meek, slim, and pretty. Even though she was from a *kolkhoz* she had modern ways. She didn't cover her hair. She wore traditional clothes that covered her from wrist to ankle, but only because her cafe-au-lait skin was marred by white, pigmentless blotches. She was getting married to a man she'd chosen for herself. Maral sucked her teeth. She disapproved.

"It used to be that boys and girls played separately and parents arranged their marriages. We didn't have love back then," she said. "These days boys and girls spend time together and marry for love."

"Everything's changing," she continued, staring out the window. "Couples are even having fewer kids. They used to have eight, nine, maybe even 10. Now it's more like three or four. There's no work. Families can't feed 10 kids anymore."

For the rest of the morning Maral filled out forms and I colored "Drink Only Boiled Water" signs. Around noon, I woke Islam. We all filed out the door and went home for lunch. I walked over the plank across the irrigation ditch at the edge of the clinic's yard, passed the little brick mosque, crossed the street, and rounded the corner of my house. Seven boys were standing by the door, waiting for their advanced English class. They wore their good school clothes: black slacks and white button-down shirts. The school was too small so the students were split into morning and afternoon sessions. My boys were on afternoons. After class with me, they would run down the street to school.

I opened the front window, reached through, and unlatched the door from the inside. The boys scrambled into the living room, sat down on the floor cross-legged, and unpacked their notebooks and pens. They were about 12 years old, which, in a little village like Nurana, meant they were still very much children. For them, the only thing girls were good for was teasing. They were in awe of adults, polite and deferential.

We were playing bingo when Dowlet's best friend, Azat, dropped by looking for Jeren. I would call out a number in English. The boys would find it among the 25 numbers written into the grids on their bingo boards, and cover it with a scrap of paper. When one of them covered five numbers in a row, he would yell "bingo" and then – stammering and blushing – struggle to read the numbers back in English. I told Azat that Jeren wasn't around. He lingered for a while, watching the boys finish their lesson. When I gave him a bingo board and tried to pull him into the lesson, though, he got shy and left.

That evening, when Döwlet's car chugged into the driveway and shuddered to a stop, Azat was in the passenger seat. He came inside, sat down at the *klionka*, and gave me his best, jaunty English "hello," and a crooked grin. He stayed for *plov*. Jeren apologized, insisting she'd over-salted it, but she was just being modest. We all ate until there were only a few bites left on our plates, drowned in cotton seed oil. Then we scraped the remains to one side and tilted our plates to the other, to drain the oil before finishing. As we sipped our tea, full and content, Azat started telling a story in Turkmen. I heard my name.

"What are you saying about me, Azat?" I asked.

"I'm telling them about your class today," he said.

"You should have seen Sam," he told Döwlet and Jeren. "He was just like a kid, playing games with the students on the floor."

"You're a *viliki dushni chilovek* [big-souled person]," he told me, smiling.

Someone tapped on the door. Döwlet, sitting at the *klionka*, motioned for Jeren to answer it. When she pulled it open, she found a stocky, middle-aged man with a bristly face, wearing greasy sweatpants and a black leather cap. Döwlet put down his spoon, stood, and – still chewing – reached to shake the man's hand. In the Soviet days, the *kolkhoz* had been run by a director, who'd relied on several "brigade leaders" to make sure all the *kolkhozniks* went to the fields to plow, plant, and harvest on time.

202

The man was Döwlet's brigade leader, still hard at work despite the fall of the Soviet Union. He'd come to tell Döwlet to get his act together. It was almost time to plant the cotton and Döwlet hadn't even plowed his 2.5-acre plot.

A few days later, Döwlet came home early from his job at the electronics store. He changed into a dusty, stained pair of slacks and a wrinkled Napoleon Dynamite t-shirt. We climbed into his car and bounced out of town into the cotton fields, passing donkey carts and cars, child shepherds and herds of sheep. After the brigade leader's visit, Döwlet had hired a tractor driver to plow his land. We were going to check his work. The village disappeared in the distance behind us. We stopped next to a rectangular field so large that it would have taken 20 minutes to walk one of its long sides and 10 to walk one of its short sides.

"All this is yours?" I asked, surprised.

"No," Döwlet laughed. "Just this section here, between that sapling and that really tall mulberry tree."

"Who owns the rest?"

"Well, on the left of me is Juma. He's probably got the best plot. It produced more cotton last year than any of the others in this field. Then, to the right, there's ..."

Döwlet proceeded to tell me the owner and production history of each of the dozen or so plots in the field, which, he explained, was called the *Yeke Toot* (Lone Mulberry) field, because there used to be a single mulberry tree growing in its center. Then he moved on and told me about the surrounding fields. There was the one where an old woman had been bitten by a wolf. There was the one where the plows had once turned up human bones and gold trinkets. I had run through these fields a couple times a week since arriving in Nurana and to me, they all looked the same – dirt, trees, rocks. Döwlet, though, knew every inch of soil.

The tractor driver had done poor work, Döwlet decided. The furrows weren't straight and the field was uneven. When Döwlet opened the irrigation ditch, the water would pool in some places and would fail to reach others, drowning some plants and leaving others thirsty. He squatted on his heels at the edge of the field, a sour look on his face. I squatted next to him.

"If my father were alive, he'd make the tractor driver plow

203

it again," he said.

"You should make him redo it, whether your father's around or not."

"I can't. I'm not like that."

Döwlet's father was a strong, outgoing man. A gym teacher who used to run several miles to school every day, he was full of pithy advice for every occasion. He'd died only a few months before I arrived so I'd never met him. In my imagination he resembled the ex-wrestler grandfather Iowa Bob from John Irving's *Hotel New Hampshire*. Döwlet must have been his mother's son. He was quiet, soft-spoken, and shy. His older sisters – he seemed to have an endless supply – were louder and more confident than him. In the Azat-Döwlet partnership, Azat was the leader and Döwlet the sidekick. At home, Jeren deferred to Döwlet's judgment, as a good Turkmen wife was supposed to, but he always seemed a little afraid of her – she was fierce, he was not.

We squatted next to the Lone Mulberry field for an hour, watching the flaming orange sun set over the village. Döwlet was feeling nostalgic. He missed his dad. He missed his guidance and his presence. He missed having his help planting the kitchen garden and the cotton field. He hadn't figured out yet how to work 60-70 hours a week at the electronics store and still get everything done at home, too. He felt lonely and overwhelmed.

Döwlet also missed the *kolkhoz* days. The irrigation ditches along edges of the fields were no longer maintained properly, he said. And the system of metal gates that used to regulate the flow of water in the big canals that fed those ditches had been torn apart, their pieces sold for scrap. A decade earlier, almost all of Turkmenistan's cotton had been harvested by machine. The harvesters broke down, though, and the Turkmen were forced to go back to picking most of their cotton by hand.[93]

All this, I knew, was a symptom of a larger problem: Turkmenistan wasn't developing; it was degenerating. In the Soviet days, Russians had, to a large extent, run the country. They'd had the best educational and career opportunities and had risen to the tops of their fields, becoming directors and managers at every level, from Ashgabat to Nurana. When Russians in Moscow had given orders, in many cases it had been Russians in

Turkmenistan who made sure they were carried out. After independence, many of Turkmenistan's Russians left for Russia. The country lost many of its most experienced managers and most highly skilled workers. Those who had filled their positions had – in many cases – been unable to maintain the infrastructure the Soviets had left behind.

"I don't know what's going to happen to us," Döwlet said sadly, staring out across the field.

I didn't know whether he meant his family, his village, or his country.

* * *

When all Nurana's fields had been plowed, the brigade leaders decided that the time was right for planting. In the late afternoons, the streets were crowded with donkey carts hauling sacks of cotton seed out to the fields. Tractors grumbled along from one plot they'd been hired to plant to the next. All over the village, the men were tense. Since there were no permanent markers dividing the fields into individual plots, there were endless arguments over who owned what. Islam, my officemate, was tangled up in a dispute with the man who farmed the plot next to his. Each year, the man took another yard, Islam complained. Islam had looked the other way for years because he didn't think a yard or two was enough to fight over, but his neighbor just kept taking more and more, so Islam had appealed to the village administrator for help.

It took Döwlet a while to find time to plant. The brigade leader came by the house three times to chastise him. Then one day, Döwlet brought four sacks of cotton seed home. The sacks were as big and heavy as dead sheep. The seeds were fuzzy pellets coated in a red powder that Döwlet said was a pesticide, meant to keep critters from eating them while they lay in storage during the winter. We washed it off by dunking the sacks in the irrigation canal at the edge of our yard, where the ducklings lived. Since Döwlet's car had a flat tire and he couldn't afford to fix it, he borrowed a donkey and a cart from a neighbor.

The cart was a wood-plank platform set atop a single axle

that had car wheels fastened to either end. Two scrap metal bars connected it to the donkey's saddle. Döwlet and I loaded the wet sacks onto the cart. They dripped pink pesticide water through its cracks and into the dust below. We sat on the cart's front edge, just behind the donkey, taking turns holding the reins. The old gray beast trudged toward the fields. We rolled through a trash-strewn empty lot at the edge of the village and then past electric-green fields of young wheat and dusty brown cotton fields.

Döwlet was impatient. He whipped the donkey's flanks with a twig and yelled at it to go faster. The donkey was much better at ignoring orders, though, than Döwlet was at giving them. It continued on at its own pace. Eventually he gave up and we lounged on the cart under the cloudless sky, letting the donkey find its own way along the road, at its own speed. The temperature was well above 90 degrees, but a restless wind kept us cool. As we approached farmers returning from the fields, Döwlet would sit up and greet them. They'd offer a formulaic blessing, the same every time. I didn't understand it completely, but it was along the lines of "may your seeds grow and multiply." Döwlet would thank them, return the blessing, and lie back down.

When we reached the Lone Mulberry field, we found that we were fifth in line for the tractor driver's services. For three hours, we lay in the shade of a mulberry tree, watching the ancient Soviet "Belorus" tractor kick up dust as it roared back and forth across the field, opening the furrows, depositing the seeds, closing the furrows. Back and forth, back and forth. The donkey grazed on weeds. When our turn came, we hauled our sacks of seed to the tractor and poured them into the four funnel-shaped hoppers on the sledge it was pulling. We stood on the sledge as the tractor pulled it across the field, using sticks to stir the cotton seeds in their hoppers, to make sure they flowed smoothly so they would deposit the seeds in evenly spaced rows.

The dust swirled around us and the sledge shook and rattled like it was about to fall apart. I held on with my left hand, legs braced far apart, and stirred. I could taste the dust; I could feel the grit in my eyes. When the tractor came to the edge of the field, Döwlet and I would jump off the planter into the powdery soil. The tractor would raise the sledge, make the turn, and then lower it back to earth. As the tractor accelerated back across the field, we'd chase after it, and leap back onto the sledge.

Once, a hopper started dumping seeds in random clumps and Döwlet threw a stick at the tractor's back window. The driver stopped, climbed wearily down from the cab, and inspected the hopper. As the tractor idled, he walked back to the cab and found a curl of baling wire, a pair of pliers, and a hammer made from a lump of iron welded to a piece of pipe. He banged and tied and twisted for a few minutes and then climbed back into the cab. We were off again.

When the tractor driver finished Döwlet's plot, he paused long enough to pick up the next farmer and refill the hoppers. Then he roared away across the field again in his little tornado of dust. Döwlet and I, dirt covering our clothes and crunching between our teeth, climbed back on our donkey cart and headed home. As we approached the village, the sun was setting and we could hear the muezzin's call to prayer, amplified by the mosque's tinny old loudspeaker. I made a joke about how the muezzin kept calling and calling, but no one was listening – the mosque was usually empty. Döwlet took my joke as a personal criticism and said he was too busy to go to mosque. He told me a parable about two men. One secretly doubted God's existence but went to mosque every day so his neighbors would respect him as a pious man. The other was a drinker who never set foot in a mosque but went to bed every night asking God, in whom he fervently believed, to forgive his sins. When both men died, the pious man went to hell, the drinker to heaven.

"As long as you think of God, as long as you believe in him, you're okay," Döwlet said.

At home, we took turns in the *banya*. With cool water from the cistern, I washed the dust from my hair and skin. In the dim room, I kicked something squishy. It turned out to be a frog, which leaped into the drain and swam out to the irrigation canal behind the *banya*. While Döwlet and I were in the field, Jeren had made a giant meal. The *klionka* was loaded with spinach *somsas* and *plov* and mutton fat soup. She had even baked *yagly nan* (bread dough mixed with mutton fat, salt, and onions and baked in the *tamdur*), one of the most delicious things in the world. There were plates of sliced cucumbers, scallions, and kiwis, and a bowl of chocolate

207

cookies. We ate until we were stuffed and then lounged around the living room watching American movies dubbed into Russian (the end of *Black Rain* and the beginning of *Cobra*) until it was time for bed.

* * *

As spring deepened and the blossoms on the trees in our yard were replaced by miniature apples, apricots, plums, and pomegranates, my Turkmen lessons with Maksat started to pay off. When I met people in the street, I could ask after their families in Turkmen instead of Russian, which they seemed to appreciate. At home, I could finally talk to my little sisters, who didn't know Russian. When Altyn asked me one day to help her tie a loop of rope onto the branch of an apricot tree in our yard, I understood her. It was an epiphany. After months of mime, we had discovered language. After I'd finished with the knots, she sat in the loop and swung toward the sky, shaking the branch and bringing a few stray leaves down on her head.

"Do you have swings in America?" she asked.

"Yes," I assured her.

She was so pleased that I could understand her that she decided I should learn faster. She started quizzing me on Turkmen vocabulary, leading me around the house, pointing to objects, and demanding that I name them. It became a competition. She had joined my basic English class and was among the best students even though, at eight, she was four years younger than most of the other kids. So when she asked me for a word in Turkmen, I'd ask her for a word in English in return. The problem was, she was learning faster than I was. She taunted me mercilessly. Teachers give Turkmen students number grades (5, 4, 3, 2, 1) instead of letter grades (A, B, C, D, F). Altyn nicknamed me *birlik*, which means, roughly, "1 student," or "F student."

I tried to catch up, but, unfortunately, my Turkmen teacher had given up on teaching me Turkmen. He'd decided that I would never use the language once I returned to America. So he started teaching me about Turkmen culture, instead. Twice a week I'd walk across town to his house. Those spring evenings were warm and clear. As I crossed the bridge, a few of my students, swimming in the river below, would call out "hello, teacher" and I'd wave. I'd often stop at the store for a chocolate-covered ice cream bar. When I knocked at Maksat's gate his mutt would run around the corner and bark at me until I bent down to pet it. Hearing the racket, Maksat would appear from one of the buildings surrounding the courtyard and shake my hand. Then we'd walk over to his neighbor's mud-brick garage.

As part of my Turkmen culture lessons, Maksat was teaching me about silk production. Nurana's teachers were all required to buy 7 grams of silk worm eggs, raise the worms, and sell their cocoons to the government. This annoyed Maksat. He had enough to do already and there wasn't much money in raising silk worms. The government paid less than $1 per kilogram for even the highest quality cocoons. So he gave his eggs to his neighbor to raise. That way he'd get credit for meeting his quota and the neighbor would get the profits, such as they were.

Inside the neighbor's garage was a single, massive table, pieced together from sawhorses and stray boards, and covered with what looked like butcher paper. A gas heater warmed the garage. A light bulb hung from the underside of its straw-and-mud roof. On the table was a pile of mulberry leaves that the women of the house had chopped with knives and scissors. It was sprinkled with squirming white silk worms. They were the size of maggots when I first saw them, but slowly grew to the size off my thumb. Eventually, they would spin themselves into cocoons of long silk threads, which the neighbor would gather and sell to the government.

After checking on the worms' progress, Maksat and I would go back to his house to sit in his twin easy chairs and talk. One day he gave me a lesson on Turkmen names. Some were names of precious things: Altyn means gold, and Kümüsh means silver. Others were like prayers: if a man's wife gave birth to a series of daughters, he might name the fifth or sixth Ogulgerek, meaning, "I want a boy." If his next child were a boy, he might call him Hudayberdy, meaning, "God gave." Others were just functional. If a couple had whole series of boys, they might start numbering them: four, five, six, seven (Chary, Bashim, Alty, Yedy). So, Maksat joked, if a guy is giving you trouble and you're thinking of fighting him, ask his name. If it's Hudayberdy, you can be pretty sure he's alone, so hit him. If it's Yedy, he has six brothers, so run for your life.

On other days, Maksat told me about Turkmen artists. He showed me a book of paintings by Ayhan Hajiyev, realistic renderings of collectivization, *kolkhoz* life, and Turkmen heroes. He told me how, during the Soviet era, men like Ashyr Kuliev had studied at universities in Russia and become great composers of Western-style classical music. We also talked a lot about great Turkmen writers, and especially the eighteenth century poet Magtymguly Feraghy.

There is no writer who holds a place in American culture analogous to Magtymguly's place in Turkmen culture. Magtymguly is a national hero and sage. Every Turkmen knows who Magtymguly is and most can quote from his work. Many of his best lines are so well known that they have become proverbs.

Magtymguly studied in *madrassahs* in Bukhara and Khiva and then worked as a teacher and silversmith.[94] He wrote poetry in his free time. While most Central Asian poets at the time wrote in one of the region's literary languages (Chagatay, Arabic, and Persian), Magtymguly wrote in Turkmen, which he thought was just as beautiful. In fact, he was something of a proto-nationalist. He wrote poems decrying the tribal divisions he believed kept the Turkmen weak and disorganized. "If Turkmens would only tighten the Belt of Determination," he wrote, "they could drink the Red Sea in their strength/ So let the tribes of Teke, Yomut, Gokleng, Yazir, and Alili/ Unite into one proud nation."

All the great Turkmen writers Maksat told me about were, like Magtymguly, long dead. When I asked him who the great contemporary Turkmen writers were, he laughed.

"There's only one," he said. "The Great Turkmenbashy."

* * *

I was content in Nurana, happy. The village was beautiful, my friends and host family were kind, and my English classes kept me busy. I had to return to the Ashgabat area twice during the spring, though, and each time I was reminded why I'd been so

210

frustrated and angry for my first year and a half in Turkmenistan. There were the checkpoints clogging the roads on the way to the capital, staffed by surly guards and stuffed with impatient travelers. And there were Ashgabat's golden statues and stupid slogans: "The 21st Century is Turkmenistan's Golden Age," "People, Nation, Turkmenbashy." Within hours of leaving Nurana, I was wound up, pissed off, and full of despair for the future of the country.

The first time I returned to Ashgabat, it was for the debate tournament I'd begun planning with Mehri so many months earlier. The tournament itself went fine. Mehri and Phoebe had arranged travel and lodging for the nine debate teams that slipped quietly into Ashgabat from across Turkmenistan. The debaters met at the Peace Corps office for a series of 44-minute debates on whether it was better to deal with drug addicts through law enforcement (throw them in prison) or harm reduction (give them clean needles, put them in rehab). Each team debated four times, starting with prepared statements and working through a series of cross-examinations and rebuttals. Panels of Peace Corps Volunteers served as judges.

The kids were terrified at first, but their coaches had prepared them well, and after the second round their stage fright wore off and they dug in for battle. They'd spent weeks doing research and came armed with statistics on things like how much it cost to imprison a drug addict versus how much it cost to put him in rehab. In the final round, a team from Mary and a team from Turkmenbashy faced off in front a panel of seven judges and an audience of about 40. After it was all over, we talked to the debaters about how to start debate clubs, sent them home with debate coach handbooks, and went to the bar to celebrate.

The depressing part of the trip came after the tournament was over, when I took a *marshrutka* to Abadan to visit Ana and Sesili. The hot weather had ruined their business; their Korean salads had started spoiling before they could sell them. Then Ana's brother Andrei had gotten sick. Helping to pay his hospital bills and support his family while he was out of work had wiped out Ana and Sesili's savings. They were scraping by on the money that Sesili brought home from selling cabbages at the bazaar for 1,500 *manat* a piece (about 6 cents). They were so broke they couldn't even offer me dinner. We drank tea together for a while and then I excused myself. I left a roll of cash on the bathroom sink with a note that said: "Don't argue with me, just take it." On my way out, I stopped to check on my garden. Nothing had sprouted.

The second time I returned to Ashgabat was to speak at a conference on tourism in Turkmenistan organized by the Organization for Security and Cooperation in Europe (OSCE). It was held at the glitzy new President Hotel.[95] Most of the 50 or so conference participants were employees of either government ministries or state-run tourism agencies. They spent a lot of time congratulating each other on what a good job they were all doing. A couple European tourism experts gave speeches on how to make budding tourism industries like Turkmenistan's flourish. When it was my turn, I gave a slideshow of some of the tourist attractions I'd visited in Turkmenistan: Merv, Margush, Dekhistan, and Yekedeshik. Turkmenistan had a fascinating history that tourists would pay to come see, I told the audience.

"The problem," I said, "is that you make it so hard for tourists to come here and see all these wonderful things. I visited Thailand recently. At the airport, a customs official checked my passport, issued me a visa, and wished me well. It took about five minutes. Then I was free to go anywhere and see anything."

"If an American tourist wants to come to Turkmenistan, he needs a Turkmen organization to apply to the Turkmen government for a letter of invitation, which takes weeks. After he gets the letter, he has to apply to the Turkmen embassy in Washington for a visa. Then, once he arrives in the country, in most cases, he can travel only to certain places and only under the supervision of a 'guide' provided by one of the state tourism agencies."

As I spoke, the audience began to shift in their chairs, shuffle papers, and harrumph. When I was done, a middle-aged suit raised his hand and told me I was wrong – that it was easy for foreigners to visit Turkmenistan. Perhaps he meant it was easier than it had been in the Soviet era. After my talk, there was a break before the next session. I went to the hotel bar for a cup of coffee. I wanted a minute to unwind; I'm uncomfortable speaking in public.

A suave young man from the Ministry of Foreign Affairs drifted over to where I was sitting. He spoke good English and had a warm, easy manner. He wore a suit with a shiny gold pin on his lapel that depicted Niyazov's head. His black hair was cut short and his face was clean shaven, all in accordance with Niyazov's decree that Turkmen men should not wear long hair or beards.[96]

"Now why did you have to say that?" he asked me, smiling. "You offended people."

"I didn't mean to offend anyone," I said. "But somebody needed to say it."

After the conference was over, I packed my bags and headed back to Nurana. I stopped by the Peace Corps office on the way out of town to check my mailbox. In the hallway, I ran into Sachly, my supervisor.

"Sam, have you been traveling a lot?" she asked.

"Not really," I said. "Why?"

"Because I hear they're asking a lot of questions about you in Mary. I don't know why, but I thought it might be because you were traveling a lot."

In the taxi home, I seethed. Once again, I'd run head on into the Turkmen government's refusal to acknowledge reality. There was no hope that things would improve as long the government continued to insist that everything was already perfect, that the country was already in a "Golden Age." And the police or the KNB was on my case again.

As I waited through checkpoint after checkpoint, I was sorry I'd left Nurana and visited the other part of Turkmenistan – the ugly, absurd, fucked up, government-controlled part. I was pissed off for days. It took a long, sunny afternoon of sitting under a mulberry tree playing my guitar and teaching Döwlet a Woody Guthrie song while Kümüsh and Altyn gathered sun-warmed apricots and plums nearby, the smell of simmering *plov* drifting over from the kitchen, to remind me why I'd come to love Turkmenistan.

213

30.
Boating the Karakum

With only about a month left, I decided to check another item off my list of places to see before leaving Turkmenistan. I still hadn't figured out which permits I needed to legally go see the dinosaur footprints in Kugitang Nature Reserve – much less how to get them. Instead of wading through bureaucratic nonsense for weeks to figure it out, though, I decided to outsmart the system. After all, I'd managed to visit Yekedeshik without any permits.

The normal way to get from Murgab to Kugitang would have been to bump north for three hours along the black highway through Mary to Turkmenabat and then hang a right and follow the Amudarya southeast for about five hours to the reserve. That route was choked with checkpoints – impossible without permits. Lying on the living room floor one afternoon, studying a map, though, I noticed that there was another route. A thin red line on the map ran east from Mary through the desert to Kugitang. It was so small and remote that surely no one would be guarding it, I thought.

I convinced my friends Kelly and Alei to join me in my ill-advised, permit-less attempt to reach Kugitang. We took the main highway north from Mary, as if we were going to follow the standard route. But we got out of our taxi at Ravnina, a black blip on the map at the beginning of the red line that led through the desert to Kugitang. I'd expected a town, or maybe a village. Ravnina turned out to be a few houses sprinkled over some drifting sand dunes. The sun beat down on us and a constant wind spread sand and dust over everything. There was an ancient two-ton truck parked near the spot next to the highway where our taxi had left us. We walked over and asked its driver to take us to Kugitang. He looked at us like we were crazy.

"It's too far," he said. "And the road's terrible. It's just sand."

"Take us part way. Take us to Nichka. We'll find someone there to take us the rest of the way," I said.

"Just come in and have lunch with me and then go home," he said.

"You'd rather sit here all day and do nothing than take us to

Nichka and make some money?" I asked.

"Yes," he said.

Defeated, we walked over to a *chaikhana* (teahouse), near the road. It was the only business in Ravnina as far as I could tell. We were its only customers. We sat outside on a shaded *tapjan* and ordered *manty* with sour cream. We told the owner we were looking for a ride to Nichka. She sent a little boy running off across the sand to look for someone willing to take us. We sat and ate the lamb-and-onion filled dumplings with our hands and watched the sand blow, the sun burn, and the cars roll by on the highway. We sweated.

After a half-hour, the boy hadn't returned, so Kelly and I took a walk through the village to find another truck and try to convince its owner to take us to Nichka – or even to Kugitang. Alei stayed on the *tapjan* with the leftover *manty* and a big, Russian-style 3.5-ounce shot of vodka. There was another truck parked outside a sun-bleached brick house, but we couldn't find its owner. A group of older men squatted on their heels nearby, smoking and talking. When I joined them, they told me that the owner of the truck was out of town and said I would have better luck finding a ride from a nearby town called Zakhmet. It wasn't at the beginning of the road I wanted to travel on, but at least it was a decent sized town, with more than two trucks.

Kelly and I walked back to the *chaikhana*, wilting under the angry sun, and woke Alei from his nap. We paid our bill, walked to the highway, and – after a few attempts – managed to flag down a *marshrutka* to Zakhmet, which turned out to be a proper town of pleasant one-story homes with sunflowers growing in their yards. I asked the first person I saw where I could hire a truck to take me to Nichka. He leaned out the window of his beat up white Lada.

"A truck? You should take the boat," he said.

At first, I thought he was mocking me. We were standing in the middle of a desert. But he didn't look like he was kidding. It dawned on me that we were close to the massive Karakum Canal, a Soviet-era irrigation canal that was longer than Europe's longest river, the Rhine. It hadn't occurred to me that boats might travel along the canal, though I knew it was plenty big enough – 800 feet wide in some places.[97] I consulted my map. The canal appeared to

215

run straight to Kugitang. I pictured myself bouncing along a sandy road in the sweltering cab of a 20-year-old truck. Then I pictured myself lounging on the deck of a ferry, the cool wind blowing off the canal, the miles drifting by.

"Where can I catch the boat?" I asked.

"See those cranes? That's the port."

We started walking. The roads were dirt and the houses were surrounded by fences made from scraps of lumber so sun-bleached that they looked like driftwood. The sunflowers towered over us. Their drooping heads, too heavy to face the sun, looked disapprovingly down at us. Camels munched on thorns and shrubs in front yards, but we were the only people outside. It was mid-day. No one else was foolish enough to take a beating from the sun.

The port was a ramshackle, rusted, Soviet relic. Towering over it were two massive cranes, which must have been 100 feet tall and were encased in rust. Three boats were tied up at the edge of the canal. It was unclear which of them had been junked (maybe all of them) and which of them were still in use (maybe all of them). At the base of the cranes, a couple of dockworkers were frying potatoes and mutton in a cast-iron cauldron over a wood fire. They told us that one of the boats was due to leave for Nichka that evening and its captain, Berdy, might agree to take us along.

I set off across town, following the dockworkers' directions to Berdy's house, while Kelly and Alei waited in the shade of the cranes. After a half an hour of searching, though, I gave up. No one seemed to know – or be willing to tell me – which house was Berdy's. And I couldn't take the sun anymore. It was boring into my head, cooking my brain. I was starting to feel woozy. I took off my button-down shirt and covered my head with it as I walked back to the port.

Kelly and Alei had disappeared from their spot under the cranes. When I asked where they'd gone, the dockworkers, eating their potatoes and mutton, pointed toward a wooden shack. Inside the shack, there were two rooms. I poked my head in the first one and found a gray-haired man in raggedy clothes sitting by the window, smoking a cigarette. He was the port's watchman; the shack was his home. Drawing on his cigarette, he inclined his head toward the other room. I followed his cue and found Kelly and Alei sitting in rickety metal chairs against the wall of the second room while a fat policeman wearing his open uniform jacket over a dirty white undershirt examined their passports.

I introduced myself, handed the policeman my passport, and sat down next to my friends. The policeman had heard about our arrival and had come to find out who we were and what we were doing in his town. At first, he found it hard to believe that we were teachers from America who wanted to take the boat to Nichka for fun. He sweated. He paged through our passports again and again. After a few minutes, though, he returned our documents to us, wished us luck, and left.

Once the policeman was gone, I rifled through my backpack to find a bottle of water. As I poured as much of it as I could down my throat, the watchman appeared in the doorway. He offered us hot tea, which I accepted, and invited us to stay and rest for a while. When the sun had fallen a little and the temperature had dropped below 110 degrees, the watchman took us across town to Berdy's house. He banged on the door and Berdy appeared, a fit and serious man of about 40, with heavy, black eyebrows. He'd been sleeping when we knocked and was still pulling on his t-shirt (backwards) as he invited us in. We sat cross-legged on the carpeted floor of his living room and drank tea while we talked. After two cups, he'd agreed to take us to Nichka and we'd settled on a price. He told us to meet him at the port in two hours. We would motor upstream all night and arrive in the morning.

We left Berdy to get his t-shirt on forwards and pack his things. On the way back to the port, we ducked into a tiny store and bought vodka, pickles, bread, cheese, and dried sausage from its half-empty shelves. Berdy appeared at the port exactly on time. He climbed onto his boat, started the engines, cast off, and motioned for us to hop aboard. The boat, which was painted blue and white, was about 25 feet long. It had a pilothouse amidships and a *tapjan* on the bow, shaded by an awning made from reed mats. Below deck there was a cabin with four saggy bunks. The boat hummed and vibrated under my feet. It smelled like diesel. Kelly, Alei, and I climbed onto the *tapjan*, dropped our backpacks and plastic shopping bags of food, and settled in for the long trip.

The boat chugged upstream, parting the massive canal's

muddy waters with its bow, leaving a trail of bubbles behind. We passed under a highway bridge and waved to some boys swimming near the shore. Then we left the houses and sunflowers of Zakhmet behind and entered the open desert. By boat. It was a strange feeling. I sat on the bow, my feet hanging over the side, the bow wave frothing below me, watching the sand-dune-and-scrub desert roll by. Kelly listened to her iPod nearby and Alei napped on the *tapjan*. Berdy stood in the pilothouse, hands on the wheel, eyes on the canal.

* * *

When the Russians conquered Turkmenistan, they thought it would be a good idea to turn it into a cotton colony, but found that although it had good soil and plenty of sunshine, it didn't have enough water. So they decided to build a canal for irrigation. They couldn't find investors for the project, though. When the Soviets took control, they had the same idea, but they were delayed for a while by the civil war, collectivization, and World War II. It wasn't until after the war that they started construction.[98] The Soviets, of course, didn't need to look for investors.

The canal began near Turkmenistan's southeast corner, branching off the Amudarya and following the bed of the long-dead Kelif Uzboi River.[99] It stretched west through the Karakum, along the base of the Kopetdag Mountains, passing through Mary and Ashgabat. The further it got from the Amudarya, the narrower it became until it eventually got small enough to fit into a pipe. The pipe reached the Caspian shore at Krasnovodsk in 1986. The completed canal was 851 miles long, making it the longest irrigation canal in the world. It can take 30 days for water to travel from one end to the other.[100]

The Karakum Canal siphons vast amounts of water out of the Amudarya to quench the thirst of Turkmenistan's cotton and wheat fields. By the 1970s, Soviet scientists had realized that the canal, combined with all the other irrigation projects in the Amudarya basin, would eventually kill the Aral Sea. After all, the sea, which straddled the Uzbek-Kazakh border and was roughly the size of West Virginia at the time, got 75 percent of its water from the Amudarya. If the river's water fed cotton fields instead of replenishing the sea, the sea would evaporate like a puddle in a summer parking lot. They proposed saving the sea by diverting a few Siberian rivers to fill it back up again,[101] but they never got around to it.

By 2007, the Aral Sea had lost three-quarters of its volume and more than half its surface area. It had split into three puddles. (Two continued to dry up. One was dammed off and began slowly to refill.) As the sea withered away, it left behind 5,000 square miles of salty wasteland – an area almost as big as Connecticut. "The shriveling sea bequeathed poisonous sandstorms, chronic health problems, dead fishing grounds and unemployment" to the areas in Uzbekistan and Kazakhstan that surrounded it. The slow death of the Aral Sea has been called one of the worst ecological disasters of the twentieth century.[102]

As I floated through the Karakum Desert on water that should have been filling the faraway Aral Sea, I passed several rusty old barges, which looked like they were held together with old twists of wire and bits of welded tin cans. They were dredging barges, sucking sand off the bottom of the canal, and spitting it out onto the shore, to keep the canal deep and straight. In the Soviet days, a staff of 1,700 had tended the canal, which was crucial to producing food for local consumption and cotton for export. By 1996, the Soviet Union had fallen and there were only 640 workers still on the job.

Although engineers use computers to manage water flow through most major irrigation systems in the world, the remaining workers on the Karakum had to make do with more primitive technology. They monitored water levels with a series of what were essentially giant rulers. Workers noted how high the water was on the rulers and called the data in to a central office in Ashgabat – when the phones were working.[103] Using this scanty information, engineers had to keep the water in the canal flowing fast enough so that sediment didn't have time to settle to the bottom of the canal, but not so fast so fast that it ripped up the sandy bed of the canal and carried it downstream.[104] They also had to balance the canal's needs with the farmers' needs, making sure that enough water flowed out of the main canal and into the fields to produce a good harvest.

Under these difficult circumstances, the staff often pulled far too much water out of the Amudarya and into the Karakum Canal system. So, even as the Aral Sea was dying of thirst, engineers were dumping excess water into the desert and farmers in Turkmenistan were over-watering their fields, "which has led to widespread land degradation in the Karakum Canal zone. Rising groundwater tables and soil salinization now [have become] endemic and ... resulted in large tracts of land being abandoned and a significant reduction in crop yields"[105]

The water table in Murgab was so high that when Döwlet's brother-in-law was working in his courtyard garden, it took only two big shovels-full of dirt to dig a hole that would fill with water from underground. All over the Murgab oasis, from Mary to Bayramali to Murgab, I saw vast tracts of land covered in what looked like a sprinkling of snow; when I tasted it, it turned out to be a crust of salt.

Despite the environmental disaster that the Karakum Canal had helped to cause in the Aral Sea and in Turkmenistan, the Soviet government looked on the bright side. A 1977 report from the USSR Academy of Sciences pointed out that the canal created a micro-climate that was slightly cooler and wetter than the standard Karakum Desert climate and, as a result, was more comfortable for people to live in. The report also pointed out that the canal had created a huge swath of new habitat for fish, birds, and plants.[106] That much was true. The canal was swarming with life. In some places, the desert sloped gently into the water and the shoreline was choked with reeds taller than our boat. In others, the sand dunes dropped straight down into the canal, creating sandy cliffs, where birds dug holes for their nests. As we passed, they soared over us, diving and swooping. Though I couldn't see any fish swimming in the murky water, I did see fishermen standing next to the canal now and then, selling fish as big as my thigh.

The trip was peaceful. The chugging of the boat's engine was the only sound that broke the silence. I saw a few people on shore: shepherds watching herds of sheep from the backs of donkeys and beekeepers tending to stacks of white bee boxes. But mostly we were alone under an electric blue sky with a few high, wispy clouds. We lounged on the *tapjan* reading, listening to music, and watching the desert drift by. Berdy stopped the boat in the late afternoon so we could jump into the water and cool off. The canal was about 10 feet deep, warm, and muddy. Lying on the deck afterwards, it took only a few minutes to dry out. As the sun dipped below the sand dunes to our stern, a crescent moon appeared, hanging precariously from the navy blue fabric of the sky. Then the sky faded from navy blue to black, and the stars began to appear, first by the dozen, then by the thousand.

After finishing a half-liter bottle of vodka with Alei, I fell asleep on the *tapjan*. Sometime in the middle of the night, Berdy pulled the boat over into the reeds and threw an anchor ashore. A swarm of mosquitoes woke me by trying to suck as much blood as possible from my face, hands, and ankles. I wrapped myself in the carpet covering the *tapjan* and went back to sleep. I woke again when the marigold sun started rising over our bow. Berdy appeared from below, pulled the anchor back on board, and started the engine. After another hour, we arrived in Nichka. The trip had taken 12 hours.

Berdy's job was to pick up his boss, the engineer in charge of overseeing the Zakhmet-Nichka stretch of the canal, and take him back to Zakhmet. The boss was waiting on Nichka's pier with a couple of assistants. He was a middle-aged Turkmen bureaucrat, overweight and greasy, with thinning hair. As soon as he laid eyes on Alei, Kelly, and I, he started yelling at Berdy for bringing us along. We were not going to Kugitang, we were going back to Zakhmet with him, he said. At first he didn't want to allow us ashore even for a moment, but after Berdy put in a word for us, he told us we could go into Nichka to find a bathroom and buy some food, but we'd better hurry. We left the two men arguing on the waterfront and slipped into town.

Nichka's houses were weathered but well-kept, its yards were planted with vegetables and carefully weeded, its streets were sandy and clean. There were no cars in sight. In the sandy village square, there was a 30-foot-long model of the canal. When we asked for directions to the bazaar, we learned that it had been closed for the day because of a mild sandstorm. So we found a tiny shop that an old woman was running out of her house and bought what she had: orange soda and cookies. She let us use her outhouse, too, which was built from weathered scrap wood and was listing to one side. Then we hurried back to the boat.

Berdy cast off as soon as we were on board, and turned the boat around, pointing it downstream toward Zakhmet. While the boss brooded on the bow, I ducked into the pilothouse to apologize to Berdy for getting him in trouble and to try to find out what we'd done wrong. It turned out that two KNB men had visited Berdy's boss the previous week and warned him not to allow any strangers on the canal. Since it began within spitting distance of Afghanistan and was barely monitored by the police, it had become an opium smuggling route. The boss was convinced that we were either smugglers or spies and that he was going to end up in jail because we'd appeared on the canal on his watch.

The authorities in Turkmenistan have been trying for at least a century to stem the flow of opium across their southern border. Raw opium has been used in Turkmenistan for centuries, both as a panacea to cure everything from aches and pains to diarrhea and coughing, and also used recreationally. When the Russians conquered the Turkmen lands, large quantities of opium were being imported from Afghanistan and Iran.[107] The Russians and then the Soviets and then the independent Turkmen government fought this flow of drugs and failed.

But it seemed the boss was determined to do his bit in this endless war on drugs by turning us in to the police. On the long ride back to Zakhmet, we took turns trying to smooth things over with him, to convince him we were neither smugglers nor spies. He immediately hated Alei, who asked him what was wrong and how we could fix things. He tolerated my questions about the plants and birds of the canal zone. He liked Kelly. Of the three of us, she spoke the best Turkmen. She was also young and pretty and had good Turkmen manners. He was charmed. The atmosphere on the boat began to thaw.

After a few hours, we stopped at a dredging barge so the boss could bark some orders at its crew. While the boss was acting important, Berdy bought a three-foot-long fish from a man sitting on a nearby sand dune. He hung it from the awning over the *tapjan* where it dripped fish juice from its tail onto the deck, its mouth gaping at the sky.

Around lunchtime, a freeway bridge appeared ahead of us, arching over the canal. The boss told Berdy to tie the boat up underneath it. Then the two of them jumped ashore and disappeared into the desert. Once they were out of sight, I climbed to the top of the bridge. There was no freeway, just a bridge. There was no town in sight, just the canal, and a whole lot of scrub-covered sand dunes. I went back to the boat to wait.

A half-hour later, Berdy and his boss reappeared out of the desert with two bottles of vodka and a giant bowl of fish stew. Berdy refused to eat with the boss – he was still offended at being yelled at. He stayed in the pilothouse while Kelly, Alei, and I ate fish stew with his boss on the *tapjan*. The fish has been fried in batter and cut into chunks before being simmered in a salty broth with potatoes, green peppers, and onions. We ate it with stale *chorek* that we'd bought the day before in Zakhmet. It was delicious, much better than the orange soda and cookies I'd had for breakfast, and by the end of the second bottle of vodka, we are all friends with the boss. He had nothing against us. He was just scared.

On the outskirts of Zakhmet, the boss told Berdy to pull the boat close to shore. He wasn't going to drag us into the police station and tell them we were smugglers or spies with fake passports. Much better to just make the problem disappear, he'd decided. He told us to jump ashore and get lost. We didn't argue. We grabbed our bags and leaped. From the shoreline, I waved goodbye to Berdy as he steered the boat back out into the channel and headed for the port.

We hiked through the desert toward the highway, which we could see in the distance. A man appeared ahead of us, standing among the thorn bushes. He wore a suit and stood with his arms clasped behind his back. He was about 30 and hadn't shaved for a couple days. His suit was dusty and had lost its creases. He looked too bedraggled to be a KNB man, but still, it was an odd place for a guy to be standing.

"Did you just get off that boat?" he asked.

"Why?" I asked.

"Was that Berdy's boat?"

"Why?"

"He's my cousin. He said he was going to bring me a fish. Do you know if he has it?"

Relieved, I told him Berdy had the fish. Then Alei talked him into giving us a ride up the highway to Bayramali. We piled into the car, covered in sand, exhausted from nearly 24 hours on the boat. I was still a little drunk from lunch. We bounced across the desert to the highway, dodging thorn bushes, and then turned south. Between potholes, I wrote a note to Berdy in my awkward, looping Russian cursive, apologizing for getting him in trouble and wishing him well. His cousin promised to deliver it.

31.
Mugged

In exchange for speaking at its tourism conference in Ashgabat, the OSCE had paid for a room for me in the President Hotel. It was one of the best hotels in the country, with five stars from someone or other, marble-floored lobbies, bathrobe warmers in all the bathrooms, and a price tag of $95 a night – more than my monthly salary. I stayed one night, but felt out of place. I don't like fancy hotels and restaurants, where things look too delicate and clean to touch and people dote on me. So I moved across town to the Syyhat Hotel, a seedy flophouse where I'd stayed before. For $2.50, I got a single bed in a double room. As I was falling asleep, my roommate Anamurat and his friend Ashyr showed up and sat down on Anamurat's bed. They couldn't have been more than 19 or 20 years old, long-necked and pimple-faced.

"You have to get out of here for a little while," Anamurat said. "We're supposed to do Natasha here."

"You're going to have to do Natasha somewhere else," I said. "It's 11. I have to be up early. I'm going to sleep."

"Come on …" Ashyr pleaded.

"Why don't you guys do Natasha in *your* room?" I asked him.

Annoyed, they left. I closed the door and turned off the light. I was just falling asleep when someone opened the door (there was no lock) and flipped the light on. I opened my eyes and saw a pretty Russian girl in a short black skirt standing by the switch.

"You called?" she asked.

"No, Anamurat called. He went to his friend's room down the hall," I told her. "Could you turn off the light on your way out?"

I went back to sleep. Sometime later, the light went on again. I rolled over and squinted at the door. There were two girls standing by the light switch this time. One was a Turkmen girl in tight jeans and a low-cut red shirt. The other was another Russian girl in another short black skirt and way too much makeup.

"Anamurat?" the Russian girl asked.

"No, he's down the hall in Ashyr's room, I think," I said. "Turn off the light."

She looked around the room.

"Well, as long as we're here, do you want to ..." she trailed off and made one of the internationally recognized hand signs for "fuck."

"No. I want to sleep. Turn off the light."

"Come on, let him sleep," the Turkmen girl said, turning off the light and pulling the Russian girl out the door.

Apparently three girls were enough for Anamurat and Ashyr, because no one else woke me up that night. It wasn't the best night's sleep I'd ever had. The upside, though, was that I'd saved myself the equivalent of a month's salary. I decided to use the money, combined with some other money I'd saved by living way out in the country where there was nothing to buy, for tourism development. It seemed only fitting. I planned a four-day seminar designed to teach young adults from the Mary area how to be tour guides at Merv and Margush. That way, if the Turkmen government ever decided to start welcoming tourists into the country, a few local guys would know how to make some money off them.

I found five English students who wanted to come to my seminar. Begench was a geeky 18-year-old kid, socially awkward, and much too old for his age. Kakajan was an effeminate 20-year-old wedding singer who wore a goatee, a bandana, and a white tank-top. His friend Juma was a Tupac fan and wannabe gangster with arms covered in homemade tattoos that looked like Japanese characters but meant nothing – he'd made them up. Muhammad, only 16, was painfully shy and quiet. Oraz was a big, rowdy country boy and at 22, the oldest of the group. I convinced Alei to join us.

During the seminar, we stayed at the Bayramali sanatorium. The place had once been famous; people from all over the USSR used to visit for its famous melon cure. Its shabby concrete dormitories and hospital buildings were crumbling, but its gardens were still gorgeous, filled with luscious red roses and orange cosmos. A grove of evergreen trees shaded its grounds. Crotchety

Turkmen grandparents and white-coated doctors roamed the shady paths between the buildings. My boys were easily 40 years younger than any of the other guests. The old women took a liking to them. There was a lot of "you boys are so handsome" and "you're so skinny, you need to eat more" and "you remind me of my grandson."

Every day, we went on a field trip. First, we visited the museum in Mary, where a beautiful Turkmen girl in a *koynek* gave us a tour. At first, the boys' constant flirting flustered her. She was sassy, though, and soon put them in their places so she could finish telling them about the ceramics, jewelry, and figurines that had been dug from the deserts of Turkmenistan, dusted off, and set on the museum's glass shelves. When we went to Merv, the director of the national park there gave us free admission and a free guide. At the end of the day, he talked to the boys about how to get into the tourism industry.

The next day, our guide from Merv, Jumageldy, took us to see Margush. The van was old and full of holes. The last hour of the trip was on sandy roads through the desert. Our tires kicked up a cloud of dust that blew in through the holes and filled the van. We had to hold our shirts over our faces to keep from choking. We wandered the ruins, an endless maze of knee-high mud-brick foundations that were probably built before Stonehenge. The desert wind whipped a cloud of sand across the abandoned city.

Kakajan and Juma sang all the way back to the sanitorium. It's what they were good at. They were an aspiring pop duo. Every day they dressed alike: white wife-beaters, blue bandanas, baseball caps tilted just so. Any time we had to wait for something – lunch, a guide, a taxi – the rest of us would find a bench to sit on or a curb to squat on. Kakajan and Juma used the time to choreograph dance routines. Alei suggested we call them Menudo, after the Puerto Rican boy band. Oraz called Juma "Michael" and Kakajan "Jackson." In the van, they sang anything the other boys requested, from Turkmen pop songs, to Fergie, to Eminem. Everyone got into it except Begench, who sat apart, looking at them like they were all morons.

As we were passing an old pile of bricks that Jumageldy said was a centuries-old Nestorian Christian church, an argument broke out in the van. I missed the beginning of it because it was in

227

Turkmen, but when I caught on, Oraz was maintaining that the *kulan*, a type of wild Turkmen donkey, could live for 700 years. The other boys were mocking him, insisting that no animal could live that long. He held his ground, though, maintaining that he'd read it in a Magtymguly poem so he was sure it was true.

"If *kulans* lived for 700 years, scientists would know about it," Juma said.

"How? Scientists don't live for 700 years," Oraz said. "Besides, even if scientists knew, it doesn't mean we would know."

No one could convince Oraz that Magtymguly might have been mistaken.

* * *

On the last day of the seminar we packed our things, left the sanatorium, and took a *marshrutka* south to the Hindukush Dam, which stemmed the flow of the Murgab River near Yolotan, creating a massive, swampy reservoir. The tsarist government had built the dam in 1895 as part of its effort to irrigate more land for cotton cultivation.[108] By the time we arrived, the downstream side, where an enthusiastic stream of whitewater rushed out of the dam and into a shallow pool surrounded by sandy beaches and shade trees, had become a popular spot for picnicking and swimming. We were planning to eat lunch, listen to the boys' final presentations, go swimming, and then go home.

To make sure the boys would have an audience for their presentations, Alei and I had invited other Peace Corps Volunteers. Ngai and Kelly came. Two of Kelly's friends from Yolotan came, too – an Uzbek girl named Umida and her father Omar. Hindukush was crowded. Boys in their underwear and girls in their dresses played in the water. Families sat under trees, eating and napping. We found a shady spot and settled down to eat *somsas*, fending off armies of ants. When we were all full, the boys took turns standing in front of our little group and pretending to be tour guides, telling us about the sites we'd visited at Merv and Margush.

After the presentations, we scattered. Some stayed at Hindukush to swim and lounge. Others walked up to the road to find a taxi. Soon only the four Peace Corps Volunteers, Begench, and Umida remained. We lazed around until the sun started to get low in the sky. Then we packed our things and walked up the sandy path to the road to find a taxi home. Begench disappeared for a minute and then reappeared, running up the path after us, carrying a plastic Coke bottle full of cloudy, yellow water. Six boys in their late teens who were wearing nothing but the white briefs they'd been swimming in were chasing him, yelling insults.

Begench ran past us, putting us between him and the underwear posse. From the yelling and cursing and Begench's breathless explanation, I gathered that Begench had gone to a nearby spring to fill his bottle with sulfur water that he thought might help his acne. The posse had been hanging out near the spring and had insisted Begench pay them for the water. Begench, charming guy that he was, told them to fuck themselves and then ran to hide behind Alei and I. If they hadn't already been ready to beat him up for taking "their" water without paying, they were ready to whip him for what he'd said while he was running away.

I stepped in to try to calm things down, apologizing to the posse on Begench's behalf. But I was speaking Russian and they were country boys – they didn't understand me very well, which annoyed them even more. So Alei tried to defuse things in Turkmen. That didn't help either.

"Why don't you talk to us in Russian? You think we're too stupid, we don't understand Russian?" one of them yelled.

They closed in around us and started pushing and cursing. Alei and I told Ngai, Kelly, Umida, and Begench to go up to the road and find a taxi. They moved a little way up the path, and lingered there, not wanting to leave us behind. A short, wiry man in his 30s with a black beard appeared from somewhere and started urging the teenagers to attack us. One of the boys, thinking he was Jean-Claude Van Damme but forgetting I had four or five inches on him, tried to kick me in the head. I leaned back and his heel whizzed past my chest. Another leaned in and threw a sloppy punch at me, which I also managed to avoid.

While I was distracted, the man with the beard, the ringleader, darted into the fray, ripped my backpack off my shoulder and ran away. I chased after him and tried to grab it back. I pulled on one shoulder strap and he pulled on the other, our feet braced in the sand.

"You're not going to get out of here alive," he hissed at me.

All of a sudden my head lit up and I lost track of things for a second. One of the boys had snuck up behind me and punched me in the side of the face while I was focused on getting my bag back. When the world cleared up, I had what felt like some pebbles in my mouth. I spit them on the ground and yanked my backpack out of the bearded man's hands. He slunk away to a safe distance. I walked up the hill to where Alei was still trying to fend off the posse. They were going after his backpack, too, but he didn't seem worried.

"Look, you can have the backpack," he said calmly. "Just let me grab my passport out of it first, okay?"

Attracted by the posse's yelling and cursing, a crowd of picnickers started to gather around us. I weighed my options. If Alei and I fought the boys, we'd almost certainly lose. We might even get our faces smashed in with the bricks and rocks the boys were starting to collect. On the other hand, there was nowhere to run. So I just kept retreating up the path, pushing the boys back when they got too close, arguing with them in Russian.

"Aren't you a man?" they jeered.

"Won't you fight us?" they taunted.

Then, all of a sudden, Umida was next to me. She was in her late teens, strikingly beautiful, and furious.

"What's wrong with you!?" she yelled at the boys. "These are guests in our country! They're teachers! Have some respect!"

The boys paused.

"I know you," she continued, jabbing a finger at them. "I know where you live. I know your parents. You should be ashamed of yourselves."

Umida's rant didn't have much effect on the boys. When she was done, they went back to taunting and pushing and throwing looping punches and telling us they were going to kill us. Her speech had a big effect on the crowd that had gathered to watch the fight, though. On some silent cue, they formed a human shield around us. The underwear posse backed off.

Our protectors, mostly teenaged boys and girls, led us up to the road, to a spot under an apricot tree. While we waited for a ride into town, they picked apricots for us and apologized for what had happened. My body humming with adrenaline, I munched on a handful of warm, juicy apricots and paced up and down the road. There was something sharp in my mouth that kept poking the inside of my lip. I ran my tongue over my teeth. One of them had a chunk busted out of it and another had a chip missing.

Ten minutes later, we flagged down two cars and convinced them to take us to the ice cream shop in Yolotan where Umida's younger sister Malika worked. Sitting at one of the tables on the sidewalk outside the shop, eating bowls of soft-serve vanilla ice cream drizzled with home-made strawberry sauce, we told Malika what had happened. I showed her my chipped teeth. After we finished our ice cream, we all found our own ways home.

When I got back to Nurana, dinner was ready. Over *plov*, I told Jeren and Döwlet what had happened. I showed Kümüsh and Altyn my chipped teeth. Döwlet looked worried and told me he was glad I was all right. Jeren looked disappointed and told me that Alei and I should have fought the boys, should have taught them not to mess with Americans. I lay on my *dushek* for a long time that night, staring at the ceiling and thinking about whether I'd done the right thing. I decided I had. True, my pride was hurt and a couple of my teeth were chipped, but no one had gotten robbed or had their face bashed in with a brick. Things had worked out well.

32.
Going Home

Spring was wedding season. Young brides paraded through the dirt streets of Nurana, draped in silver jewelry like chain mail, their heads and shoulders covered with embroidered ceremonial jackets. They moved like silently, their mouths hidden by the tails of the kerchiefs that covered their hair. Attended by sisters, female cousins, or girlfriends, they shuffled from house to house in their grooms' neighborhoods, introducing themselves to their new communities. I was at Islam's house, watching a World Cup soccer match when three brides appeared together at the door to pay their respects to his wife. They'd decided that, since their future neighbors were obliged to lay out *klionka*s covered with food for visiting brides, they would make things easier for their hosts and visit together.

In May and June, I went to a couple of wedding parties (*toi*s) every week with Döwlet and Jeren. We would iron our clothes, shine our shoes, and drive out to some *kolkhoz* or other. Döwlet still called them by their old names: Marxism, Leninism, Communism. The *toi*s were usually outside. It wasn't going to rain, after all – it was the desert. In the dusty yard outside the groom's house, the cooks would be tending giant cauldrons of soup or *plov* that were simmering over wood fires. Rows of tables would be loaded with pastries and sweets, *chorek* and salads, vodka and soda. At first, there would be only a sprinkling of people. Women in their embroidered *koyneks*, their hair covered with their best kerchiefs, would gather inside the house or at the tables. Men in dark suits would stand in tight groups near the cauldrons, smoking, or spitting *nas*, a mysterious green powder that's rumored to include ingredients ranging from tobacco to opium, chicken shit to saksaul ashes.[109] The children would run in giggling packs around and through the house, skirting the men at their cauldrons, sneaking sweets from the tables.

By the time the *plov* was ready, the tables would be packed with two or three hundred people. We would eat before the sun went down, since there usually wasn't good outdoor lighting. Elbow-to-elbow at long banquet tables, we'd shovel food into our mouths and drink vodka toasts to the bride and groom. When it got dark, the music would start. Parked on one of the dirt roads near the house there would be a trailer – an ordinary looking metal box from a tractor-trailer rig. One of the long sides would fold up to reveal a makeshift stage inside. There, in the belly of the trailer, the wedding singer would stand among microphone cables, power cords, speakers, amps, and flashing, colored Christmas lights.

I only ever saw one wedding singer sing. Most of them just lip-synched to recordings of popular songs. Sometimes they even had fake bands – guys who pretended to play drums or tambourines. Niyazov had banned lip-synching, complaining that performers were forgetting how to sing.[110] Like many of his decrees, though, it had no apparent effect outside the cities. When the singer started the music, the guests would flow from the tables to the street to dance under the stars and the flashing lights.

Going to *toi*s was fun, but it was also challenging. Turkmen take pride in their hospitality. Some become overly enthusiastic hosts when they get drunk, forcing their guests to eat, drink, and dance more and more – whether they like it or not – and berating them if they don't cooperate. The biggest problem was vodka. To make it through *toi* season without dying of alcohol poisoning, I had to develop a strategy. I ate as much fatty meat as I could, as early as I could, and continued to eat slowly but steadily all night long. If the shots of vodka started to overwhelm the cushion of food in my stomach, I had other tricks: covertly pouring my vodka onto the ground instead of into my mouth; raising my glass to toast but only sipping the shot instead of throwing it all back; and, in true crisis situations, simply offending my hosts by refusing to drink more.

Once I learned the tricks, I really enjoyed *toi*s. So when Cennet, a Peace Corps Volunteer who lived in Murgab, said she wanted to have a *toi* before she returned to the US, I latched onto the idea. I had wanted to do something nice for my friends from Nurana before I left. I would throw them a giant party. I'd seen how much they liked *toi*s. I talked it over with Jeren at dinner one evening and she thought it was a great idea: she was full of advice, which I wrote down; she even helped me plan and price out a menu. In fact, she got her whole extended family involved (and several Peace Corps Volunteers pitched in, too). Cennet also played an important role. She agreed to be the bride, fake-marrying her friend Cam. We set the date: June 14. A week before the event, the local government began to complain that we didn't have permission to throw a party. We ignored them.

I started shopping two days before the party. I'd take a taxi into Murgab and head to the bazaar, where merchants hawked everything from basil to books, from peanuts to matches. I'd wade through the cars and the crowds, browsing. I bought so many shopping bags full of onions, potatoes, green peppers, tomatoes, scallions, herbs, beets, cabbages, cotton seed oil, rice, and beans that I had to hire a boy with a cart to haul it all to Jeren's parents' house, near the bazaar. I left some of the groceries there. Others, I delivered to a woman in Murgab who I'd hired to make four different kinds of salads for the party.

On the day of the *toi*, I woke early, had a cup of coffee at the *klionka*, and then climbed into the car with Döwlet. The sun was rising. We rattled along the road, Döwlet fighting with his old Lada to keep it moving. It was a quirky machine that required its radiator to be refilled after every 15 or 20 minutes of driving and stalled if its driver lifted his foot from the gas even for a moment, even when he was shifting or braking. We left Nurana and bumped past farm fields to a popular fishing spot on the Murgab River.

There were two single-wide trailers there that served as stores. When men caught more fish with their cane poles than they needed for their dinners, they sold them to the owners of the stores, who stashed them in baskets floating in the river. We bought everything they had in their baskets, two squirming grocery bags full – about 20 pounds of fish. Back at the house, I squatted under a pomegranate tree and scaled and cleaned the fish. Altyn came over and offered to help. I gave her a small fish with thick, golden scales and she went to work. Kümüsh squatted nearby and giggled. When the fish were all naked and empty, we cut them into chunks, floured them, and left them with Jeren, who promised to fry them.

Then Döwlet and I drove to Murgab. The temperature was already over 90 and, even with the windows down, I was sweating.

Döwlet had to go to work. I had to go to the butcher. Jeren's father went with me. He was a crusty, shambling old man who wore a furry, Russian-style *shapka*. His face was a rough-hewn, dark walnut color, but his balding head, underneath his hat, was a light pine. As we walked from his house to the bazaar, he told me about life in Turkmenistan during World War II: "The lucky ones ate grass; the rest starved."

The butcher's shop was under the bazaar's patchwork canvas roof. A man with an axe stood behind a table groaning under sections of lamb and cow carcasses, covered in cheesecloth to keep the flies off. Jeren's dad helped me choose 45 pounds of lamb and beef. He would point to a section and the butcher would sling it onto a stump and hack it to pieces with his axe. We hauled the meat back to the house in dripping plastic grocery bags.

It took two hours for Jeren's brother-in-law Maksat and I to de-bone, cube, and salt it all. Maksat worked happily, chatting with me through a mouthful of *nas*. "Eaten any mushrooms, lately?" he asked, using a Turkmen euphemism for sex that I always found strange since most Turkmen men claim they don't give oral sex. We'd only finished 20 pounds or so when my right hand got so blistered I couldn't use it anymore. I switched to my left. By the time we were done, both of my hands were red and swollen.

By early afternoon, Jeren was at the wedding hall I'd rented, with a crew of its employees and her family members, chopping and peeling. I'd hired a cook, a man from Nurana who worked as a cut-rate doctor, delivering medicines and advice on his bicycle. He was the head chef, standing over a massive black cauldron behind the wedding hall, supervising everything. I did some chopping and peeling, but mostly I ran errands, fetching more cottonseed oil, more soda, more vodka, more bread. Meanwhile, Cennet was getting her hair done and trying on her wedding dresses. We'd planned a bi-cultural wedding, so she had rented both a colorful Turkmen-style dress and a white Western-style dress.

People started to file into the hall about 6:30. We were expecting 150 – a small *toi*. Oraztach, Islam, and the rest of the doctors and nurses from the clinic came. A group of the boys from one of my English classes came. Umida and Malika came with

Kelly. Altyn and Kümüsh were there, dressed like princesses in clouds of white taffeta and lace, their hair sprayed into place and sprinkled with glitter. Peace Corps Volunteers came from all over the country. My extended host family was there, and so was Cennet's. They all took their seats and started snacking and drinking. I was still solving last minute problems.

Kakajan, one of my future tourist guides, had agreed to be our wedding singer. He had promised to actually sing, unlike the lip-synchers at most weddings. But he hadn't shown up. I ran across the street to the post office, placed a few phone calls, and managed to track him down. He claimed he was on his way. Even if he did arrive soon, though, we weren't ready for him. Döwlet's friend Shokhrat had agreed to lend us his sound system. But Shokhrat hadn't shown up, either.

Since Shokhrat had no phone, Döwlet and I climbed into the old Lada and rumbled off to his *kolkhoz* to find him. We banged on his door until he woke up. He apologized, explaining that the guy who had promised to give him a ride to the *toi* hadn't shown up so he'd decided to take a nap, figuring we'd come get him eventually. We packed him into the car with all his speakers and amps and hurried back to Murgab, stopping only once to refill the radiator from a stream.

Back at the wedding hall, we set up the sound system. Azat, our master of ceremonies, grabbed the microphone, welcomed everyone to the *toi*, and thanked them for coming. The cook, half-drunk, staggered in and announced that dinner was ready. "How 'bout a hand for the cook?" he slurred at the gathered guests, who obliged him. The wedding hall staff served *plov* and lamb stew and the vodka started flowing in earnest. Cennet and Cam sat quietly on a couch at the front of the room, at a table piled with fruit and cookies and bottles of soda and champagne – the happy couple on display. I moved from table to table, drinking toasts with friends and picking at plates of *plov*. A videographer, a necessity at any *toi*, recorded everything.

Guests took turns at the microphone. They made toasts to the lovely couple and their fake marriage. They made toasts to me, wishing me luck in America. There were wedding gifts, hugs, and tearful speeches. Jeren took the microphone and dragged Döwlet,

Altyn, and Kümüsh up to the front of the room and presented me with a carpet they'd had woven for me that said: "In memory of our son Sam from Döwlet, Jeren, Altyn, Kümüsh. 14.06.2006." Kakajan got up and sang a couple songs and he was great – the crowd loved him. Then the dancing and the toasts, the vodka and the food, all started to blur. I'd been too busy running errands and saying goodbyes to follow my *toi* drinking strategy.

At some point, Cennet went downstairs and changed into her white dress. She re-entered the banquet hall to the sound of the Peace Corps Volunteers all humming "dum, dum, da dum." Cam joined her and they took their fake vows in front of a Peace Corps Volunteer pretending to be a minister. Then it was time for more dancing, Cennet whirling across the dance floor in a blur of white. Almost everyone danced except the older Turkmen women, who thought it would be improper to join in. Around midnight, the power went out. It was getting late anyway, so the owner took the opportunity to usher the last of us out the door.

I climbed into the front seat of Döwlet's car, three more guests climbed into the back, and we headed back to Nurana. My window was open and the wind was cool and soft. The countryside was silver in the starlight. I was far too drunk. I leaned out and puked – probably all over the side of the car. At home, I slept outside on the *tapjan,* so I could vomit into the garden if necessary. Döwlet checked on me now and then, bringing me water, rubbing my back.

When morning came, I was deeply embarrassed, but too hung over to worry about it much. I apologized to Döwlet and Jeren, who said they were just glad I was feeling better. When Jeren came home from work that afternoon, she told me the wedding hall owner wanted to see me about some damage we'd caused. I peeled myself off the floor and taxied into Murgab to pay for our wedding party's sins: a broken glass, a smashed chair, a tear in one of the wedding dresses.

As I walked from the wedding hall back to the taxi stand, a car pulled up and the driver called me over. He said we'd met at a *toi*, but I suspected he was lying because he tried to talk to me in Turkmen. Anyone who'd traded a few words with me knew my Russian was better. Still, when he offered me a ride to Nurana, I

237

accepted. A free ride is a free ride. On the way, we stopped to get gas. The driver bought me a bag of salted pistachios and then turned the car around and headed the wrong direction– away from Nurana.

"Do you want to see a secret military base?" he asked. "My friend works there and they've got missiles so secret that they don't even let *him* see them."

It was a bizarre offer. People usually suspected I was a spy and were too nervous to talk to me about politics until after they'd known me for a while. I decided the driver was either insane or setting me up.

"Uh-uh. No way," I said. "If it's secret, I don't want to go near it. Everyone here already thinks I'm a spy. I don't need to be hanging around secret military bases."

He wouldn't give up. He kept trying to convince me to go with him. I wanted to go; I was dying of curiosity. Not about the base, but about where the whole thing was headed, whether it was a setup. I decided it was too risky to find out, though, so I started acting angry and yelling at him to pull over and let me go. He turned around and drove me home to Nurana. It was a long, silent ride.

* * *

In the weeks following the *toi*, my friends and acquaintances – and even strangers – hounded me for the tape the videographer had made. Döwlet even took a copy to work and held screenings of it on the big TVs he was supposed to be selling. I don't know why the video was so popular. I think it was just the right combination of the familiar and the exotic. Every Turkmen couple had a *toi* video. I'd watched Döwlet and Jeren's three times. But this video was something a little different. For starters, the whole *toi* was a game. No one was really getting married. Then there were the Americans making toasts in Russian and Turkmen and English, the Americans dancing funny, and the American wedding.

The days slipped by. I'd said all my goodbyes. I'd given away everything I couldn't take home on the airplane. I started packing my bags. Jeren stood in the doorway and watched.

"I don't know what I'm going to do when you leave," she said. "Every day when I come home it will be like something's missing. And I'll be so bored."

The morning I left, Jeren gave me two loaves of fresh *chorek* for the journey. We all climbed into Döwlet and Azat's cars with my bags and drove to Murgab. We said our goodbyes in a parking lot there. Jeren cried a little and gave me a hug. Döwlet shook my hand, warned me that if I didn't write he'd come to America and give me a beating, and then tried to laugh. Azat took a photo of us all together.

Since Döwlet and Jeren had to go to work, Azat drove me to Mary, where I would find a taxi to Asghabat. I stared out my open window, watching the cotton fields roll by. The countryside was lush and green, the cotton high. Two shepherds wallowed in an irrigation canal as their sheep, fat and wooly, grazed nearby. Then checkpoints began to appear, manned by surly policemen. We passed the charred remains of two cars. Concrete buildings and empty lots replaced the farm fields. Dust and smog blew in my window. We entered the city.

The taxi to Ashgabat followed the familiar highway along the base of the Kopetdag range. In the capital, I found a hotel, and then went to the Peace Corps office to start filling out paperwork. That night, I called Geldy and we arranged to meet at a bar. I'd barely heard from him since leaving Abadan. I'd invited him to the *toi*, but he'd begged off, saying he didn't have time to make the trip. At the bar, I ordered myself a beer and Geldy ordered a coffee. He said he'd quit drinking. He was still smoking, though. He lit one of his slim cigarettes.

"So how have you been?" he said. "You're such a bitch. You never call. You never visit."

"I'm the bitch?" I said. "You didn't come to my going away party."

"It was all the way out on the ... *kolkhoz*," he said with distaste.

We talked about what I was going to do when I got back to America. Then we ran out of things to talk about. We'd lost track of each other's lives. We didn't know the right questions to ask anymore, the secret passwords to conversations worth having. He smoked his cigarette. I sipped my beer.

"Did you know I left Red Crescent?" he asked.

"It's about time. What are you doing now?"

"I sell ice cream. I like it. It's honest work, not like humanitarian aid."

Then his friends Aka, Mehri, and Nastya drifted into the bar and joined us. We made the "oh, I haven't seen you in so long" noises, and then I told them I was leaving for America so we made the "don't forget to write, it's been so great to know you" noises. Then Geldy walked me out. I gave him a hug and left.

When I went to Abadan the next day to say goodbye to Ana and Sesili, I found them in the garden picking lettuce, peppers, strawberries, and scallions. The seeds I'd planted had finally sprouted. Inspired, they'd planted the strawberries and the peppers themselves. The garden was weeded and watered. The porch was freshly painted. The refrigerator was full. Andrei had recovered, and with him, the family's finances.

We cooked a big meal together: fried chicken and potatoes, cucumber and tomato salad, wine and cake. I told them about Nurana. I think they were a little hurt to hear that I'd been so happy there, when I'd been so unhappy in Abadan. Ana packed me some pickled eggplant and a loaf of *chorek* for my trip to America. Then they walked me to the *marshrutka* stop and waved goodbye as my minivan trundled away toward Ashgabat.

My flight to America left after midnight. I spent the evening at a bar with friends and then loaded my bags into a car and headed for the airport. The capital's white marble buildings, monuments, and fountains, were all lit up, but the streets were deserted. Only a few taxi drivers roamed the city's wide boulevards, looking for fares. The windows of the apartment buildings were dark, the restaurants and stores were closed.

"I'm so jealous of you," the driver told me. "I'd love to leave this country. You must be really happy."

We left the city center and started passing row after row of identical apartment buildings – the concrete dominoes I'd known so well. I thought about Abadan, about being robbed by Olya, being blackmailed by Aman, being stonewalled by city hall, being hounded by the KNB. In my memory, it was all winter. It was all mud and slush. It was all frustrating, absurd, and ugly. Then I thought about spring in Nurana, about eating warm apricots off the trees, planting cotton with Döwlet, working in the vineyard with Jeren, hanging the swing for Altyn, and singing Kümüsh to sleep. I thought about my English students and my conversations with Maksat. I thought about all my friends who had come to say goodbye at my going-away *toi*.

"No," I told the taxi driver, "I'm going to miss it."

Notes

1. Economist. (2003). "The World's Worst: Turkmenistan." The World in 2004. London.

2. I saw the pit on a return visit a few weeks after my original visit.

3. "The Turkmen nation has traced marks as magnificent as those of Great Britain, of the Great Indian Nation, and of the Great Chinese Nation." Niyazov, Saparmurat. (2005). Rukhnama: Reflections on the Spiritual Values of the Turkmen. Ashgabat: Turkmenistan, p. 60.

4. Agence France Presse (Aug. 25, 2005). "Placing Book in Orbit, Turkmenistan Aims for the Stars."

5. "Between the 17th and 19th centuries, some states diffused wicked propaganda in pursuit of their own national interests. They falsely represented the nation of Turkmen as pillagers and merciless slaughterers, and described them as a wild community who kill each other, living in tents, an ignorant, uneducated and nomadic nation," wrote Niyazov, Rukhnama, p. 44.

6. Hughes, Langston (1956). I Wonder as I Wander. New York: Hill & Wang, p. 102.

7. Koestler, Arthur (1954). The Invisible Writing. New York: The MacMillan Company, p. 111.

8. Allworth, Edward (Ed.) (2002). Central Asia: 130 Years of Russian Dominance, A Historical Overview. London: Duke University Press.

9. Shifrin, Avraham (1980). The First Guidebook to the Prisons and Concentration Camps of the Soviet Union. New York: Bantam, pp. 268-269.

10. U.N. Development Program (2007). Human Development Report. Retrieved Feb. 23, 2007, from http://hdr.undp.org/hdr2006/statistics/countries/data_sheets/cty_ds_TKM.html.   CIA (2007). The World Factbook – Turkmenistan. Retrieved February 23, 2007, from https://www.cia.gov/cia/publications/factbook/geos/tx.html.

11. Estimates on the size of Turkmenistan's natural gas reserves vary considerably, which is not surprising given the difficulty in obtaining reliable information from the Turkmen government. Energy economist James P. Dorian offered one of the more conservative estiimates in his 2006 article in the journal Energy Economist: "Turkmenistan ... will play a critical role in the future of world energy markets, as it ranks 11th in world reserves of gas, above Iraq. Some analysts place reserve amounts at much higher levels [p.546]." Nancy Lubin offered a more optimistic estimate in her contribution to the 2000 book Energy and Conflict in Central Asia and the Caucasus, ranking Turkmenistan's reserves as "third in the world after only Russia and Iran [p.108]."

12. Levine, S. and R. Corzine. (Aug. 22, 1995). Turkmenistan: A Catalogue of Promises Unfulfilled, in The Financial Times. London.

13. Global Witness (2006). "It's a Gas: Funny Business in the Turkmen-Ukraine Gas Trade." London: Global Witness, p. 4.

14. Polo, Marco (1931). The Travels of Marco Polo. London: G. Routeledge & Sons, p. 20.

15. Tzareva, Elena (1984). Rugs and Carpets from Central Asia. Leningrad: Aurora Art Publishers. Schurmann, Ulrich (1969). Central Asian Rugs. Frankfurt Am Main: Verlag Osterrieth.

16. Annanepesov, M. (2003). The Turkmens, in History of Civilizations of Central Asia: Volume V. Paris: UNESCO Publishing, p. 138.

17. Edgar, Adrienne Lynn (2004). Tribal Nation: The Making of Soviet Turkmenistan. Princeton and Oxford: Princeton University Press, pp. 2-3.

18. Dawisha, Karen and Bruce Parrott (1997). Conflict, Cleavage, and Change in Central Asia and the Caucasus. Cambridge: Cambridge University Press, pp. 320-321.

19. Olcott, Martha Brill (2005). Central Asia's Second Chance. Washington DC: Carnegie Endowment for International Peace, p. 251.

20. Heritage Foundation. "Index of Economic Freedom." 2008. http://www.heritage.org/research/features/index/.

21. Cummings, Sally (2002). Power and Change in Central Asia. New York: Routledge.

22. Hopkirk, Peter (1992). The Great Game: The Struggle for Empire in Central Asia. New York: Kodansha International, pp. 388, 402-407.

23. Hiebert, Fredrik Talmage (2003). A Central Asian Village at the Dawn of Civilization, Excavations at Anew, Turkmenistan. Philadelphia: University of Pennsylvania Museum of Archaeology and Anthropology, pp. 24-25.

24. Pumpelly, Raphael. (1908). Explorations in Turkestan, Expedition of 1904. Washington DC: Carnegie Institution of Washington, pp. 320-321.

25. Hiebert. A Central Asian Village, p. 9.

26. Pumpelly, My Reminiscences, p. 732.

27. Golombek, Lisa and Wilber, Donald (1988). The Timurid Architecture of Iran and Turan. Princeton: Princeton University Press, pp. 291-292.

28. The Soviet government initially reported that the death toll was 10,000. In his 1990 book published in Ashgabat, The Ashgabat Catastrophe, Shokhrat Kadyrov suggests that the proper number is closer to 35,000. In the Rukhnama, Niyazov writes that there were 198,000 people in Ashgabat at the time of the earthquake and that 176,000 of them were killed (p. 41).

29. US Geological Survey. (Accessed June 2, 2007)."Most Destructive Known Earthquakes on Record in the World." earthquake.usgs.gov/regional/world/most_destructive.php.

30. Kadyrov, Shokhrat. (1990). Ashkhabadskaia katastrofa: istoriko-demograficheskii ochek krupneishego zemletriasenia. XX v. Ashgabat: Turkmenistan, p. 34.

31. Niyazov, Rukhnama, pp. 41-42.

32. Curzon, George. "The Transcaspian Railway." Proceedings of the Royal Geographical Society, 1889. Vol. 2, No. 5, p. 275.

33. Curzon took notes during his trip and then wrote a 478-page report on the railway and its significance to the Great Game, called Russia in Central Asia and the Anglo-Russian Question (according to Hopkirk). Eleven years later, Curzon would become Viceroy of India, from which post he would pursue the Great Game for years to come. He later became a member of the House of Lords and Foreign Secretary (1919-1924).

34. Curzon, "The Transcaspian Railway," pp. 273-295, 279.

35. Morris, L.P. "British Secret Missions in Turkestan, 1918-1919." Journal of Contemporary History, 1977. Vol. 12, No. 2, pp. 363-379. Sargent, M. (2004). British Involvement in Transcaspia (1918-1919). Swindon: Conflict Studies Center, Defence Academy of the UK.

36. Morris, "British Secret Missions," p. 365.

37. To Christians, this is the story of Abraham and Isaac.

38. According to a 2000 World Bank report, "the share of income derived from self-employment or entrepreneurial activities has increased ... to more than 50 percent in the poorer republics of the Transcaucasus and Central Asia." World Bank. "Making Transition Work for Everyone." Washington DC: World Bank, pp. 152.

39. Olcott, Central Asia's Second Chance, p. 251.

40. Committee to Protect Journalists. "North Korea tops CPJ list of '10 Most Censored Countries.' May 2, 2006.

41. Reporters Without Borders. "Worldwide Press Freedom Index." 2006.

42. In March 2005, Niyazov ordered the country's rural libraries closed, saying that rural Turkmen didn't read anyway. In my experience he was right. Few Turkmen I met outside of Ashgabat used books for anything except toilet paper. (Of course, that doesn't mean the libraries should have been closed).

43. Olcott Central Asia's Second Chance, p. 184.

44. Ibid, p. 67.

45. International Merv Project. (1996). The Ancient Cities of Merv, Turkmenistan: A Visitor's Guide. London: The International Merv Project.

46. Herrmann, Monuments of Merv, p. 16.

47. Ibid, p. 121.

48. Ibid, pp. 31-32.

49. Ibid, pp. 17, 125.

50. Sevin, A. (1992) The Seljuqs and the Khwarazm Shahs in History of Civilizations of Central Asia Volume I: The Dawn of Civilization: Earliest Times to 700 BC, A.H. Dani.and V.M. Masson (eds.). UNESCO Publishing: Paris, pp. 147.

51. Ibid, p. 155.

52. LeStrange, Guy (1977). The Lands of the Eastern Caliphate: Mesopotamia, Persia and Central Asia from the Moslem Conquest to the Time of Timur. Lahore: Al-Biruni, p. 401.

53. Hermann, Monuments of Merv, p. 126.

54. Le Strange, Lands of the Eastern Caliphate, p. 402

55. Herrmann, Monuments of Merv, pp. 127-128.

56. Le Strange, Lands of the Eastern Caliphate, pp. 402-403.

57. Herrmann, Monuments of Merv, p. 82.

58. Gall, Carlotta (Nov. 21, 1998). "Winged Gods of the Desert." The Financial Times.

59. Maslow, Jonathan (1994). Sacred Horses: Memoirs of a Turkmen Cowboy. New York: Random House, pp. 113.

60. Gall, "Winged Gods of the Desert."

61. Associated Press (Dec. 27, 1999). "Turkmenistan Bans Smoking in Public Places."

62. Brice, W.C. (1978). The Environmental History of the Near and Middle East Since the Last Ice Age. Academic Press: London, p. 329.

63. LeStrange, Lands of the Eastern Caliphate, p. 457.

64. Morgan, E.D. and C.H. Coote (Eds.) (1967). Early Voyages and Travels to Russia and Persia by Anthony Jenkinson and Other Englishmen. New York: Burt Franklin Publishers, p. 68.

65. LeStrange, Lands of the Eastern Caliphate, p. 403.

66. United Press International (March 2, 2005). "President Closes Down Nation's Hospitals."

67. CIA. "World Factbook: Turkmenistan." Retrieved July 4, 2007, from https://www.cia.gov/library/publications/the-world-factbook/geos/tx.html.

68. Most of Turkmenistan's GDP comes from exports. About 80 percent of Turkmenistan's exports are "fuels and mining products" and 10 percent are "agricultural products." The first category includes mostly gas and oil, while the second is mostly cotton. World Trade Organization (2007). "Country Profiles: Turkmenistan." World Bank (2007). "Turkmenistan Data Profile."

69. Allworth, Central Asia, p. 127, and Whitman, John. "Turkestan Cotton in Imperial Russia." American Slavic and East European Review, 1956. Vol. 15, No. 2, pp. 190-205.

70. Allworth, Central Asia, pp. 284-289. Whitman, "Turkestan Cotton."

71. Curtis, Glenn. (1996). Turkmenistan: A Country Study. Washington: GPO for the Library of Congress. Retrieved on July 25, 2007 from http://countrystudies.us/turkmenistan/

72. U.N. Committee on the Rights of the Child (June 2, 2006). "UN Committee on the Rights of the Child: Concluding Observations, Turkmenistan." CRC/C/TKM/CO/1. Retrieved June 27, 2007 from www.unhcr.org/cgi-bin/texis/vtx/refworld/rwmain?docid=45377ee50.

73. US Department of State (2004). "Country Reports on Human Rights Practices, 2003: Turkmenistan." Retrieved on July 1, 2007 from http://www.state.gov/g/drl/rls/hrrpt/2003/27870.htm.

74. Agence France Presse. (Nov. 5, 2003). "Turkmen Traffic Cops Round Up Drivers to Gather Cotton Harvest: Report."

75. Gelb, Michael, "An Early Soviet Ethnic Deportation: The Far-Eastern Koreans." Russian Review, 1995. Vol. 54, pp. 389-412. Kho, Songmoo (1987). Koreans in Soviet Central Asia. Helsinki: Finnish Oriental Society.

76. Gelb, "The Far-Eastern Koreans," p. 401.

77. US Commission on International Religious Freedom (2004). "Countries of Particular Concern: Turkmenistan." Retrieved on July 2, 2007, from http://www.uscirf.gov/countries/countriesconcerns/Countries/Turkmenistan.html.

78. Conolly, Arthur (2001). Journey to the North of India Overland from England Through Russia, Persia and Afghanistan. New Delhi and Madras: Asian Educational Services, p. 76.

79. LeStrange, Lands of the Eastern Caliphate, pp. 379. Though the remains of Dekhistan now sit in the middle of the desert, the Caspian coast is actually not that far away. It's possible that either the sea's level was higher in Hawqal's time, so that it extended further inland than it does today, or that Dekhistan was once a sprawling region that stretched all the way to the coast.

80. Kharin, Vegetation Degradation,pp. 40-41.

81. Edgar, Tribal Nation, p. 213.

82. Ibid, p. 206.

83. Ibid, p. 209.

84. Olcott, Martha Brill. "The Basmachi or Freemen's Revolt in Turkestan 1918-1924." Soviet Studies, 1981. Vol. 33, No. 3, p. 353.

85. Edgar, Tribal Nation, p. 212.

86. Lerman, Zvi and Karen Brooks (2001). Turkmenistan: An Assessment of Leasehold-Based Farm Restructuring. Washington DC: World Bank, pp. xi-xii. Pomfret, Richard. "Turkmenistan: From Communism to Nationalism by Gradual Economic Reform." MOCT-MOST, 2001. Vol. 11, p. 170.

87. For men, life expectancy at birth in Turkmenistan is 65. For women, it's 72. CIA, World Factbook – Turkmenistan, retrieved on July 17, 2007 from https://www.cia.gov/library/publications/the-world-factbook/geos/tx.html.

88. Masson, V.M. (1992). The Decline of Bronze Age Civilization and Movements of the Tribes, in History of Civilizations of Central Asia Volume I: The Dawn of Civilization: Earliest Times to 700 B.C., A.H. Dani and V.M. Masson (eds.). UNESCO Publishing: Paris, pp 342.

89. Marri, Mir Khuda Bakhsh. (1997). Searchlight on Baloches and Balochistan. Lahore: Ferozsons, Ltd, pp. 17-21. By 1997, there were some 40,000 –50,000 living in the area.

90. Hopkirk, The Great Game, pp. 425-429.

91. De Laesso, F. 1885. "The Caves and Ruins at Penjdeh." Proceedings of the Royal Geographical Society and Monthly Record of Geography, New Monthly Series, Vol. 7, No. 9 (Sep. 1885), p. 584.

92. Hopkirk, The Great Game, p. 429.

93. US Foreign Agricultural Service. (2004). "Crop Production in the Cotton Region of the Former Soviet Union." Retrieved on July 25, 2007 from http://www.fas.usda.gov/remote/soviet/country_page/fsuasia_text.htm.

94. Aldiss, Songs from the Steppes, p. 5.

95. This hotel was home to a handful of American "gas-and-go" guys, who serviced the American military aircraft that regularly stopped off to refuel at the Ashgabat airport on the way from Europe to Afghanistan. This operation has been in place since the US invaded Afghanistan after the terrorist attacks of Sept. 11, 2001. See Balancing Military Assistance with Human Rights in Central Asia, a hearing in front of the Senate Foreign Relations Committee on June 27, 2002.

96. United Press International. (March 1, 2004). "Men Get Makeovers in Turkmenistan." Niyazov justified his decree by claiming that, "excess hair gives outsiders the 'wrong impression' of the country and is 'unhygienic.'"

97. Hannan, Tim and Sarah O'Hara. (1998). "Managing Turkmenistan's Karakum Canal: Problems and Prospects." Post-Soviet Geography and Economics, Vol. 39, No. 4, p. 227.

98. Ibid," p. 227.

99. Allworth, Central Asia, p. 117.

100. Hannan, "Managing Turkmenistan's Karakum Canal," p. 231.

101. Brice, Environmental History, p. 348.

102. Finn, Peter. (July 10, 2007). "Aral Sea's Return Revives Withered Villages." Washington Post.

103. Hannan, "Managing Turkmenistan's Karakum Canal," pp. 230-231.

104. Ibid, pp. 230-231.

105. Ibid, p. 232.

106. USSR Academy of Sciences. (1977). The Remaking of Nature under Socialism: Desert Development in the V.I. Lenin Karakum Canal Zone. Moscow: USSR Academy of Sciences.

107. Kerimi, Nina. "Opium Use in Turkmenistan: A Historical Perspective." Addiction, 2000. Vol. 95, No. 9, pp. 1319-1333.

108. Allworth, Central Asia, p. 274.

109. A half-pencil-sized cellophane tube of nas costs only a few cents and can be found at most bazaars. Recipes vary, but they can include tobacco leaves, lime (purportedly from chicken shit), vegetable oil, pomegranate rind, and saksaul ashes. When I tried it, it wasn't much fun – it made me dizzy and a little queasy. Niyazov banned it in 2004, claiming it caused cancer and tuberculosis. Still, the sidewalks in most Turkmen cities were stained with green splotches, where men had spit their nas goop.

110. Associated Press. (August 23, 2005). "Turkmen President Bans Lip Synching Performances."

Index

Made in the USA
Las Vegas, NV
25 March 2022

46294500R00144